Key Labor Market Indicators

OTHER TITLES IN THE ADePT SERIES

ADePT

Simulating Distributional Impacts of Macro-dynamics: Theory and Practical Applications (2014) by Sergio Oliveri, Sergiy Radyakin, Stanislav Kolenikov, Michael Lokshin, Ambar Narayan, and Carolina Sánchez-Páramo

Analyzing Food Security Using Household Survey Data: Streamlined Analysis with ADePT Software (2014) by Ana Moltedo, Nathalie Troubat, Michael Lokshin, and Zurab Sajaia

A Unified Approach to Measuring Poverty and Inequality—Theory and Practice: Streamlined Analysis with ADePT Software (2013) by James Foster, Suman Seth, Michael Lokshin, and Zurab Sajaia

Health Equity and Financial Protection: Streamlined Analysis with ADePT Software (2011) by Adam Wagstaff, Marcel Bilger, Zurab Sajaia, and Michael Lokshin

Assessing Sector Performance and Inequality in Education: Streamlined Analysis with ADePT Software (2011) by Emilio Porta, Gustavo Arcia, Kevin Macdonald, Sergiy Radyakin, and Michael Lokshin

For more information about Streamlined Analysis with ADePT software and publications, visit www.worldbank.org/adept.

STREAMLINED ANALYSIS WITH ADePT SOFTWARE

Key Labor Market Indicators

Analysis with Household Survey Data

Ina Pietschmann
Steven Kapsos
Evangelia Bourmpoula
Zurab Sajaia
Michael Lokshin

WORLD BANK GROUP

ISBN (paper): 978-1-4648-0784-8
ISBN (electronic): 978-1-4648-0785-5
DOI: 10.1596/978-1-4648-0784-8

ILO ISBN (paper): 978-92-2-130354-1
ILO ISBN (electronic): 978-92-2-130355-8

Cover images: foreground image: brick worker Ricaute Morales, © Scott Wallace/World Bank; *background image:* © iStockphoto .com/Olga Altunina. Images used with permission. Further permission required for reuse.
Cover design: Kim Vilov

Library of Congress Cataloging-in-Publication Data has been requested.

Contents

Contents

Boxes

Figures

Contents

Screenshots

Contents

Tables

Acknowledgments

This book, and the ADePT software module that accompanies the book, is the result of collaboration between the International Labour Organization (ILO) and the World Bank. The authors are grateful to Rosina Gammarano, Francisco Guerreiro, Richard Horne, Phu Huynh, Kee Beom Kim, Devora Levakova, Akiko Minowa, Yves Perardel, Marie-Claire Sodergren, Theo Sparreboom, and Christian Viegelahn for key inputs and assistance throughout the process of developing the software module and producing the manuscript.

The authors thank Lynne Butler, Antonio Junior Indart, Owais Parray, and Roberto Pes for organizing a training session on the ADePT ILO Labor Market Indicators Module in Dili, Timor-Leste, and Makiko Matsumoto and Bolormaa Purevsuren for organizing a training session in Ulaanbaatar, Mongolia. Moreover, the authors thank the participants at these training sessions, from national statistical offices, and labor and planning agencies, whose inputs and insights led to improvements and further development of the module.

The authors also express their gratitude to Rafael Diez de Medina, Director of the ILO Department of Statistics, and Ritash Sarna, Chief of the Department's Management Support Unit, for their strong support of this project.

Abbreviations

HIES	household income and expenditure survey
ICLS	International Conference of Labour Statisticians
ICSE	International Classification of Status in Employment
ILO	International Labour Organization
ISCED	International Standard Classification of Education
ISCO	International Standard Classification of Occupations
ISIC	International Standard Industrial Classification of All Economic Activities
KILM	Key Indicators of the Labour Market
LFS	labor force survey
LLL	lifelong learning
LMI	labor market information
LMIA	labor market information and analysis
LSS	living standards survey
MDGs	Millennium Development Goals
NEET	not in education, employment, or training
NSCO	National Standard Classification of Occupations
NSO	National Statistics Office

Abbreviations

PPP	purchasing power parity
R	South African rand
SDGs	Sustainable Development Goals
SNA	System of National Accounts
Tog	Mongolian tughrik

Introduction

Plan of the Book

ADePT is a software platform for automated data tabulation, designed and maintained by the World Bank. The software produces sets of predefined analytical results (tables and graphs) based on household survey data. This book aims to provide the essential guidelines in using the ADePT ILO Labor Market Indicators Module and explain its background methodology. It is organized into five chapters:

- Chapter 1 provides a brief introduction to labor market information and analysis (LMIA).
- Chapter 2 provides an overview of core concepts and definitions of the variables used as inputs and the indicators produced in output tables.
- Chapter 3 provides a short analysis based on country-specific examples from Greece, Mongolia, South Africa, and Timor-Leste to illustrate the interpretation and use of the tables.
- Chapter 4 provides guidelines on the construction of the variables used to produce the labor market indicators.
- Chapter 5 explains how to install and use ADePT-LMI.

What Is the Purpose of Labor Market Analysis and a Labor Market Information System?

Countries, whether developed or developing, typically face a wide range of challenges in the labor market. Insufficient employment generation, under-employment, skills mismatches, working poverty, and labor market dis-crimination are just a few of the many challenges faced by countries across the development spectrum. Timely, relevant, and accurate labor market information and analysis are essential for planning, implementing, moni-toring, and evaluating policies to address these and other challenges while promoting decent, adequate, and productive employment for both men and women (Sparreboom 2013). That is, for countries to be able to effectively address priority areas in their labor markets, it is essential for them to have a well-functioning LMIA system.

Definition, Sources, Components, and Functions of LMIA Systems

An LMIA system is a network of institutions, persons, and information with agreed roles to produce, analyze, and disseminate labor market information (LMI). LMIA systems are not only about statistics (see figure 1.1). While statistics, and in particular labor statistics, are crucial, sound analysis of the available LMI, along with a mechanism for communicating the findings of this analysis, are required for policy formulation, monitoring, and evaluation of labor market policies and programs. An LMIA system can provide data on

Figure 1.1: LMIA and Statistics

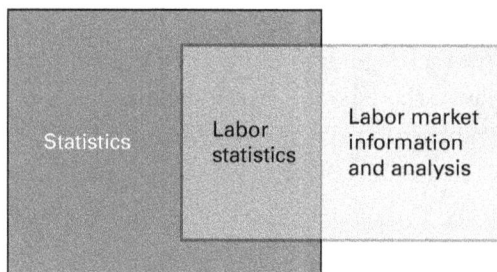

Note: LMIA = labor market information and analysis.

2

the balance of labor demand and supply, the current labor market situation (stock), and developments (trends) over time. An LMIA system also identifies priority issues and target groups in the labor market to evaluate and help formulate appropriate policies.

There are various sources of labor statistics: (a) censuses and surveys of households ("persons"), such as population censuses, labor force surveys (LFSs), and household income and expenditure surveys (HIESs); (b) surveys of establishments ("companies"), such as establishment surveys, employment and earnings surveys, and occupational employment and vacancy surveys; and (c) administrative data ("records"), such as educational enrollment data, migration records, and employment services records. As table 1.1 shows in detail, each source of information has strengths and limitations. Taking these into consideration, a fully developed LMIA system incorporates information from a variety of sources. For example, from an establishment survey one can easily surmise where the vacancies in the labor market are (which sectors, which occupations, etc.). But only from a household survey can one identify which subcategory of the population might be interested and has the right skills to fill those vacancies.

Table 1.1: Strengths and Limitations of Primary Sources of Labor Market Information

Information sources	Strengths	Limitations
Household surveys	– Comprehensive coverage of population – Detailed questioning permits precise measurement of statistical concepts for short reference periods	– Sampling prevents reliable estimates for small groups – Lower quality of data on sensitive, income-, and employer-related topics – Cannot provide estimates of vacancies, training needs, etc.
Establishment surveys	– Comprehensive coverage of larger businesses – Payroll records provide consistent and reliable data for income and employment by industry – Only source for data on vacancies, training needs, etc.	– Typically poor coverage of very small and unregistered businesses – Requires constant updating of registers (births and deaths) – Difficult identification of small or informal units – High nonresponse rates – Sampling prevents reliable estimates for small groups – Data items are limited by the information in establishment's registers
Administrative records	– Total count allows maximum detail – Inexpensive to compile statistics	– Often poor coverage – Often not up to date – Data quality may be questionable

3

The strengths and limitations of the various statistical sources imply that there is no single data source that can meet all needs in an LMIA system. Therefore, it is crucial to use all available information sources and to understand the strengths and limitations of different types of surveys and other data sources.

LMIA systems have three main functions (figure 1.2):

- Producing and disseminating labor market information and analysis
- Monitoring and reporting on employment and labor policies
- Providing a mechanism to exchange information and coordinate different actors and institutions that produce and utilize LMIA.

Figure 1.2: Functions and Components of an LMIA

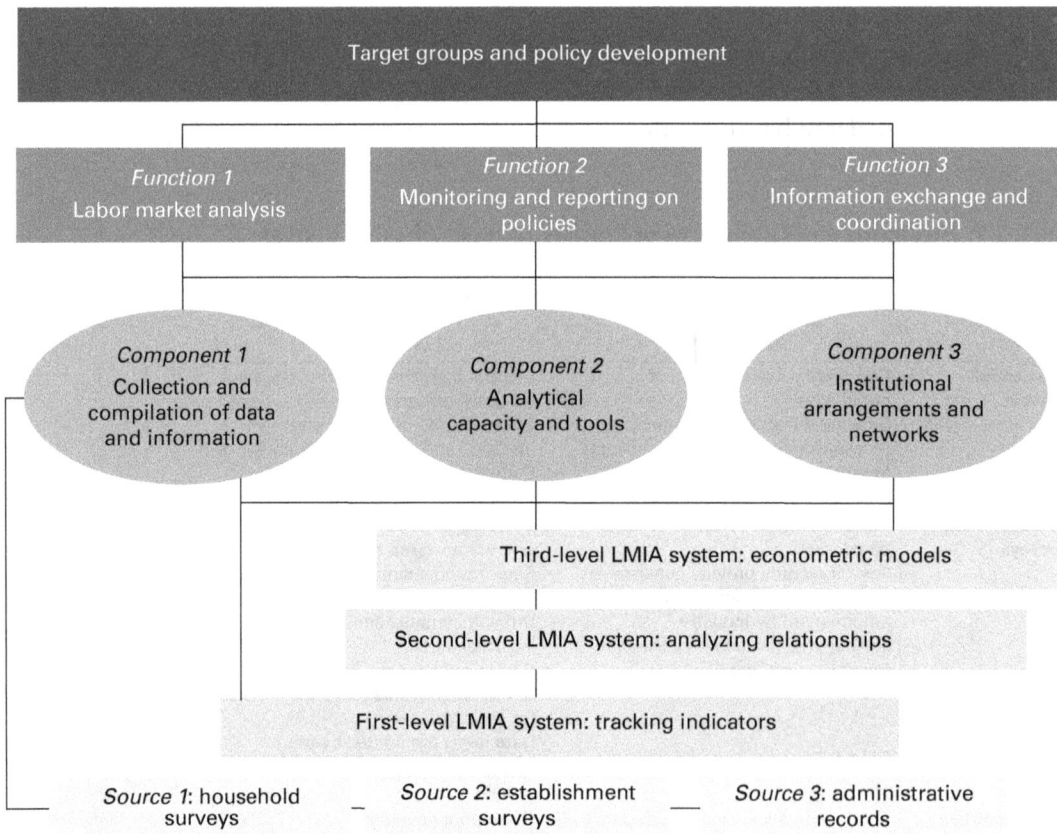

Target groups and policy development

Function 1
Labor market analysis

Function 2
Monitoring and reporting on policies

Function 3
Information exchange and coordination

Component 1
Collection and compilation of data and information

Component 2
Analytical capacity and tools

Component 3
Institutional arrangements and networks

Third-level LMIA system: econometric models

Second-level LMIA system: analyzing relationships

First-level LMIA system: tracking indicators

Source 1: household surveys

Source 2: establishment surveys

Source 3: administrative records

Note: LMIA = labor market information and analysis.

4

LMIA systems also have three main components (figure 1.2):

- *Collection and compilation of data and information.* Policy makers often use a standard set of indicators, such as the International Labour Organization's (ILO's) Key Indicators of the Labour Market[1] (KILM) or the Millennium Development Goals (MDGs) employment indicators,[2] now succeeded by the Sustainable Development Goals (SDGs) employment-related indicators.
- *Analytical capacity and tools.* Policy makers use appropriate tools to detect labor market trends and challenges and relate them to policies and other elements of the broader economy that play an important role in shaping the state of the labor market. The analytical capacity within LMIA systems can be designed at three levels:
  - Monitoring labor markets and developing a set of indicators
  - Analyzing relationships between variables and indicators
  - Creating econometric models to produce estimates and projections of key labor market indicators.
- *Well-defined institutional arrangements and networks.* Coordination and cooperation among agencies and actors involved in the LMIA system, such as governmental departments and employers' and workers' associations, are essential for facilitating the smooth functioning of the LMIA system.

Features of an LMIA System

There are many considerations in developing an effective LMIA system. For example, an LMIA system has to be *relevant* with respect to the needs of end users; it must provide *timely* information, meaning that it works efficiently enough to, for example, minimize the time lag between conducting surveys and releasing data and related reports. It must provide *accurate* and *reliable* information, and be *accessible* to all end users. Moreover, the LMI produced within the LMIA system must be well documented (e.g., clear metadata, sources, definitions, and descriptions of the methodologies) to be easily used by expert and nonexpert users alike.

The basic framework for labor market analysis is often similar across countries and over time. Labor market analysis needs to be current to present an analytically comprehensive picture of the labor market and to inform policy makers. For any government agency (e.g., national statistical office or ministry of labor), international organization, or research institute, there is a considerable upfront cost to establish a standardized framework for labor market analysis. This includes development of expertise in advanced statistical software packages, coding and processing datasets, outlier detection, and producing tabulations from survey data. In addition, there must be staff development in the area of labor market indicator concepts and definitions.

How Does the ADePT-LMI Module Contribute to LMIA Systems?

The ADePT-LMI module is a powerful tool to strengthen LMIA systems by significantly *simplifying* and *standardizing* the calculation of key labor market indicators. It allows for standardized analysis of internationally recognized key labor market indicators, greatly *reduces* the time lag between surveys being conducted and dissemination of results, and can free up resources for deeper analysis of survey data. Furthermore, it can be easily used by different agencies in an LMIA system.

Benefits of the ADePT-LMI module:

- Does not require expertise in statistical software programs
- Introduces advanced statistical and econometric tools to a wider audience
- Minimizes human errors
- Allows for standardized analysis of internationally recognized key labor market indicators based on international standards and classifications
- Requires minimal data preparation from users
- Provides extensive diagnostics of possible problems with the data
- Provides localized versions (software available in many languages)
- Is free of charge.

Notes

1. The KILM is a comprehensive database of country-level data on 17 key indicators of the labor market from 1980 to the latest available year. The KILM can serve as a tool for policy makers and researchers in monitoring

and assessing many of the pertinent issues related to the functioning of labor markets (ILO, "Key Indicators of the Labour Market [KILM] 2015," www.ilo.org/kilm).

2. ILO, "Millennium Development Goals (MDGs) Employment Indicators," http://www.ilo.org/empelm/what/WCMS_114244/lang--en/index.htm.

Reference

Sparreboom, T. 2013. "Labour Market Information and Analysis." In *Perspectives on Labour Economics for Development*, edited by S. Cazes and S. Verick. Geneva: International Labour Organization.

Chapter 2

Concepts and Definitions

Introduction

Labor market information (LMI) produced with the ADePT ILO Labor Market Indicators Module measures characteristics of the population and labor force; the quantity, structure, and quality of employment; the extent of labor underutilization; and the extent of poverty among workers, among others.

This chapter provides an overview of core concepts and definitions of the variables used as inputs into the module, and the indicators produced in output tables. A sound understanding of the underlying concepts and standards is the precondition for correctly using ADePT to produce information from household surveys, and for correctly interpreting the ADePT tables.

All information in the following sections corresponds to international statistical standards. The labor statistics concepts were adopted during sessions of the International Conference of Labour Statisticians (ICLS), which is convened every five years by the Governing Body of the International Labour Organization (ILO).

Over the years, the ILO has developed a number of analytical and research instruments and tools that apply the adopted labor standards, such as the ILO Key Indicators of the Labour Market (KILM; ILO 2013b), the ILO Decent Work Indicators (ILO 2012), and the ILOSTAT database.[1] This chapter draws heavily from these databases and related publications.

Underlying Concepts of the ADePT-LMI Module

This section presents the standard definitions used for the key underlying concepts of the ADePT-LMI module, as well as relevant explanations related to these concepts. Some of the main underlying concepts of the ADePT-LMI module refer to households, while others refer to individuals. Both are included in this section.

Household Variable Concepts

In order to use and accurately interpret the tables obtained through the ADePT-LMI module, it is important to understand the main underlying concepts, beginning with a description of the household variable concepts.

Welfare Aggregate

Welfare aggregates are a measure of living standards across households. The continuous variable *Welfare aggregate* is usually constructed based on aggregated monetary welfare indicators, such as measured consumption or income. But they can also relate to nonmonetary indicators such as an assets index, a basic needs index, or a welfare ratio (ratio of consumption to poverty line) defined at the household or individual level.

Welfare measures constructed on the basis of household surveys usually refer to aggregated consumption as a summary measure of household living standards. They are essential to establish poverty lines, to conduct poverty analysis and inequality research, to assess changes in living standards over time, and to monitor the impacts of policies and programs related to poverty and inequality.

Welfare aggregates are widely used to determine the income of individuals who are likely to benefit from or be adversely affected by different policies or programs, such as social protection schemes, taxes, or subsidies.

In the context of the ADePT-LMI module, welfare aggregates typically refer to monthly household consumption per capita, measured in local currency units (Deaton and Zaidi 2002).

Poverty Line

The binary variable *Poverty line* displays the minimum level of consumption or income deemed necessary to achieve an adequate standard of living in a given country. National poverty lines are thresholds defined at the country level, below which a person is deemed to be poor. For international comparisons, a poverty line of $1.25 a day is used—measured at 2005 international dollars and adjusted for purchasing power parity (PPP).

According to Ravallion (1992), there are two main ways of setting poverty lines—relative or absolute:

- *Relative poverty lines*. Defined in relation to the overall distribution of income or consumption in a country; for example, the poverty line could be set at 50 percent of the country's mean or median per capita income or consumption.
- *Absolute poverty lines*. Reflect the absolute standards of what households should "have" to meet basic needs. In terms of monetary measures, absolute poverty lines are often based on estimates of the cost of basic food needs (e.g., the cost of a nutritional basket considered minimal for the healthy survival of a typical family) to which a provision is added for nonfood needs.

Consistent with the poverty measurement methodology used for the Millennium Development Goals (MDGs) and with ILO estimates of the working poor, the module produces poverty and welfare indicators on the basis of absolute poverty lines (ILO 2013a; Kapsos and Bourmpoula 2013).

Labor Force Framework

The backbone of labor statistics and their analysis is the labor force framework, which splits the population into categories that thereafter can be examined in more detail.

Labor Force Status Concepts

A crucial subset of the underlying concepts of the ADePT-LMI module are the concepts pertaining to individuals' labor force status. Definitions of these concepts are provided in the following paragraphs.

Working-Age Population

The population can be divided into populations below and above the working age. The minimum age limit for defining the working age varies among countries and depends on such national circumstances as the compulsory schooling age, the minimum age for admission to employment, and the extent of child labor. However, it is common to define *working-age population* as the population ages 15 and older (ADePT's default working-age population). Nevertheless, this can be changed in ADePT's parameters, as explained in chapter 4.

Internationally, *youth* is defined as persons ages 15–24, which is the default setting in ADePT. However, as with the working-age population, users can adjust the lower- and upper-age boundaries for the youth cohort to be in line with national definitions and practices. The lower age limit for young people is usually determined by the minimum legal working age. The upper age limit for youth targeted in national policies and programs varies greatly among countries, and this parameter needs to be set according to the analytical needs and national circumstances.

The working-age population is broken down into (a) those in the labor force and (b) those not in the labor force.

Labor Force

The labor force comprises the employed and the unemployed, while the remainder of the working-age population is outside the labor force (figure 2.1).

Employment

According to the resolution adopted by the 19th ICLS (ILO 2013c), the concept of work comprises any activity performed by persons of any sex and age to produce goods or to provide services for use by others or for own use. This concept is aligned with the general production boundary as defined in the System of National Accounts (SNA) 2008 (SNA 2008).[2] Five mutually exclusive forms of work are identified for separate measurement, as follows:

- Own-use production work comprising production of goods and services for own final use
- Employment comprising work performed for others in exchange for pay or profit
- Unpaid trainee work comprising work performed for others without pay to acquire workplace experience or skills

Figure 2.1: Labor Force Framework

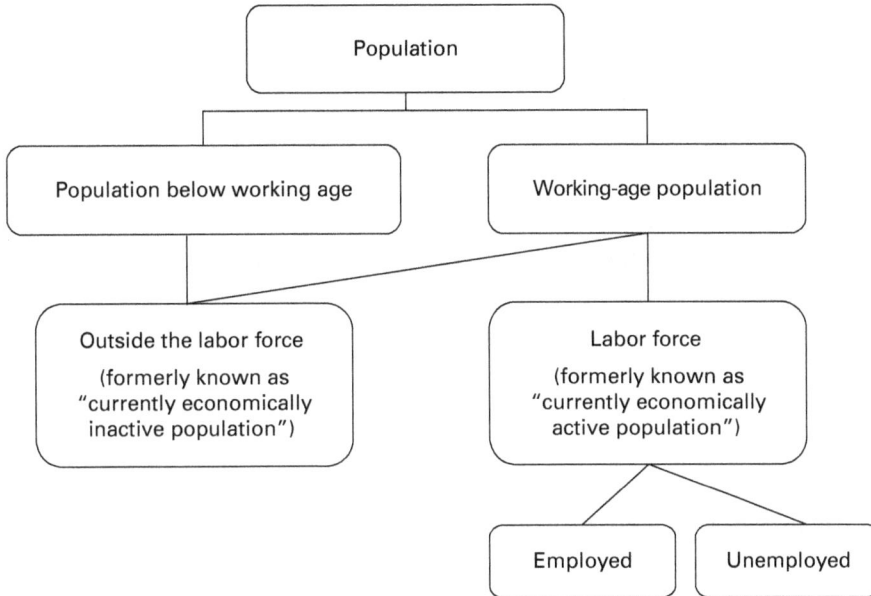

- Volunteer work comprising noncompulsory work performed for others without pay
- Other work activities (not defined in the resolution).

According to the resolution, *persons in employment* is defined as all those of working age who, during a short reference period, were engaged in any activity to produce goods or provide services for pay or profit. They comprise the following:

- Employed persons "at work," that is, who worked in a job for at least one hour during the reference period
- Employed persons "not at work" during the reference period due to temporary absence from a job or to working time arrangements (such as shift work, flextime, and compensatory leave for overtime).

The ADePT-LMI module is mostly concerned with employment, leaving aside the other forms of work.[3]

Unemployment

The resolution adopted by the 19th ICLS defined *persons in unemployment* as all those of working age who were not in employment, carried out activities to seek employment during a specified recent period, and were currently available to take up employment given a job opportunity, where

- "Not in employment" is assessed with respect to the short reference period for the measurement of employment; and
- "Seek employment" refers to any activity when carried out, during a specified recent period comprising the last four weeks or one month, for the purpose of finding a job or setting up a business or agricultural undertaking. This includes also part-time, informal, temporary, seasonal, or casual employment within the national territory or abroad.

Included in "unemployment" are the following:

- Future starters, defined as persons "not in employment" and "currently available" who did not "seek employment" because they had already made arrangements to start a job within a short subsequent period (set according to the general length of waiting time for starting a new job in the national context but generally not greater than three months)
- Participants in skills training or retraining schemes within employment promotion programs, who, on that basis, were "not in employment," not "currently available," and did not "seek employment" because they had a job offer to start within a short subsequent period (generally not greater than three months)
- Persons "not in employment" who carried out activities to migrate abroad to work for pay or profit but who were still waiting for the opportunity to leave.

Potential Labor Force

Potential labor force is a new concept introduced in the resolution adopted by the 19th ICLS. It is defined as all persons of working age who, during the short reference period, were neither in employment nor in unemployment and (a) carried out activities to "seek employment," although they were not "currently available" but would become available within a short subsequent period established in the light of national circumstances (i.e., unavailable jobseekers); or (b) did not carry out activities to "seek employment" but wanted employment and were "currently available" (i.e., available potential jobseekers).

Among those who did not carry out activities to seek employment, it may be useful to categorize "discouraged jobseekers," comprising those who did not seek employment for labor market reasons. These reasons may include past failure to find a suitable job; lack of experience, qualifications, or jobs matching the person's skills; lack of jobs in the area; and considered too young or too old by prospective employers.

Outside the Labor Force

Persons in the potential labor force constitute a subgroup of all persons outside the labor force (i.e., persons who are neither employed nor unemployed). Besides labor market–related reasons, there are many other reasons for not seeking employment, being unavailable for employment, or not wanting employment. These include personal reasons (own illness, disability, studies); family-related reasons (pregnancy, presence of small children, refusal by family); lack of infrastructure (assets, roads, transportation, employment services); other sources of income (pensions, rents); and social exclusion.

Unemployment Concepts

This subsection presents the definitions behind the categories in the ADePT-LMI module of the unemployed by duration of unemployment.

Duration of Unemployment

Duration of unemployment refers to the length of time (typically measured in months) during which a person has been continuously unemployed. Researchers commonly define the duration as short-term if the spell of unemployment is less than six months. Unemployed persons with continuous periods of unemployment extending for a year or longer are generally referred to as long-term unemployed. Depending on the national policy measures or programs to be monitored, categories that capture the duration of unemployment may differ from country to country.

In general, short periods of joblessness can be of less concern, especially when unemployed persons are covered by unemployment insurance schemes or similar forms of social protection. Short-term unemployment may even be viewed as desirable when it allows time for jobless persons to find optimal employment. In addition, in employment systems in which workers can be temporarily laid off and then called back, short spells of unemployment allow employers to weather temporary declines in business activity (see KILM 11).[4] Long-term unemployment, on the other hand, represents a serious distortion in the labor market, with potential detrimental effects on aggregate productivity and on people's well-being. Prolonged periods of unemployment bring with them many undesirable effects, particularly loss of income and diminishing employability of jobseekers.

Employment Concepts

This subsection provides the definitions underlying the categories in the ADePT-LMI module for persons in employment.

Status in Employment

Status in employment captures the distribution of the employed according to their category of status in employment, which provides a statistical basis for describing workers' conditions of work and for defining an individual's socioeconomic group (KILM 3). According to the International Classification of Status in Employment (ICSE) (ILO 1993), the basic criteria used to define the status groups are the types of economic risk that workers face (an element of which is the strength of institutional attachment between the person and the job) and the type of authority over establishments and other workers that the jobholder has or will have as an explicit or implicit result of the employment contract (KILM 3).

Although international recommendations for the status in employment classification have existed since before 1950,[5] the 1993 revisions retained the existing major categories but attempted to improve (a) the conceptual basis for the distinctions made and (b) the distinction between wage employment and self-employment. The 1993 ICSE categories and extracts from their definitions follow:

- *Employees* are all those workers who hold "paid employment jobs," where the incumbents hold explicit (written or oral) or implicit employment contracts that give them a basic remuneration that is not directly dependent upon the revenue of the unit for which they work.
- *Employers* are those workers who, working on their own account or with one or a few partners, hold "self-employment jobs" (i.e., jobs where the remuneration is directly dependent upon the profits derived from the goods and services produced), and, in this capacity, have engaged, on a continuous basis, one or more persons to work for them as employee(s).
- *Own-account workers* are those workers who, working on their own account or with one or more partners, hold "self-employment jobs" and have not engaged on a continuous basis any employees.
- *Members of producers' cooperatives* are workers who hold "self-employment jobs" in a cooperative producing goods and services.
- *Contributing family workers* are those workers who hold "self-employment jobs" as own-account workers in a market-oriented establishment operated by a related person living in the same household.
- *Workers not classifiable* by status include those for whom insufficient relevant information is available or who cannot be included in any of the preceding categories.

The sum of own-account workers and contributing family workers constitutes the broader category of vulnerable employment as defined for the MDGs. These two groups of workers have a lower likelihood of having formal work arrangements and are at risk of lacking adequate social security and a voice at work (KILM 3).

Occupation

Occupation is a categorical variable that captures the occupational categories in which employed people are engaged. Occupational classifications categorize all jobs into groups, which are hierarchically structured in a number of levels. Analysis of employment by occupation informs economic and labor policies in areas such as educational planning and employment services. Changes in the occupational distribution of an economy can be used to identify and analyze stages of development (KILM 5).

The following are the major groups of the International Standard Classification of Occupations (ISCO) adopted in 2008:[6]

1. Managers
2. Professionals
3. Technicians and associate professionals
4. Clerical support workers
5. Service and sales workers
6. Skilled agricultural, forestry and fishery workers
7. Craft and related trades workers
8. Plant and machine operators and assemblers
9. Elementary occupations
10. Armed forces occupations
X. Not elsewhere classified.

National classifications of occupations can differ compared to those in the ISCO. While serving as a model, ISCO-08 is *not intended* to replace any existing national classification of occupations, since the occupation classifications of individual countries should fully reflect both the structure of the national labor market and information needs for nationally relevant purposes (KILM 5).[7] The occupational categories can be very detailed. According to ISCO-08, under each major group, there are submajor groups, minor groups, and, finally, unit groups. Hence, there are four different levels of detail.

Sector of Economic Activity and Broad Sector

Sector of economic activity is a categorical variable that captures the sector of economic activity of employed persons. Sectoral information is particularly useful in identifying broad shifts in employment and stages of development (KILM 4). Sectoral information can provide insights into a range of policy questions, for example: Which sectors are seeing increasing employment and which are declining? How do shifts in employment from one sector to the other relate with shifts in productivity? To what extent is the labor market segregated? Are men and women distributed equally across sectors, or are they concentrated in certain sectors? How does segregation correlate with other labor market outcomes?

Based on the most recent revision (Revision 4, 2008) of the International Standard Industrial Classification of All Economic Activities (ISIC)[8] there are 21 major sectors (categories). These sectors are further disaggregated into divisions, groups, and classes.

Sectors of ISIC Revision 4 are:

A. Agriculture, forestry and fishing
B. Mining and quarrying
C. Manufacturing
D. Electricity, gas, steam and air conditioning supply
E. Water supply; sewerage, waste management, and remediation activities
F. Construction
G. Wholesale and retail trade; repair of motor vehicles and motorcycles
H. Transportation and storage
I. Accommodation and food service activities
J. Information and communication
K. Financial and insurance activities
L. Real estate activities
M. Professional, scientific, and technical activities
N. Administrative and support service activities
O. Public administration and defence; compulsory social security
P. Education
Q. Human health and social work activities
R. Arts, entertainment and recreation
S. Other service activities
T. Activities of households as employers; undifferentiated goods- and services-producing activities of households for own use
U. Activities of extraterritorial organizations and bodies
X. Not elsewhere classified.

As with the occupational classification, national classifications of industries may have different categories than those in the ISIC. While serving as a model, ISIC revisions are *not intended* to replace any existing national classification of sectors. In other words, the sectoral classifications of individual countries should fully reflect the structure of the national labor market and information needs for nationally relevant purposes.

A *Broad sector* variable is also a categorical variable that derives from the sector of economic activity variable. It aims to capture the more aggregate categories of economic activity where employed people are found. The most common broad sectoral categories are agriculture, industry, and services. Information on employment by broad economic activity can be very useful for comparisons across countries and for broad structural shifts in the economy.

The main activities under the agricultural sector are agriculture, hunting, forestry, and fishing (category A in ISIC 4), and the industry sector comprises mining and quarrying, manufacturing, construction, and public utilities (electricity, gas, steam, and air conditioning supply and water supply; sewerage, waste management, and remediation activities). Based on ISIC 4, this means that industry includes categories B to F. Finally, the services sector consists of wholesale and retail trade; restaurants and hotels; transport, storage, and communications; finance, insurance, real estate and business services; health and education; arts; and community, social, and personal services. Based on ISIC 4, the broad sectoral category for services includes categories G to U (KILM 4).

Public Sector Employment

The variable *Public sector employment* captures the number and share of people working in the public sector. The public sector refers to the general government sector as defined in the SNA plus any resident, publicly owned enterprises and companies operating at central, state (or regional), and local levels of government.[9] A person who is employed directly by those institutions, without regard for the particular type of employment contract, is defined as "employed" in the public sector.

The distinction between public and private wage employment can help in analyzing the dynamism of the private sector in terms of generating employment. A high incidence of public employment can indicate a lack of decent opportunities in the private sector.

Type of Contract

The variable *Type of contract* captures the type of employment contract held by workers, which is intended to provide insights into the legal relationship between workers and employers. The types of contracts reported in household surveys vary substantially from country to country, but in general these should distinguish between permanent, fixed-duration, or no contract governing the employment, with further breakdowns possible, such as apprentice or trainee, probationary period, among others. The type of contracts can be analyzed concurrently with the "Status in employment" indicator to capture a more complete picture of workers' conditions of work.

Earnings

Earnings is a continuous variable that captures the reported earnings of the employed. This variable may correspond to either wages or earnings and may be reported on a monthly, weekly, daily, or hourly basis.

Wage or salary rates are the rates paid for normal time of work, comprising basic wages and salaries, cost-of-living allowances, and other guaranteed and regularly paid allowances. The following should be excluded: overtime payments, bonuses, and gratuities; family allowances; other social security payments made by the employer directly to employees; and ex gratia payments in kind, supplementary to normal wage and salary rates.

Earnings include some elements of remuneration such as overtime and some bonuses not counted as part of wage rates. Earnings are the remuneration in cash and in kind paid to employees, at regular intervals, for time worked or work done, together with remuneration for time not worked, such as for annual vacation, other paid leave, or holidays. They include those elements of earnings usually received regularly, before any deductions are made by the employer in respect of taxes, contributions of employees to social security, and pension schemes, life insurance premiums, union dues, and any other obligations of employees. The following should be excluded: contributions paid by employers on behalf of employees to social security and pension schemes, and benefits received by employees under these schemes; severance and termination pay; and irregular bonuses such as year-end and other one-time bonuses that accrue over a period longer than a pay period (ILO 2013b).

Information on earnings is important for the analysis of trends and levels of workers' purchasing power and standard of living. It is particularly useful to analyze data on earnings alongside information on labor productivity, which provides insights into the extent to which workers are sharing in the overall gains from their labor.

Hours of Work

Hours of work is a continuous variable that captures the reported number of hours worked by the employed during the reference period. Depending on the formulation of the relevant survey question or questions, this variable may capture data on actual hours, usual hours, hours paid for, or other measurements of hours of work. It is typically measured as the number of hours worked per week, but can also be reported on a monthly or daily basis.

The number of hours worked has an impact on the health and well-being of workers, as well as affecting workers' productivity and the labor costs of establishments. Measuring the level and trends in working time in a society, for different groups of persons and for individuals, is important for monitoring working and living conditions and for analyzing economic and social developments (KILM 7).

In 2008, the ICLS adopted the "Resolution Concerning the Measurement of Working Time" (ILO 2008b). The resolution revised the existing standards on statistics of hours of work ("Resolution Concerning Statistics of Hours of Work," adopted by the 13th ICLS, 1962) to reflect the working time of persons in all sectors of the economy and in all forms of productive activity toward the achievement of decent work for all. It also provided measurement methodologies and guidelines on a larger number of measures than previously defined internationally, thereby enhancing the standard's usefulness through its technical guidelines and the consistency and international comparability of related statistics.

The resolution provides definitions for seven concepts of working time:

A. *Hours actually worked*, the key concept of working time defined for statistical purposes applicable to all jobs and to all working persons;
B. *Hours paid for*, linked to remuneration of hours that may not all correspond to production;
C. *Normal hours of work*, refers to legally prevailing hours for collective groups of workers;
D. *Contractual hours of work*, individuals are expected to work according to contractual relationships as distinct from normal hours;
E. *Hours usually worked*, most commonly in a job over a long observation period;
F. *Overtime hours of work*, performed beyond contracts or norms; and
G. *Absence from work hours*, when working persons do not work.

The resolution also provides definitions for two concepts of working time arrangements that describe the working time in a job, namely the *organization* and *scheduling* of working time, regardless of type of job, and formalized working time arrangements that comprise specific combinations of those characteristics and that have legal recognition.

Hours *"usually worked"* per week identifies the most common weekly working schedule of a person in employment over a selected period. The internationally agreed statistical definition of *usual hours of work* refers to the hours worked in any job during a typical short period such as one week. The definition is applicable to all types of jobs, even those for which the worker does not possess a working contract (e.g., in small-scale or family enterprises and self-employed workers). *Hours usually worked* includes overtime that occurs systematically every day or week and excludes time not worked on a usual basis. This measure is not affected by unusual absence or by irregular or unusual overtime, whether worked for premium pay, regular pay, or without compensation (ILO 2013b).

For some countries, data are available only according to *hours actually worked.* This measure includes time spent at the workplace on productive activities ("direct hours") and on other activities that are part of the tasks and duties of the job concerned ("related hours"). The latter can include, for example, cleaning and preparing working tools and certain on-call duties. The concept also includes time spent at the place of work when the person is inactive for reasons linked to the production process or work organization ("down time"), since during these periods paid workers, for example, still remain at the disposal of their employer, while the self-employed may continue working on other tasks and duties. *Hours actually worked* also includes "resting time," or short rest periods spent at the place of work since they are necessary for human beings and because they are difficult to distinguish separately (even if paid workers, for example, are not "at the disposal" of their employer during those periods). Explicitly excluded are lunch breaks if no work is performed, since they are normally sufficiently long to be easily distinguished from work periods. The international definition relates to all types of workers, whether in salaried or self-employment, paid, or unpaid work, and carried out in any location, including the street, field, or home (KILM 7).

Willing to Work More Hours

The variable *Willing to work more hours* is important when combined with the *Hours of work* variable because it can produce estimates of *Time-related underemployment* (see the following subcategory). *Time-related underemployment* is defined as a person in employment who is working below a specified threshold number of hours (often the cutoff is "less than 30 hours") and is willing and available to work additional hours.

Time-Related Underemployment

Underemployment in general reflects the underutilization of the productive potential of workers and thus can be related to "inadequate" working time (time-related underemployment), income, and occupational skills. Capturing a complete picture of underutilization requires a careful examination of a set of indicators that includes (but is not limited to) labor force participation rates and inactivity rates (such as discouraged workers and other inactive persons available for work), employment-to-population ratios, and other subcategories of employment (e.g., time-related underemployed, vulnerable employment, employed with low earnings, working poverty, employed with underutilized skills, and labor productivity).

Currently, time-related underemployment is the only underemployment concept that has been agreed upon and properly defined for statistical measurement within the international community and therefore is adopted in the module. It measures underutilization of the productive capacity of the employed population in terms of hours of work.

Time-related underemployed comprises all persons in employment, as defined in current international guidelines regarding employment statistics, who satisfy the following three criteria during the reference period used to define *employment* (ILO 1952): (a) willing to work additional hours (or jobs), (b) available to work additional hours, and (c) worked less than a threshold relating to working time.

Secondary Employment

The variable *Secondary employment* captures whether an employed person, during the reference period, had a second job for pay or profit (or pay in kind) besides the primary job.

A high incidence of employed people holding a secondary job may indicate a lack of adequate utilization of the labor supply (e.g., in terms of time) and insufficient remuneration.

Status in Employment in Secondary Job

The variable *Status in employment in SJ* (secondary job) identifies the *Status in employment* type of employed persons in their secondary job. The definitions and the categories are discussed in the variable *Status in employment* earlier in this chapter.

Contributions to Social Security

According to the ILO, minimum standards of social security comprise nine categories: medical care, sickness, unemployment, old age, employment injury, family, maternity, invalidity, and survivors' benefits (ILO 1952).

ILO standards on social security provide different social security coverage under different economic systems and stages of development. Especially in times of heightened economic risks, there is growing consensus that social security coverage can buffer (at least for some time) many of the negative effects of crises.

The categories and levels of minimum benefits (social security coverage) are usually determined at the national level with reference to the level of development of the country concerned.

Trade Union Membership

The concept of trade union membership requires a clear definition of what constitutes a trade union and who can be defined as a member.

Currently, there are no international standards available on trade union membership statistics. However, according to the ILO (2008a), a trade union is an independent organization consisting predominantly of employees, with principal activities including the negotiation of rates of pay and conditions of employment for its members. Excluded from the definition are nonoperating unions or branches, that is, those that have no members at the time the data are being collected.

Trade union membership connects to one of the Decent Work Indicators related to social dialogue, aims to reflect freedom of association, and is at the core of the fundamental principles and rights at work.

Trade union concepts differ largely between countries and over time and often refer to national legislation such as labor codes or trade union acts used for union registration. These definitions might have changed over time in line with new laws or regulations adopted in this field.

Working Poverty

The term *working poor* is defined as the proportion of employed persons living in a household whose members are living below the internationally or nationally defined poverty line. In many developing countries, unlike in most of the developed world, social security schemes and social safety nets often do not cover large segments of the workforce and population. Thus, people have to work to survive. These people are often engaged in low-quality jobs that are of low productivity and work for low wages (ILO 2011).

Working poverty therefore gives an indication of the lack of decent work: if a person's work does not provide an income high enough to lift them and their families out of poverty, then these jobs, at the very least, do not fulfill the income component of decent work. In addition, it is likely that other components are not being fulfilled, either.

The *working poor* definition shows the intersection of individuals' situation regarding poverty and their situation regarding employment. By combining LMI with poverty data, working poverty estimates clarify the relationship between poverty and employment and thereby complement standard poverty data.

The number of working poor is calculated on the basis of cross-tabulations from household survey datasets that include variables on both poverty status and labor force characteristics. An individual is classified as working poor if he or she is (a) employed and (b) living in a household with per capita consumption or income below the poverty line. The working poverty rate is the proportion of working poor in total employment: working poverty rate = number of employed persons living in a household with per capita consumption or income below the poverty line/total employment * 100.

The poverty line needs to be established before one can estimate the number and proportion of the working poor. Countries use different methods. For example, surveys on household consumption expenditure or, in some cases, household income can provide information on household consumption expenditure. However, household consumption data are usually preferred since they tend to be more reliable and give a better reflection of the real current living standards of households. A level of household consumption expenditure (or income) is then set, below which the person or household is considered to be poor.

Since this indicator requires a cross-tabulation of employment and poverty status on the basis of household survey data, both sets of information must be derived from the same source (typically household income and expenditure surveys [HIESs] or living standards surveys [LSSs]). However, as these surveys often do not have probing questions related to employment as in a typical labor force survey (LFS), the employment data derived in the cross-tabulation should be compared with other survey- or census-based estimates of employment to identify potential biases in the estimates. If large differences are observed, working poverty rates derived from an HIES can be applied to employment estimates from an LFS to obtain an estimate of the total number of working poor in a country.

Individual Variable Concepts

The ADePT-LMI module implies the use of numerous underlying concepts pertaining not to households but to individuals (other than those presented in the previous section regarding the labor force status of persons). These other individual variable concepts are presented below.

Enrollment

Enrollment data in household surveys usually refer to all persons living in the household that are enrolled and/or registered in an education program. Enrollment information indicates the capacity of national education systems to enroll students of a particular age group or sex.

In many countries, enrollment data show the general degree of participation in a given level of education, indicating the capacity of the educational system to enroll students of a particular age group (UNESCO 2009).

Enrollment information is central for measuring the share of the population that is not in education, employment, or training (NEET). The incidence of NEET in the youth population provides a measure of potential youth labor force participants and gives insights into youth discouragement or lack of opportunities for access to education or training.

Educational Attainment

Educational attainment generally refers to the highest grade of education completed within the educational system of the country where the education was received, that is, the highest grade of *education completed* (successfully).

However, educational attainment data in many household surveys and countries are presented as the highest grade attended (UN 1984).

The International Standard Classification of Education (ISCED) is a three-stage classification with a coding system for five digits, providing successive subdivisions from level to field to program group (UNESCO 2009). The level of education (ISCED 1-digit code) represents the broad categories within a country's educational system. These categories range from very elementary to more advanced and complex learning experiences, recognizing all fields and program groups that people can attain.

Notes

1. ILOSTAT database, www.ilo.org/ilostat.
2. See also the resolution concerning statistics of work, employment, and labor underutilization, adopted by the 19th International Conference of Labour Statisticians, http://www.ilo.org/global/statistics -and-databases/standards-and-guidelines/resolutions-adopted-by -international-conferences-of-labour-statisticians/WCMS_230304 /lang--en/index.htm.
3. Nevertheless, many of ADePT's labor market indicators are equally relevant when produced on the basis of work as defined according to the 1982 "Resolution Concerning Statistics of the Economically Active Population, Employment, Unemployment and Underemployment," adopted by the 13th ICLS and replaced by the 19th ICLS resolution. See http://www.ilo.org/global/statistics-and-databases/standards-and -guidelines/resolutions-adopted-by-international-conferences-of-labour -statisticians/WCMS_230304/lang--en/index.htm.
4. In this chapter, sections that draw on the ninth edition of the KILM include a reference in brackets (KILM) followed by the number corresponding to the KILM indicator.
5. The Sixth International Conference of Labour Statisticians (1947) and the 1950 Session of the United Nations Population Commission made relevant recommendations for statistics on employment and unemployment and on population censuses, respectively.
6. Information about the ISCO-08 structure and preliminary correspondence with ISCO-88 can be found at http://www.ilo.org/public/english /bureau/stat/isco/isco08/index.htm.

7. However, countries whose occupational classifications are aligned to ISCO-08 in concept and structure will find it easier to develop the procedures to make their occupational statistics internationally comparable (KILM).

8. Full details on the latest revision and links to crosswalks between previous revisions are available at http://unstats.un.org/unsd/cr/registry/isic-4 .asp.

9. Full definition can be found at http://laborsta.ilo.org/applv8/data /sectore.html. See also http://unstats.un.org/unsd/nationalaccount/docs /SNA2008.pdf.

References

Deaton, A., and S. Zaidi. 2002. "Guidelines for Constructing Consumption Aggregates for Welfare Analysis." Living Standards Measurement Study Working Paper 135, World Bank, Washington, DC.

ILO (International Labour Organization). 1952. "ILO C102–Social Security (Minimum Standards) Convention, 1952 (No. 102)." Convention adopted Geneva, June 28. http://www.ilo.org/dyn/normlex/en/f?p=1000 :12100:0::NO::P12100_ILO_CODE:C102.

———. 1982. "Resolution Concerning Statistics of the Economically Active Population, Employment, Unemployment and Underemployment." Resolution adopted by the 13th International Conference of Labour Statisticians, Geneva.

———. 1993. "Resolution Concerning the International Classification of Status in Employment." Resolution adopted by the 15th International Conference of Labour Statisticians, Geneva, January. http://www.ilo.org/global/statistics-and-databases/standards-and -guidelines/resolutions-adopted-by-international-conferences-of-labour -statisticians/WCMS_087562/lang--en/index.htm.

———. 2008a. Decent Work Indicators for Asia and the Pacific: A Guidebook for Policy-Makers and Researchers. Bangkok: ILO. http://www.ilo.org/asia /whatwedo/publications/WCMS_099163/lang--en/index.htm.

———. 2008b. "Resolution Concerning the Measurement of Working Time." Resolution adopted by the 18th International Conference of Labour Statisticians, Geneva, November–December. http://www .ilo.org/global/statistics-and-databases/standards-and-guidelines

/resolutions-adopted-by-international-conferences-of-labour-statisticians /WCMS_112455/lang--en/index.htm.

———. 2011. *Key Indicators of the Labour Market.* 7th ed. Geneva: ILO.

———. 2012. *Decent Work Indicators: Concepts and Definitions.* Geneva: ILO. http://www.ilo.org/wcmsp5/groups/public/---dgreports/---integration /documents/publication/wcms_229374.pdf.

———. 2013a. *Guide to the Millennium Development Goals Employment Indicators.* 2nd ed. Geneva: ILO. http://www.ilo.org/wcmsp5/groups /public/---ed_emp/---emp_elm/documents/publication/wcms_208796.pdf.

———. 2013b. *Key Indicators of the Labour Market.* 9th ed. Geneva: ILO. http://www.ilo.org/kilm.

———. 2013c. "Resolution Concerning Statistics of Work, Employment and Labour Underutilization." Resolution adopted by the 19th International Conference of Labour Statisticians, Geneva, October. http://www.ilo.org/global/statistics-and-databases/standards-and-guidelines /resolutions-adopted-by-international-conferences-of-labour-statisticians /WCMS_230304/lang--en/index.htm.

Kapsos, S., and E. Bourmpoula. 2013. "Employment and Economic Class in the Developing World." ILO Research Paper No. 6, International Labour Organization, Geneva. http://www.ilo.org/wcmsp5/groups /public/---dgreports/---inst/documents/publication/wcms_216451.pdf.

Ravallion, M. 1992. "Poverty Comparisons: A Guide to Concepts and Methods." Living Standards Measurement Study (LSMS) Working Paper LSM88, World Bank, Washington, DC. http://documents .worldbank.org/curated/en/1992/02/437897/poverty-comparisons-guide -concepts-methods.

SNA (System of National Accounts). 2008. http://unstats.un.org/unsd /nationalaccount/docs/SNA2008.pdf.

UN (United Nations). 1984. *Handbook of Household Surveys.* Rev. ed. Studies in Methods, Series F, No. 31. New York: UN.

UNESCO (United Nations Educational, Scientific and Cultural Organization). 2009. *Education Indicators: Technical Guidelines.* http:// www.uis.unesco.org/Library/Documents/eiguide09-en.pdf.

Further Reading

ILO (International Labour Organization). 1990. *Surveys of Economically Active Population, Employment, Unemployment and Underemployment: An ILO Manual on Concepts and Methods*. Geneva: ILO.

———. 1998. "Resolution Concerning the Measurement of Underemployment and Inadequate Employment Situations." Resolution adopted by the 16th International Conference of Labour Statisticians, Geneva, October. http://www.ilo.org/global/statistics-and-databases/standards-and-guidelines/resolutions-adopted-by-international-conferences-of-labour-statisticians/WCMS_087487/lang--en/index.htm.

———. 2012. International Standard Classification of Occupations (ISCO-08). http://www.ilo.org/wcmsp5/groups/public/---dgreports/---dcomm/---publ/documents/publication/wcms_172572.pdf.

Sparreboom, T. 2013. "Labour Market Information and Analysis." In *Perspectives on Labour Economics for Development*, edited by S. Cazes and S. Verick. Geneva: International Labour Organization.

UN (United Nations). 1997. *Handbook for Producing National Statistical Reports on Women and Men: Social Statistics and Indicators*. New York: UN.

UNESCO (United Nations Educational, Scientific, and Cultural Organization). 2011. *International Standard Classification of Education: ISCED 2011*. Montreal: UNESCO Institute for Statistics. http://www.uis.unesco.org/Education/Documents/isced-2011-en.pdf.

Chapter 3

Analyzing Labor Statistics with the ADePT-LMI Module

Introduction

When carefully analyzed, the output tables created with the ADePT ILO Labor Market Indicators Module can contribute to a better understanding of developments in national labor markets (e.g., the quantity of jobs, distribution of employment across industries and occupations, and trends in employment quality). By identifying key labor market issues and decent work challenges, governments and employers' and workers' organizations will be better equipped to develop and implement labor market policies and action plans. Sixty tables can be produced in the current version of the module. However, the number of tables that can be generated depends on the nature of the input datasets and the variables available in the respective surveys.

The primary source for labor market information (LMI) used in the module is the labor force survey (LFS). An LFS is a household sample survey designed to divide individuals of working age into three mutually exclusive categories: (a) employed, (b) unemployed, and (c) persons outside the labor force. The LFS collects detailed data on various key employment indicators to monitor the quantity and quality of work. In addition, the LFS is a major source of information on personal characteristics of the working-age population, including age, sex, educational attainment, and family characteristics. Usually the LFS is carried out on an annual, quarterly, or monthly basis.

For some indicators—namely the working poor and labor force status by household consumption—an LFS may not have the necessary information on household income or consumption. These indicators are typically produced on the basis of household income and expenditure survey (HIES) or living standards survey (LSS) datasets. Analysts use these surveys, conducted at the household level, for measuring and understanding poverty in developing countries. They may provide data for national accounts and are used to study general income and expenditure patterns of households.

ADePT produces two types of tables: output information tables and data output tables, which are described in the pages that follow. This chapter provides country-specific examples from Greece, Mongolia, South Africa, and Timor-Leste to illustrate ADePT's tables. It also offers examples to assist in interpreting and analyzing output tables.

Output Information Tables

ADePT generates output information tables that are automatically produced in formatted Excel workbooks. Each Excel workbook contains three types of output information tables (spreadsheets): (a) content table, (b) notification table, and (c) original data report table.

Content Table

The first sheet in the Excel file contains the table of contents, which lists all the tables produced by the particular run of the ADePT-LMI module. By clicking on the tables, users can easily navigate between them. If selected in the ADePT user interface, each indicator output table has a corresponding table with a standard errors (SE) tab and a frequencies (FREQ) tab (screenshot 3.1).

Notification Table

During the computation of tables, error messages occur in the system message window in the lower right corner of the ADePT interface.

Screenshot 3.1: Example of ADePT-LMI Content Table

	A	B	C	D	E	F
1		ADePT ILO Labour Market Indicators: Table of Contents				
2						
3						CPU time
4	Notifications	Errors, Warnings and Notifications generated by data checking process				
5	Original Data Report	Original Data Report				0.94
6	Summary 1	Summary table 1: Labour market summary table				1.03
7	Summary 2	Summary table 2: Labour market summary table, by sex				1.06
8	Table 1	Table 1: Population by sex and age group	TABLE_SE	TABLE_FREQ		5.47
9	Table 2	Table 2: Population by sex and region	TABLE_SE	TABLE_FREQ		3.76
10	Table 3	Table 3: Population living in urban and rural areas by sex	TABLE_SE	TABLE_FREQ		1.45
11	Table 4	Table 4: Working-age population by sex	TABLE_SE	TABLE_FREQ		0.61
12	Table 5	Table 5: Working-age population by sex and region	TABLE_SE	TABLE_FREQ		3.90
13	Table 6	Table 6: Labour force and labour force participation rate, by sex and age group	TABLE_SE	TABLE_FREQ		9.24
14	Table 7	Table 7: Labour force and labour force participation rate, by sex and region	TABLE_SE	TABLE_FREQ		10.37
15	Table 8a	Table 8a: Labour force by educational attainment, by age group	TABLE_SE	TABLE_FREQ		5.11
16	Table 8b	Table 8b: Labour force by educational attainment, by sex and age group	TABLE_SE	TABLE_FREQ		15.94
17	Table 9	Table 9: Labour force by educational attainment, by region	TABLE_SE	TABLE_FREQ		9.37
18	Table 12	Table 12: Employment and employment-to-population ratio, by sex and age group	TABLE_SE	TABLE_FREQ		4.61
19	Table 13	Table 13: Employment and employment-to-population ratio, by sex and region	TABLE_SE	TABLE_FREQ		9.42
20	Table 14a	Table 14a: Status in employment by age group	TABLE_SE	TABLE_FREQ		3.24
21	Table 32	Table 32: Time-related underemployment, by sex and age group	TABLE_SE	TABLE_FREQ		9.39
22	Table 35	Table 35: Unemployment and unemployment rate, by sex and age group	TABLE_SE	TABLE_FREQ		2.41
23	Table 36	Table 36: Unemployment and unemployment rate, by sex and region	TABLE_SE	TABLE_FREQ		3.53
24	Table 39	Table 39: Share of youth in total unemployment and share of youth unemployed in youth population, by sex and region	TABLE_SE	TABLE_FREQ		9.07
25	Table 40	Table 40: Ratio of youth-to-adult unemployment rate, by sex and region				0.45
26	Table 41	Table 41: Youth not in education, employment or training (NEET), by sex and region	TABLE_SE	TABLE_FREQ		3.78
27	Total time (seconds)					114.13

Contents   Notifications   Original Data Report   Summary 1   Summary 2   Table 1   **Table 1_SE**   Table 1_FREQ   ... ⊕

All system messages indicated by the ADePT software while preparing the output Excel file are stored in the notification table, which presents error, warning, and notification messages. To alert users about problems that occurred during the production of content tables, the color of the notification sheet changes to yellow for warnings and to red for error messages.

The notifications produced by the system have *no impact* on the content of tables. They alert users to potential problems (e.g., identifying outliers) and remind users of parameters or values applied by the software that were not sufficiently specified in the input dataset, but reflect users' assumptions of output tables. For example, the system assumes that value 1 of the variable *Sex* in the input dataset is "male."

Other examples are included in screenshot 3.2.

Screenshot 3.2: Example of ADePT-LMI Notification Table

1	**Errors, Warnings and Notifications generated by data checking process**
3	
4	Checking variables in Data1:
5	Urban — Note: in variable urban value 1 was assumed to mean "Urban"
6	Gender — Note: in variable sex value 1 was assumed to mean "Male"
7	**Status in employment** — **Suspected outliers with code(s): 5 - in variable status**
8	Contributing family workers — In variable status value 1 was assumed to mean "Yes"
9	**Status in employment in SJ** — **Suspected outliers with code(s): 5 - in variable second_status**
10	**Age** — **some respondents might be too young for education level - Secondary**
11	
12	
13	

Contents | **Notifications** | Table 1 | Table 2 ... ⊕

Original Data Report Table

The original data report table provides a useful overview on the input datasets loaded into the ADePT-LMI module. The original data report lists all the variables used to produce the output tables, along with the sample size (denoted "N"), the average value of each variable (mean), the minimum and maximum values for each variable values for the 1st, 50th, and 99th percentiles (p1, p50, p99, respectively). The column labeled "N_unique" shows the total number of observations with unique identifiers. The example in screenshot 3.3 shows 3,308

Screenshot 3.3: Example of ADePT-LMI Original Data Report

		N	mean	min	max	p1	p50	p99	N_unique
1	Original Data Report								
3	Data1 I:\COMMON\A6 Microdatasets_ADePT_HIES2 for ADePT.dta								
4	identif (Household ID)	14,789	2,615,383.0	1,000,201.0	4,124,708.0	1,003,902.0	3,014,108.0	4,119,908.0	3,308
5	wta_hh (Household weights)	14,789	161.9	34.9	776.7	36.8	155.3	327.5	76
6	urban (Urban)	14,789	1.4	1.0	2.0	1.0	1.0	2.0	2
7	region (Regions)	14,789	3.1	1.0	5.0	1.0	3.0	5.0	5
8	age (Age)	14,789	26.2	0.0	98.0	0.0	22.0	76.0	95
9	sex (Gender)	14,789	1.5	1.0	2.0	1.0	2.0	2.0	2
10	educ (Education completed)	12,416	3.4	1.0	7.0	1.0	3.0	7.0	7
11	enrolled (Enrolled in education)	11,958	2.2	1.0	3.0	1.0	3.0	3.0	3
12	lfstat	14,789	2.3	1.0	3.0	1.0	3.0	3.0	3
13	lfstat==1 (Employed)	9,584	0.5	0.0	1.0	0.0	1.0	1.0	2
14	lfstat==2 (Unemployed)	9,584	0.0	0.0	1.0	0.0	0.0	1.0	2
15	lfstat==3 (Economically inactive)	14,789	0.6	0.0	1.0	0.0	1.0	1.0	2
16	reason_inactivity (Reason for inactivity)	6,093	5.7	1.0	8.0	1.0	7.0	8.0	8
17	status (Status in employment)	3,246	1.5	1.0	5.0	1.0	1.0	3.0	4
18	status	3,246	1.5	1.0	5.0	1.0	1.0	3.0	4
19	status==3 (Own-account workers)	3,246	0.3	0.0	1.0	0.0	0.0	1.0	2
20	status==4 (Contributing family workers)	3,246	0.0	0.0	0.0	0.0	0.0	0.0	1
21	occupation (Occupation)	3,246	4.9	1.0	10.0	1.0	5.0	9.0	10
22	sector (Sector)	3,246	8.7	1.0	15.0	1.0	10.0	15.0	15
23	sector_broad (Broad sector)	3,246	2.8	1.0	4.0	1.0	3.0	4.0	4
24	secondary (Secondary job (SJ))	14,789	0.0	0.0	1.0	0.0	0.0	1.0	2
25	second_status (Status in employment in SJ)	168	2.7	1.0	5.0	1.0	3.0	3.0	4
26	public (Public sector employment)	2,348	0.7	0.0	1.0	0.0	1.0	1.0	2
27	Generated (Household size)	14,789	5.3	1.0	14.0	1.0	5.0	11.0	14
29	Note: The numbers in this table are unweighted								
30									
31									

Contents | Notifications | **Original Data Report** | Summary 1 | Summary 2 ... ⊕

Source: Mongolia Living Standards Measurement Survey 2002–2003.

households with unique identifiers. Users should review the original data report before starting analysis.

Data Output Tables

ADePT data output tables cover six broad categories of demographic and labor market indicators:

- Population
- Labor force
- Employment
- Unemployment and labor underutilization
- Working poverty
- Earnings.

Population Indicator Tables (Five Tables)

Population indicators provide information on the population size and structure, the distribution of the population across regions and in rural versus urban areas, and the proportion of the population that is of working age (which provides an indication of the potential workforce). Changes in a country's population structure can also influence aggregate changes in labor market indicators. For instance, as labor force participation and unemployment rates and employment-to-population ratios often vary significantly across age groups and by sex, changes in the demographic structure of a country can lead to changes in the value of these indicators over time.

Table 1: Population by Sex and Age Group

Table 1 (screenshot 3.4) provides an overview of the distribution of the population by age cohorts and sex. The table's data are benchmark data for the calculation and analysis of key labor market indicators.

Screenshot 3.4 shows that Mongolia's population is very young, with more than half of the population aged 29 or younger in 2009. The distribution by sex indicates a particularly high share of young men (11.6 percent) and women (10.4 percent) ages 15–19 in the population. This information is important

Screenshot 3.4: Table 1: Population by Sex and Age Group, Mongolia, 2009

		Male	Female	Both sexes	Male	Female	Both sexes
1	Table 1: Population by sex and age						
2	Mongolia LFS 2009						
3		Male	Female	Both sexes	Male	Female	Both sexes
4	Population ('000s)				Population distribution (%)		
5	0-4	92.0	95.9	187.9	8.1	8.1	8.1
6	5-9	105.5	100.0	205.5	9.3	8.4	8.9
7	10-14	123.3	108.9	232.2	10.9	9.2	10.0
8	15-19	131.6	123.1	254.7	11.6	10.4	11.0
9	20-24	108.3	119.1	227.4	9.6	10.0	9.8
10	25-29	96.5	100.1	196.6	8.5	8.4	8.5
11	30-34	87.5	95.8	183.3	7.7	8.1	7.9
12	35-39	83.6	98.1	181.7	7.4	8.3	7.8
13	40-44	78.7	85.4	164.1	6.9	7.2	7.1
14	45-49	71.6	83.4	155.0	6.3	7.0	6.7
15	50-54	52.4	58.9	111.4	4.6	5.0	4.8
16	55-59	31.6	35.6	67.2	2.8	3.0	2.9
17	60-64	24.3	26.9	51.1	2.1	2.3	2.2
18	65-69	20.2	24.5	44.7	1.8	2.1	1.9
19	70-74	12.9	13.2	26.1	1.1	1.1	1.1
20	75-79	9.3	10.0	19.3	0.8	0.8	0.8
21	80-84	2.5	4.6	7.1	0.2	0.4	0.3
22	85-89	1.4	3.4	4.7	0.1	0.3	0.2
23	90-94	0.2	1.6	1.8	0.0	0.1	0.1
24	95-	0.1	0.3	0.4	0.0	0.0	0.0
25	Total	1,133.5	1,188.7	2,322.2	100.0	100.0	100.0

Source: Mongolia Labour Force Survey 2009.

for policy makers and planners since these young people may require jobs that suit their set of skills when entering the labor force or may need further education and training opportunities. Additional policy measures might try to match the labor supply and demand of young people in the country.

Table 2: Population by Sex and Region

Table 2 (screenshot 3.5) presents data on the distribution of the population across a country's regions. This example shows that the majority of Mongolians live in the capital, Ulaanbaatar (36.6 percent in 2009).

Screenshot 3.5: Table 2: Population by Sex and Region, Mongolia, 2008 and 2009

	Mongolia LFS 2008			Mongolia LFS 2009			Change		
	Male	Female	Both sexes	Male	Female	Both sexes	Male	Female	Both sexes
Population ('000s)									
West region	188.8	184.7	373.5	183.8	181.3	365.1	-5.0	-3.5	-8.4
Khangai region	253.2	257.2	510.4	256.5	266.7	523.2	3.3	9.5	12.9
Central region	196.1	206.5	402.6	198.8	199.4	398.1	2.7	-7.2	-4.4
East region	82.3	89.5	171.8	94.7	90.3	185.0	12.4	0.7	13.2
Ulaanbaatar	378.5	418.0	796.5	399.7	451.1	850.8	21.2	33.1	54.3
Total	1,098.8	1,156.0	2,254.8	1,133.5	1,188.7	2,322.2	34.7	32.7	67.4
Population distribution (%)									
West region	17.2	16.0	16.6	16.2	15.2	15.7	-1.0	-0.7	-0.8
Khangai region	23.0	22.3	22.6	22.6	22.4	22.5	-0.4	0.2	-0.1
Central region	17.8	17.9	17.9	17.5	16.8	17.1	-0.3	-1.1	-0.7
East region	7.5	7.7	7.6	8.4	7.6	8.0	0.9	-0.2	0.3
Ulaanbaatar	34.4	36.2	35.3	35.3	37.9	36.6	0.8	1.8	1.3
Total	100.0	100.0	100.0	100.0	100.0	100.0	0.0	0.0	0.0

Sources: Mongolia Labour Force Surveys 2008 and 2009.

Further, comparing columns reveals that the Mongolian population increased from 2.25 million to 2.32 million between 2008 and 2009 (shown in the column "Change").

Screenshot 3.5 also shows that between 2008 and 2009, major population shifts occurred from the western and central regions to Ulaanbaatar. Geographic population shifts may be an indication of labor migration. Joint analysis of tables 2, 3, and 13 (which pertains to South Africa) provides additional insights on this topic (screenshots 3.5, 3.6, and 3.18, respectively).

Table 3: Population Living in Urban and Rural Areas by Sex

Table 3 (screenshot 3.6) seeks to understand changes in population distribution and population growth patterns in countries. The industrialization process usually accompanies shifts in the distribution of the population from rural to urban centers since industrial production centers are often based in urban areas.

As seen in screenshot 3.6, the distribution of the population in Mongolia changed between 2008 and 2009 due to population growth and other social factors. The share of the urban population increased from 56.8 percent to 57.5 percent while the rural population decreased from 43.2 percent to 42.5 percent between 2008 and 2009 (numbers in the table are rounded).

Screenshot 3.6: Table 3: Population Living in Urban and Rural Areas by Sex, Mongolia, 2008 and 2009

	Table 3: Population living in urban and rural areas by sex					
	Mongolia LFS 2008			Mongolia LFS 2009		
	Urban	Rural	Total	Urban	Rural	Total
Population ('000s)						
Male	613.5	485.3	1,098.8	639.3	494.2	1,133.5
Female	666.9	489.0	1,156.0	695.3	493.4	1,188.7
Both sexes	1,280.4	974.3	2,254.8	1,334.6	987.6	2,322.2
Population distribution (%)						
Male	55.8	44.2	100.0	56.4	43.6	100.0
Female	57.7	42.3	100.0	58.5	41.5	100.0
Both sexes	56.8	43.2	100.0	57.5	42.5	100.0

Sources: Mongolia Labour Force Surveys 2008 and 2009.

Table 4: Working-Age Population by Sex

The working-age population indicator in table 4 (screenshots 3.7 and 3.8) gives an estimate of the total number of potential workers within an economy. Each country may have a different definition for the working age, but the ages of 15 and above are commonly used. This definition is the default working age in the ADePT-LMI module and is the standard for this user guide.

Working-age population estimates for Greece in 2008 (screenshot 3.7) show a significantly higher share of females (51.2 percent) in the working-age population as compared to men (48.8 percent). These differences are

Screenshot 3.7: Table 4: Working-Age Population by Sex, Greece, 2008

Table 4: Working-age population by sex	
	Greece LFS 2008
Working-age population ('000s)	
Male	4,504.7
Female	4,729.3
Both sexes	9,234.1
Working-age population distribution (%)	
Male	48.8
Female	51.2
Both sexes	100.0

Source: Greece Labour Force Survey 2008.
Note: The data refer to the average of Q1 to Q4 of the quarterly LFS for 2008.

Screenshot 3.8: Table 4: Working-Age Population by Sex, Timor-Leste, 2010

1	**Table 4: Working-age population by sex**
2	Timor-Leste, LFS 2010
3	**Working-age population ('000s)**
4	Male 317.6
5	Female 310.8
7	Both sexes 628.3
9	**Working-age population distribution (%)**
10	Male 50.5
11	Female 49.5
13	Both sexes 100.0

Source: Timor-Leste Labour Force Survey 2010.

mainly driven by unequal life expectancies for men and women. According to the Eurostat estimates for 2010, Greek women live 82.3 years on average, while men live to be 77.7 on average.[1]

In the case of Timor-Leste (screenshot 3.8), the distribution of the working-age population shows a slightly higher share of men (50.5 percent) than women (49.5 percent) of working age, which is due to low life expectancy particularly for women, as well as high infant mortality (World Bank 2008). If one sex is more likely to emigrate from a country in search of work, this would also affect the relative shares of men and women in the working-age population.

Table 5: Working-Age Population by Sex and Region

The distribution of the working-age population by sex and region can help to determine areas with the most human resources. Table 5 (screenshot 3.9) considers all individuals of working age in a region, without differentiating between individuals who are working and those who are unemployed or outside the labor force.

For example, in Timor-Leste (screenshot 3.9) the majority of the working-age population (24.6 percent in 2010) are in the capital, Dili. Increasing shares of working-age people in urban centers are very common, especially in emerging economies that follow the development pattern in which workers shift out of agriculture and into the industry and services sectors. It is often the case that young people disproportionately move from rural to urban areas to find nonagricultural jobs.

Screenshot 3.9: Table 5: Working-Age Population by Sex and Region, Timor-Leste, 2010

	Table 5: Working-age population by sex and region Timor-Leste, LFS 2010		
	Male	**Female**	**Both sexes**
Working-age population ('000s)			
Ainaro	17.6	17.4	34.9
Aileu	12.4	10.5	22.9
Baucau	33.6	30.9	64.5
Bobonaro	25.7	26.0	51.6
Covalima	17.8	18.1	35.9
Dili	78.7	75.6	154.3
Ermera	30.4	30.4	60.8
Liquica	22.1	21.1	43.2
Lautem	16.3	18.2	34.4
Manufahi	14.5	13.9	28.4
Manatuto	12.0	10.6	22.6
Oecusse	19.4	20.1	39.5
Viqueque	17.2	18.1	35.3
Total	317.6	310.8	628.3
Working-age population distribution (%)			
Ainaro	5.5	5.6	5.6
Aileu	3.9	3.4	3.6
Baucau	10.6	9.9	10.3
Bobonaro	8.1	8.4	8.2
Covalima	5.6	5.8	5.7
Dili	24.8	24.3	24.6
Ermera	9.6	9.8	9.7
Liquica	7.0	6.8	6.9
Lautem	5.1	5.8	5.5
Manufahi	4.6	4.5	4.5
Manatuto	3.8	3.4	3.6
Oecusse	6.1	6.5	6.3
Viqueque	5.4	5.8	5.6
Total	100.0	100.0	100.0

Source: Timor-Leste Labour Force Survey 2010.

Labor Force Indicator Tables (Seven Tables)

The labor force indicators provide information on a country's working-age population that engages actively in the labor market (e.g., the employed and those seeking employment). These provide an indication of the relative supply of labor available to engage in the production of goods and services, with tables also providing information on the educational levels of different segments of the labor force. Additional information is provided by the breakdown of the labor force by sex and age group.

Table 6: Labor Force and Labor Force Participation Rate by Sex and Age Group

Table 6 (screenshot 3.10) contains labor force participation rate estimates according to the following standardized age groups: 15–19, 20–24, 25–29, 30–34, 35–39, 40–44, 45–49, 50–54, 55–59, 60–64, and 65+.

One way of eliminating the confounding effect of a changing age distribution of a population on changes in aggregate labor force participation is to focus *not* on changes in the participation rate of the entire population, but on changes in the participation rate of specific age groups. Therefore, table 6 (screenshot 3.10) compares, for example, the participation rate of those ages 15–19 with the rate of those ages 25–29. Thus, users can analyze trends in participation across groups (e.g., age- and sex-specific) in addition to examining summary measures of participation for a society.

Labor force participation rates are typically lower for females than for males in each age category. One classic reason is the difference in life cycles of women and men still observed in many parts of the world, whereby women in the prime age tend to leave the labor force to give birth and raise children and men work to secure an income for the family.

Analysis of table 6 (screenshot 3.10) shows significant differences in labor force participation rates between women and men throughout all age groups in Timor-Leste in 2010. Large discrepancies might reflect the lack of social security schemes and social values and norms that keep women out of the labor force. However, child-rearing is also an important factor, since the most significant gender-based participation gaps are estimated for 30- to 34-year-olds, whereby the participation rate for men, at 87.1 percent, is more than double the rate for women (35.8 percent). In general, when mothers reenter the labor market after

Screenshot 3.10: Table 6: Labor Force and Labor Force Participation Rate by Sex and Age Group, Timor-Leste, 2010

	Table 6: Labour force and labour force participation rate, by sex and age group Timor-Leste, LFS 2010		
	Male	Female	Both sexes
Labour force ('000s)			
15-19	4.6	2.7	7.3
20-24	13.4	7.3	20.7
25-29	20.1	9.4	29.5
30-34	20.6	9.8	30.4
35-39	28.9	11.5	40.4
40-44	25.4	11.5	37.0
45-49	19.1	10.5	29.6
50-54	14.2	7.3	21.5
55-59	10.4	5.6	16.0
60-64	12.1	5.0	17.1
65+	9.5	3.8	13.4
Total	178.4	84.3	262.8
Labour force participation rate (%)			
15-19	7.6	4.6	6.1
20-24	31.6	19.0	25.6
25-29	69.3	28.1	47.3
30-34	87.1	35.8	59.5
35-39	86.4	37.1	62.7
40-44	87.2	42.4	65.6
45-49	85.4	47.0	66.3
50-54	77.8	40.4	59.2
55-59	77.5	46.4	62.8
60-64	62.3	25.3	43.6
65+	36.7	16.5	27.2
Total	56.2	27.1	41.8

Source: Timor-Leste Labour Force Survey 2010.

their children are older, they do so at a much lower rate than that of men in the same age group.

In developed economies (e.g., Greece) or former communist states (e.g., Mongolia), the profile of female labor force participation is often more similar to that of males, with greater equality in terms of job opportunities in the labor market (table 3.1).

Table 3.1: Comparison of Results from ADePT Output, Table 6

Labor force participation rate (%)	Male	Female	Gender gap
Timor-Leste LFS 2010			
15–19	7.6	4.6	3.0
20–24	31.6	19.0	12.6
25–29	69.3	28.1	41.2
30–34	87.1	35.8	51.3
35–39	86.4	37.1	49.3
40–44	87.2	42.4	44.7
45–49	85.4	47.0	38.4
50–54	77.8	40.4	37.4
55–59	77.5	46.4	31.1
60–64	62.3	25.3	37.1
65+	36.7	16.5	20.1
Total	56.2	27.1	29.0
Mongolia LFS 2009			
15–19	17.7	14.8	2.9
20–24	56.3	43.3	13.0
25–29	83.6	68.2	15.5
30–34	85.4	76.1	9.3
35–39	87.4	77.7	9.7
40–44	86.4	79.9	6.5
45–49	82.6	74.8	7.7
50–54	75.2	59.6	15.7
55–59	63.9	35.4	28.5
60–64	32.9	20.0	12.9
65+	18.3	8.9	9.4
Total	63.5	53.8	9.6
Greece LFS 2008			
15–19	10.6	7.1	3.5
20–24	55.6	45.0	10.6
25–29	90.7	76.8	13.8
30–34	97.2	73.5	23.7
35–39	97.1	73.1	24.0
40–44	96.9	72.7	24.2
45–49	95.2	65.2	30.0
50–54	88.6	54.5	34.1
55–59	76.5	37.8	38.7
60–64	45.4	19.8	25.6
65+	7.1	2.1	5.1
Total	64.9	42.6	22.3

Sources: Labor force surveys of the respective countries.
Note: The gender gap is the difference between the male and female labor force participation rates in percentage points.

Table 7: Labor Force and Labor Force Participation Rate by Sex and Region

Table 7 (screenshot 3.11) presents labor force figures and participation rates broken down by region and sex so users can analyze regional disparities in the female and male labor force. Analysis of LFS data for Timor-Leste illustrates the varied labor force participation among Timor-Leste's regions, with the highest participation rates in the very remote and rural Ainaro (56.2 percent in 2010) and Ermera (55.4 percent in 2010) regions, and significantly lower participation rates in urban hubs such as Dili (41.4 percent in 2010).

The divide between rural and urban labor force participation rates is very common in less developed countries and less pronounced in more developed economies. One theory behind this is that economic development can be associated with shifts from labor-intensive agriculture to more urban manufacturing and service-oriented economic activities. The shifts usually go hand-in-hand with a rise in earning opportunities, particularly for the prime working-age group (25–54). The increased income of heads of urban households allows members with lower earning potential to choose not to work or to continue with education and training (which is also available through better educational and training facilities in urban centers). When combined, these factors tend to lower the overall labor force participation rate for both men and women in urban areas.

Table 8a: Labor Force by Educational Attainment and Age Group

Tables 8a, 8b, and 9 (screenshots 3.12, 3.13, and 3.14, respectively) reflect the levels and distribution of the knowledge and skills base of the labor force in a country. Overall, the analysis of educational attainment of the labor force can provide an indication of the available human capital of countries to achieve social and economic goals.

Analysis of the labor force by educational attainment and age group in Timor-Leste (screenshot 3.12) shows that out of 100 employed or unemployed persons, 44.1 percent had no education in 2010. To be in the labor force without education was particularly common among the older Timorese generation: 76 percent of those ages 55–64 and 90.4 percent of persons ages 65 and above did not complete pre-primary education While younger generations have higher levels of educational attainment, large shares of workers have less than a secondary-level education.

Screenshot 3.11: Table 7: Labor Force and Labor Force Participation Rate by Sex and Region, Timor-Leste, 2010

	Table 7: Labour force and labour force participation rate, by sex and region		
1			
2	Timor-Leste, LFS 2010		
3	Male	Female	Both sexes
4	**Labour force ('000s)**		
5 Ainaro	12.3	7.3	19.6
6 Aileu	7.1	4.2	11.2
7 Baucau	10.7	4.8	15.5
8 Bobonaro	17.9	9.7	27.7
9 Covalima	11.4	4.0	15.4
10 Dili	43.8	20.0	63.8
11 Ermera	21.5	12.2	33.7
12 Liquica	11.3	4.8	16.1
13 Lautem	8.0	3.7	11.7
14 Manufahi	10.0	5.6	15.5
15 Manatuto	6.7	1.8	8.5
16 Oecusse	11.4	4.2	15.6
17 Viqueque	6.4	2.0	8.4
18			
19 Total	178.4	84.3	262.8
20			
21	**Labour force participation rate (%)**		
22 Ainaro	70.1	42.1	56.2
23 Aileu	56.8	39.8	49.1
24 Baucau	31.7	15.6	24.0
25 Bobonaro	69.9	37.5	53.6
26 Covalima	63.9	22.3	42.9
27 Dili	55.7	26.4	41.4
28 Ermera	70.5	40.3	55.4
29 Liquica	51.3	22.7	37.3
30 Lautem	49.0	20.4	33.9
31 Manufahi	68.9	40.0	54.7
32 Manatuto	56.2	17.0	37.7
33 Oecusse	58.9	20.9	39.5
34 Viqueque	37.0	11.1	23.7
35			
36 Total	56.2	27.1	41.8

Source: Timor-Leste Labour Force Survey 2010.

Screenshot 3.12: Table 8a: Labor Force by Educational Attainment and Age Group, Timor-Leste, 2010

	Pre-primary	Primary	Pre-secondary	Secondary	Technical Secondary	Vocational course	Polytechnic/Diploma	University	None
Table 8a: Labour force by educational attainment, by age group									
Timor-Leste, LFS 2010									
Labour force ('000s)									
15-24	1.4	6.0	4.0	8.2	0.1	0.1	0.1	0.2	7.9
25-34	1.9	12.4	7.1	19.0	0.6	0.3	1.2	2.6	14.7
35-44	3.7	15.7	8.6	16.3	1.4	0.2	1.6	2.4	27.5
45-54	2.1	10.6	2.6	5.6	0.7	0.2	0.5	0.4	28.5
55-64	1.0	3.9	1.0	1.3	0.2	0.1	0.1	0.3	25.2
65+	0.1	0.8	0.0	0.2	0.0		0.0	0.1	12.1
15+	10.3	49.4	23.4	50.6	3.1	0.8	3.6	5.9	115.8
Share of the labour force (%)									
15-24	5.1	21.3	14.3	29.4	0.5	0.2	0.5	0.5	28.2
25-34	3.2	20.7	11.9	31.8	0.9	0.5	2.1	4.3	24.6
35-44	4.8	20.3	11.1	21.1	1.9	0.3	2.0	3.1	35.5
45-54	4.1	20.7	5.1	10.9	1.3	0.3	1.0	0.8	55.8
55-64	3.1	11.8	3.1	3.8	0.7	0.3	0.3	0.8	76.0
65+	1.1	6.2	0.2	1.5	0.0	0.0	0.0	0.5	90.4
15+	3.9	18.8	8.9	19.2	1.2	0.3	1.4	2.2	44.1

Source: Timor-Leste Labour Force Survey 2010.

The results underscore the need for a national vision and comprehensive education and skills development as well as lifelong learning (LLL)[2] policies to improve the productivity and employability of Timorese, and to sustain economic and social development in the long run. National policies should ensure quality education for all while strengthening an integrated education and training system relevant to the needs of people and the labor market.

Table 8b: Labor Force by Educational Attainment by Sex and Age Group

Gender-disaggregated analysis of the labor force by educational attainment and age group, as presented in table 8b (screenshot 3.13), indicates the degree of inequality in the distribution of skills and educational resources between men and women of a certain age in the labor force. Therefore, table 8b goes beyond the information in table 8a (screenshot 3.12) and is especially useful to determine gender gaps in the labor force. Also, it reflects a gender-sensitive picture of the skill structure of a country's labor force and can support analysis of the influence of skill levels on economic outcomes and the success of policies and programs in raising the educational level of the labor force.

Table 8b (screenshot 3.13), based on the LFS 2010 for Timor-Leste, reveals large discrepancies in educational attainment between men and women in the labor force. Overall, educational attainment of the female labor force is far lower than that of men, throughout all age groups, with the most pronounced differences in the Timorese generation ages 45 years and older.

Screenshot 3.13: Table 8b: Labor Force by Educational Attainment, Sex, and Age Group, Timor-Leste, 2010

Table 8b: Labour force by educational attainment, by sex and age group
Timor-Leste, LFS 2010

	Pre-primary		Primary		Pre-secondary		Secondary		Technical Secondary		Vocational course		Polytechnic/Diploma		University		None	
	Male	Female	Male	Female	Male	Female	Male	Female	Male	Female	Male	Female	Male	Female	Male	Female	Male	Female
Labour force ('000s)																		
15-24	1.0	0.4	4.3	1.6	2.5	1.5	4.5	3.8	0.1			0.1	0.0	0.1	0.2	0.0	5.4	2.5
25-34	1.4	0.5	8.7	3.8	4.9	2.2	12.9	6.1	0.4	0.1	0.3	0.0	0.9	0.3	1.7	0.9	9.5	5.2
35-44	3.0	0.7	12.2	3.5	6.5	2.0	12.3	4.0	1.3	0.2	0.1	0.1	1.1	0.5	2.1	0.4	15.8	11.7
45-54	1.8	0.3	8.5	2.1	2.2	0.4	4.7	0.9	0.5	0.1	0.2		0.4	0.1	0.3	0.1	14.9	13.6
55-64	1.0	0.1	3.6	0.3	0.9	0.1	1.0	0.2	0.2		0.0	0.1	0.1		0.1	0.2	15.5	9.7
65+	0.1	0.0	0.8	0.0	0.0						0.0				0.1		8.4	3.7
15+	8.3	2.0	38.1	11.2	17.1	6.3	35.4	15.2	2.6	0.5	0.6	0.3	2.5	1.1	4.4	1.5	69.5	46.3
Share of the labour force (%)																		
15-24	71.0	29.0	72.9	27.1	63.1	36.9	54.1	45.9	100.0	0.0	0.0	100.0	0.0	100.0	100.0	0.0	68.2	31.8
25-34	71.1	28.9	69.7	30.3	69.1	30.9	67.7	32.3	77.7	22.3	95.5	4.5	74.6	25.4	66.7	33.3	64.7	35.3
35-44	81.0	19.0	77.8	22.2	76.4	23.6	75.3	24.7	87.0	13.0	46.3	53.7	70.3	29.7	84.8	15.2	57.5	42.5
45-54	84.8	15.2	80.0	20.0	84.1	15.9	83.8	16.2	78.2	21.8	100.0	0.0	72.9	27.1	81.8	18.2	52.2	47.8
55-64	94.6	5.4	93.3	6.7	87.5	12.5	82.1	17.9	100.0	0.0	11.8	88.2	100.0	0.0	39.2	60.8	61.6	38.4
65+	100.0	0.0	100.0	0.0	100.0	0.0	35.8	64.2			0.0	100.0			100.0	0.0	69.4	30.6
15+	80.2	19.8	77.2	22.8	73.2	26.8	70.0	30.0	84.7	15.3	67.7	32.3	70.2	29.8	75.2	24.8	60.0	40.0

Source: Timor-Leste Labour Force Survey 2010.
Note: Empty spaces reflect missing values for the particular group.

Since low educational attainment and skills levels of women often lead to large gender imbalances in decent work opportunities and high rates of informal and vulnerable employment of women in the labor market, it is in the interest of governments to support the education of women and men equally.

Table 9: Labor Force by Educational Attainment and Region

Low educational attainment generally leads to skills gaps and shortages in the labor force. The large proportion of rural people with hardly any education is of particular concern for Timor-Leste, since low educational attainment is associated with low productivity and insufficient income levels. Furthermore, illiteracy impedes the trainability of the labor force, and therefore hinders the capacity of the labor market to adapt to change. This hindrance can be reinforced if, as some research indicates, employers are less likely to provide training to their workers in countries in which the quality of education is poor (Colombano and Krkoska 2006).

Regional disaggregation of educational attainment of the Timorese labor force in 2010 shows that educational attainment was particularly low in the rural labor force (table 9, screenshot 3.14). The highest share of the labor force without formal education (69.1 percent in 2010) was in Oecusse. It was more than three times as high as the share estimated for the labor force in urban Dili (19.2 percent in 2010).

Screenshot 3.14: Table 9: Labor Force by Educational Attainment and Region, Timor-Leste, 2010

Table 9: Labour force by educational attainment, by region
Timor-Leste, LFS 2010

	Pre-primary	Primary	Pre-secondary	Secondary	Technical Secondary	Vocational course	Polytechnic/Diploma	University	None	Total
Labour force ('000s)										
Ainaro	0.4	3.4	2.1	2.8			0.0	0.2	10.8	19.6
Aileu	0.7	1.9	0.6	1.5	0.0	0.1	0.1	0.2	6.1	11.2
Baucau	0.3	3.0	1.1	2.6	1.0	0.0	0.4	0.2	6.7	15.5
Bobonaro	1.1	5.3	2.0	3.5	0.1	0.1	0.1	0.2	15.3	27.7
Covalima	0.0	2.9	2.0	3.5	0.0	0.2	0.1	0.1	6.5	15.4
Dili	2.3	12.4	8.1	22.0	0.5	0.3	1.9	3.9	12.3	63.8
Ermera	1.1	7.7	2.2	3.2			0.1	0.2	19.3	33.7
Liquica	1.9	2.2	1.1	3.2	0.1	0.0	0.1	0.2	7.3	16.1
Lautem	1.3	2.4	0.6	1.6	0.6		0.2	0.1	4.9	11.7
Manufahi	0.5	3.1	1.2	2.6			0.0	0.1	8.0	15.5
Manatuto	0.8	1.2	0.9	1.3	0.1	0.1	0.1	0.1	3.9	8.5
Oecusse	0.0	2.1	0.7	1.4	0.3		0.1	0.1	10.8	15.6
Viqueque		1.7	0.6	1.3	0.3		0.3	0.1	4.0	8.4
Share of the labour force (%)										
Ainaro	1.8	17.1	10.6	14.3	0.0	0.0	0.2	0.9	54.9	100.0
Aileu	6.3	16.6	5.2	13.3	0.1	1.1	0.8	1.9	54.5	100.0
Baucau	2.0	19.6	7.3	16.9	6.6	0.1	2.4	1.6	43.6	100.0
Bobonaro	3.9	19.2	7.2	12.8	0.3	0.3	0.2	0.8	55.3	100.0
Covalima	0.1	19.0	13.3	23.0	0.1	1.1	0.6	0.8	42.1	100.0
Dili	3.6	19.5	12.7	34.5	0.8	0.4	3.0	6.1	19.2	100.0
Ermera	3.2	22.8	6.6	9.4	0.0	0.0	0.4	0.5	57.2	100.0
Liquica	11.6	13.7	6.8	20.1	0.5	0.1	0.6	1.2	45.5	100.0
Lautem	10.8	20.2	5.6	13.4	5.3	0.0	1.9	1.1	41.7	100.0
Manufahi	3.0	20.1	7.7	16.8	0.0	0.0	0.3	0.7	51.4	100.0
Manatuto	9.8	14.5	10.2	14.8	0.6	1.5	0.9	1.7	46.1	100.0
Oecusse	0.0	13.6	4.7	9.0	1.9	0.0	0.9	0.7	69.1	100.0
Viqueque	0.0	20.5	7.5	15.7	3.9	0.0	3.4	1.6	47.4	100.0

Source: Timor-Leste Labour Force Survey 2010.
Note: Empty spaces reflect missing values for the particular group.

Table 10: Labor Force Status by Household Consumption Level

Table 10 (screenshot 3.15) is usually generated on the basis of HIES files. It shows the labor force status of individuals by the consumption quintile of their households. Households with very low per capita consumption are grouped together into the 1st quintile (Q), those with higher consumption into the 2nd quintile, and so on. Five quintiles rank households from the poorest (20 percent) to the richest (20 percent).

There is a common belief that household income or household consumption expenditure depends on the labor force status of people living in the household. In other words, if people in a household have a job they can consume more than if people in the household do not have a job. This might hold true in some developed economies; however, in developing countries, given limited social protection schemes, most of the working-age people in poverty cannot afford not to work and must do so to make a meager living. For these poor workers, the problem is typically one of poor employment quality, including low wages and low levels of labor productivity.

When looking at labor force status by household consumption quintile in Mongolia (screenshot 3.15), one can see that the share of unemployed

Screenshot 3.15: Table 10: Labor Force Status by Household Consumption Level, Mongolia, 2008

	Table 10: Labour force status by household consumption level				
	Mongolia HIES data 2008				
	Q1	Q2	Q3	Q4	Q5
Population ('000s)					
Employed	180.1	209.0	215.2	221.4	237.1
Unemployed	31.9	18.9	16.7	14.4	9.4
Inactive	114.2	117.5	135.4	147.8	156.0
Total	498.1	498.1	498.3	498.0	498.4
Share of the population (%)					
Employed	55.2	60.5	58.6	57.7	58.9
Unemployed	9.8	5.5	4.5	3.7	2.3
Inactive	35.0	34.0	36.9	38.5	38.8
Total	100.0	100.0	100.0	100.0	100.0

Source: Mongolia Household Income and Expenditure Survey 2008.
Note: Q = quintile.

was the most pronounced (9.8 percent in 2008) in the lowest household consumption quintile (Q1). In turn, the share of unemployed was the least (2.3 percent in 2008) in the highest household consumption quintile (Q5), yet the share of employed was the second highest (58.9 percent in 2008), indicating a positive relationship between household consumption and employment in Mongolia.

Higher inactivity rates among more affluent households indicates that these households were more likely to have the necessary resources to allow some household members to remain outside the labor force, perhaps including extending the education of their children or economically supporting older household members.

Table 11: Labor Force Status by Household Consumption Level and Region

Table 11 (screenshot 3.16) looks into the regional differences related to the labor force status of individuals and the consumption of households they are living in. In Mongolia, for example, the labor force status varied significantly across household consumption quintiles and regions in 2008, revealing that the share of employed persons in low-consumption households (Q1 and Q2) was predominant in the remote and rural parts of western Mongolia and in its highlands, reflecting the hardship of people in these areas who have to work but remain among the poorest in the country. See also figure 3.1.

Screenshot 3.16: Table 11: Labor Force Status by Household Consumption Level and Region, Mongolia, 2008

	Q1			Q2			Q3			Q4			Q5		
	Employed	Unemployed	Inactive	Employed	Unemployed	Inactive	Employed	Unemployed	Inactive	Employed	Unemployed	Inactive	Employed	Unemployed	Inactive
Population ('000s)															
West	41.4	7.4	18.1	48.5	3.1	18.0	42.4	2.7	17.5	33.7	1.6	15.9	20.3	0.6	10.5
Highlands	62.5	8.9	28.5	63.1	4.8	29.5	61.1	3.5	29.9	39.8	2.0	23.8	30.0	1.2	18.2
Central	31.0	4.3	14.9	40.9	2.9	16.9	43.2	2.5	20.1	53.5	3.2	23.0	56.3	1.3	23.5
East	19.7	2.6	16.3	20.2	1.5	10.4	15.9	0.9	8.5	17.2	1.0	9.8	12.5	0.4	6.5
UB	25.5	8.7	36.5	36.2	6.6	42.7	52.6	7.1	59.5	77.4	6.5	75.3	118.0	5.9	97.3
Total	180.1	31.9	114.2	209.0	18.9	117.5	215.2	16.7	135.4	221.4	14.4	147.8	237.1	9.4	156.0
Share of the population (%)															
West	23.0	23.3	15.8	23.2	16.2	15.3	19.7	16.4	12.9	15.2	11.2	10.7	8.6	6.5	6.7
Highlands	34.7	27.9	24.9	30.2	25.6	25.1	28.4	20.7	22.1	18.0	14.2	16.1	12.6	13.2	11.7
Central	17.2	13.3	13.0	19.6	15.4	14.4	20.1	15.1	14.8	24.1	22.5	15.6	23.8	13.8	15.0
East	11.0	8.1	14.2	9.7	7.9	8.9	7.4	5.3	6.2	7.8	6.7	6.6	5.3	3.8	4.2
UB	14.2	27.3	32.0	17.3	34.9	36.4	24.4	42.5	44.0	34.9	45.5	51.0	49.8	62.7	62.4
Total	100.0	100.0	100.0	100.0	100.0	100.0	100.0	100.0	100.0	100.0	100.0	100.0	100.0	100.0	100.0

Table 11: Labour force status by household consumption level, by region — Mongolia HIES data 2008

Source: Mongolia Household Income and Expenditure Survey 2008.
Note: Q = quintile; UB = Ulaanbaatar.

Figure 3.1: Labor Force Status by Household Consumption Level and Region, Mongolia, 2008

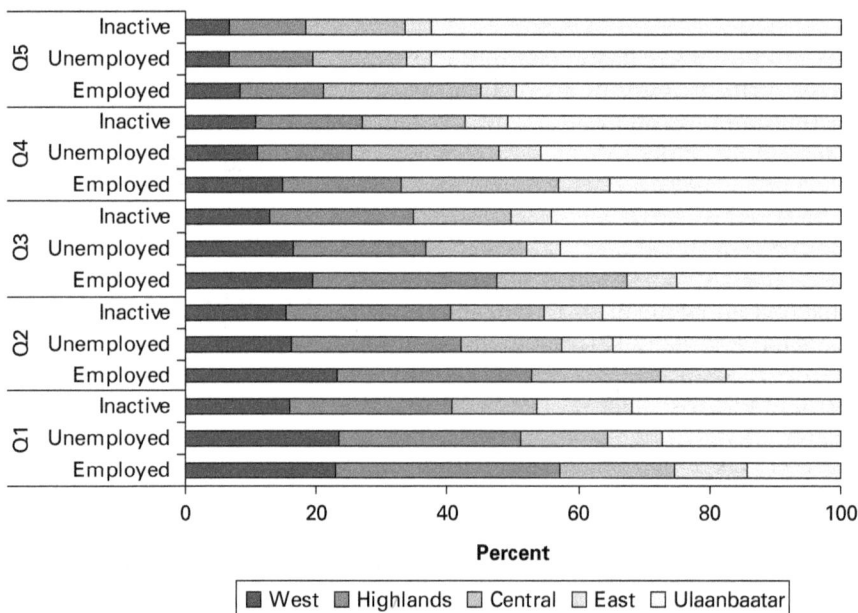

Source: Mongolia Household Income and Expenditure Survey 2008.
Note: Q = quintile.

In contrast, in the highest consumption quintile (Q5) the largest shares of employed were in the capital, Ulaanbaatar (49.8 percent), indicating that employed people in the capital are better off on average in terms of household consumption levels than the employed in remote regions.

Also, 6 out of 10 persons unemployed and outside the labor force in Mongolia lived in high-consumption households (Q5) in Ulaanbaatar, signaling that the working-age people in the capital are much better off economically when compared to their compatriots in the remaining parts of Mongolia.

Employment Tables (28 Tables)

The employment indicators, organized by key areas of employment, can help analysts monitor a range of employment issues at the country level disaggregated by sex, age cohorts, educational level, and region, among others.

Table 12: Employment and Employment-to-Population Ratios by Sex and Age Group

Absolute numbers of the employed population and employment-to-population ratios by sex and age group are shown in table 12 (screenshot 3.17). *Employment* refers to all persons of working age who worked for pay, profit, or family gain during the reference period. It also includes all persons who had a job or enterprise but were absent from that job or enterprise during that period on a temporary basis (e.g., persons who during the reference period were sick, on vacation, on maternity leave, on strike, or were temporarily laid off) (ILO 2013a; ILO 2013b).

Interpreting employment levels alone can be misleading since the number of the employed must be seen as relative to the population. Thus, the employment-to-population ratio is defined as the proportion of the working-age population that is employed. The youth employment-to-population ratio is the proportion of the youth population that is employed (ADePT's default youth category is persons ages 15–24). As an indicator, the employment-to-population ratio provides information on the ability of an economy to create jobs. In addition, it provides insights to the unemployment rate, especially in developing countries where many of the poor cannot afford to be without work. A high ratio implies that a significant proportion of a country's population is employed, while a

Screenshot 3.17: Table 12: Employment and Employment-to-Population Ratio by Sex and Age Group, Greece, 2008

	Table 12: Employment and employment-to-population ratio, by sex and age group			
1				
2			Greece LFS 2008	
3		Male	Female	Both sexes
4	**Employment ('000s)**			
5	15-24	164.4	105.8	270.3
6	25-34	722.4	500.3	1,222.7
7	35-44	795.5	547.5	1,343.0
8	45-54	662.7	424.6	1,087.4
9	55-64	367.6	182.7	550.3
10	65+	62.6	23.1	85.7
11				
12	15+	2,775.3	1,784.1	4,559.4
13				
14	**Employment-to-population ratio (%)**			
15	15-24	28.5	18.5	23.5
16	25-34	86.9	63.7	75.6
17	35-44	93.9	65.8	80.0
18	45-54	89.5	55.7	72.4
19	55-64	59.1	27.5	42.8
20	65+	7.1	2.1	4.3
21				
22	15+	61.6	37.7	49.4

Source: Greece Labour Force Survey 2008.
Note: The data refer to the average of Q1 to Q4 of the quarterly LFS for 2008.

low ratio means that a substantial share of the population is not involved directly in market-related activities, because they are either unemployed or outside of the labor force (formerly known as "inactive"). Employment-to-population ratios are of particular value when broken down by sex and age, since the ratios for men and women of a particular age group can provide information on gender differences in labor market activity in a given country.

The indicator alone is not sufficient to assess all dimensions of decent work or decent work deficits. Employment-to-population ratios do not provide any information on labor market problems such as low earnings, underemployment, poor working conditions, or the existence of a large informal sector. Therefore, the analysis of employment-to-population ratios must be done with other indicators that give more insights on the quality of employment.

For example, of the 4.6 million employed in Greece in 2008 (table 12, screenshot 3.17), men accounted for 2.8 million (60.8 percent) and women 1.8 million (39.1 percent). As calculated from the data in table 12, young people ages 15–24 comprised 5.9 percent of the total employed in 2008, and 56.3 percent of those employed were ages 25–44 in 2008.

The large differences in employment numbers between Greek men and women are also reflected in the employment-to-population ratios, whereby the ratio for men (61.6 percent in 2008) was 23.9 percentage points higher than the ratio for women (37.7 percent in 2008). The largest gender gap (33.8 percentage points) was observed for the age group 45–54 and the smallest for people 65 or older. Gender differences were far less pronounced for youth ages 15–24, with a gap of 9.9 percentage points.

The gap between male and female ratios is often a sign of gender-based differentials in the type of work, wages, and employment conditions, in turn pointing to the multidimensional nature of gender inequalities (ILO 2015).

Table 13: Employment and Employment-to-Population Ratio by Sex and Region

Table 13 (screenshot 3.18) allows users to compare the employment situation and job creation potential across regions. Besides the employed population, table 13 presents the employment-to-population ratios by sex and geographic region.

For example, table 13 (screenshot 3.18), based on Q3-2010 LFS data for South Africa, shows that the largest numbers of the 13.1 million employed South Africans were working in the Gauteng (4.0 million) and KwaZulu-Natal regions (2.4 million). On the contrary, only 0.28 million South Africans worked in the Northern Cape. However, when looking at the employment-to-population ratio, the Northern Cape had a higher ratio than the region of KwaZulu-Natal (35.8 versus 34 percent). The region of Gauteng had the highest employment-to-population ratio, at 49 percent, while Limpopo had the lowest ratio, at 25.7, indicating pronounced regional disparities in employment in South Africa.

Further, the overall employment-to-population ratio for South Africa, at 38 percent in Q3-2010, was significantly lower than the similar ratio

Screenshot 3.18: Table 13: Employment and Employment-to-Population Ratio by Sex and Region, South Africa, Q3-2010

	Male	Female	Both sexes
Table 13: Employment and employment-to-population ratio, by sex and region			
South Africa LFS 3rd Quarter 2010			
	Male	Female	Both sexes
Employment ('000s)			
Western Cape	972.1	798.6	1,770.7
Eastern Cape	699.2	625.8	1,325.1
Northern Cape	157.9	121.9	279.8
Free State	442.2	333.9	776.1
KwaZulu-Natal	1,319.9	1,108.3	2,428.3
North West	431.9	284.9	716.8
Gauteng	2,426.8	1,600.8	4,027.6
Mpumalanga	525.0	380.9	905.9
Limpopo	508.7	407.4	916.1
Total	7,483.8	5,662.7	13,146.5
Employment-to-population ratio (%)			
Western Cape	55.3	41.3	48.0
Eastern Cape	33.9	25.3	29.2
Northern Cape	44.1	28.8	35.8
Free State	45.3	32.5	38.8
KwaZulu-Natal	39.5	29.2	34.0
North West	40.5	25.6	32.9
Gauteng	58.0	39.6	49.0
Mpumalanga	45.1	29.8	37.1
Limpopo	30.9	21.3	25.7
Total	45.2	31.5	38.0

Source: South Africa Labour Force Survey third quarter 2010.

for Greece in 2008 (49.4 percent). The data indicate that a comparatively larger share of the South African population was not involved directly in market-related activities, because they were either unemployed or outside the labor force (table 12, screenshot 3.17, and table 13, screenshot 3.18).

Table 14a: Status in Employment by Age Group

The status-in-employment data in table 14a (screenshot 3.19) distinguish between three categories of employed persons: (a) those working for others and earning a wage or salary on this basis (employees); (b) those who are self-employed, either as employers who hire others to work for them or on their own account; and (c) persons who are contributing family workers (see chapter 2 for the definitions and concepts behind this categorization). This last group works without pay[3] on the family farm or in the family business and, hence, are assisting the business owner or operator in earning profits. These persons are often the spouses, sons, and daughters of the business owner or operator, but also may be members of the extended family.

Using LFS data for Greece in 2008 (screenshot 3.19), table 14a indicates that the majority of Greek workers (64.6 percent) were employed as wage and salaried workers in 2008. Self-employment was far less common, with an employment share of 29.6 percent, and just a small proportion of workers made their living as contributing family workers in 2008.

Screenshot 3.19: Table 14a: Status in Employment by Age Group, Greece, 2008

1			Table 14a: Status in employment by age group		
2			Greece LFS 2008		
3		Employee	Employer	Own-account worker	Contributing family worker	Total
4	**Status in employment ('000s)**					
5	15-24	211.1	4.5	15.9	38.7	270.3
6	25-34	921.2	55.9	176.1	69.6	1,222.7
7	35-44	896.6	126.7	264.6	55.1	1,343.0
8	45-54	660.7	116.3	258.8	51.5	1,087.4
9	55-64	241.4	69.9	201.4	37.7	550.3
10	65+	13.7	12.5	43.2	16.3	85.7
11						
12	15+	2,944.8	385.8	960.0	268.9	4,559.4
13						
14	**Share of status category in total employment (%)**					
15	15-24	78.1	1.7	5.9	14.3	100.0
16	25-34	75.3	4.6	14.4	5.7	100.0
17	35-44	66.8	9.4	19.7	4.1	100.0
18	45-54	60.8	10.7	23.8	4.7	100.0
19	55-64	43.9	12.7	36.6	6.9	100.0
20	65+	16.0	14.6	50.4	19.0	100.0
21						
22	15+	64.6	8.5	21.1	5.9	100.0

Source: Greece Labour Force Survey 2008.
Note: The data refer to the average of Q1 to Q4 of the quarterly LFS for 2008.

However, the indicator on status in employment by age group shows different distributions for the age cohorts. Wage and salaried jobs were more common among young people (ages 15–24) and for people of prime age (ages 25–54). The share of young employees in total youth employment was 78.1 percent. The corresponding share for people ages 25–54 was 67.8 percent, and for people ages 55 and above the share was 40.1 percent. More than half of the workers ages 65 and above were employed as own-account workers (50.4 percent), which indicates higher labor market vulnerabilities for the elderly in Greece (see also the table 16 section about vulnerable employment).

Economies in the early to middle stages of economic development typically have lower shares of wage and salaried workers and higher shares of own-account and contributing family workers in total employment than in a developed economy such as Greece. Both own-account and contributing family workers are viewed as more susceptible to poverty and more likely to lack social protection because of the nature of their work arrangements. Workers in these employment categories therefore require special attention by policy makers (see also the table 16 section about vulnerable employment).

Table 14b: Status in Employment by Sex and Age Group

Table 14b (screenshot 3.20) is meant to probe for gender inequalities in status in employment. Screenshot 3.20 uses LFS data for Timor-Leste in 2010. In contrast to Greece (screenshot 3.19), the majority of employed men and women in Timor-Leste were engaged in nonwage and salaried employment in 2010. Just 32.2 percent of working men and 19.9 percent of working women were working as employees (screenshot 3.20).

Further, table 14b (screenshot 3.20) uncovers significant gender gaps in the status in employment between Timorese women and men, throughout all age groups. Working women were overrepresented in the status groups of own-account workers (45.7 percent in 2010) and contributing family workers (32.4 percent in 2010) when compared to men (38.4 and 27.3, respectively). This table reveals another interesting pattern: the probability that an employed woman in Timor-Leste works as an employee declines with age, while the probability that an employed woman runs her own business increases with age until 55. Moreover, women at all ages have higher shares as contributing family workers

Screenshot 3.20: Table 14b: Status in Employment by Sex and Age Group, Timor-Leste, 2010

Table 14b: Status in employment, by sex and age group
Timor-Leste, LFS 2010

	Male						Female					
	Wage and salaried workers	Employers	Own-account workers	Contributing family workers	Not classifiable	Total	Wage and salaried workers	Employers	Own-account workers	Contributing family workers	Not classifiable	Total
Status in employment ('000s)												
15-24	4.5	0.1	5.7	5.6	0.2	16.1	3.0		1.9	2.8		7.7
25-34	16.3	0.6	13.0	8.3	0.1	38.4	5.5	0.5	7.6	4.3	0.1	18.0
35-44	20.7	1.0	19.3	12.1	0.2	53.2	4.5	0.2	10.9	6.7		22.4
45-54	10.3	0.4	14.2	8.0	0.1	33.0	2.0	0.4	9.1	5.6	0.2	17.4
55-64	3.3	0.6	9.9	8.6		22.4	0.6	0.1	5.3	4.5		10.6
65+	0.6	0.3	4.2	4.4		9.5	0.1	0.1	1.6	1.9		3.7
15+	55.6	3.0	66.3	47.0	0.7	172.6	15.8	1.4	36.5	25.9	0.3	79.8
Share of status category in total employment (%)												
15-24	27.9	0.5	35.3	34.8	1.5	100.0	39.2	0.0	24.3	36.5	0.0	100.0
25-34	42.5	1.5	33.9	21.6	0.4	100.0	30.5	3.0	42.3	23.9	0.4	100.0
35-44	38.9	1.9	36.3	22.7	0.3	100.0	20.3	1.1	48.6	30.0	0.0	100.0
45-54	31.1	1.3	42.9	24.3	0.4	100.0	11.7	2.2	52.6	32.5	1.1	100.0
55-64	14.7	2.5	44.3	38.5	0.0	100.0	6.0	0.9	50.4	42.6	0.0	100.0
65+	5.8	3.2	44.6	46.3	0.0	100.0	2.8	3.2	43.7	50.4	0.0	100.0
15+	32.2	1.7	38.4	27.3	0.4	100.0	19.9	1.7	45.7	32.4	0.3	100.0

Source: Timor-Leste Labour Force Survey 2010.
Note: Empty spaces reflect missing values for the particular group.

than men. The same holds for own-account workers for all age groups except youth (ages 15–24) and workers ages 65 and older. The largest differences between women and men (19.4 percentage points in 2010) were observed for the status in employment group of wage and salaried workers ages 45–54.

Table 15: Status in Employment by Region

Table 15 (screenshot 3.21) was calculated based on LFS data for Mongolia in 2009. The regional breakdown of status in employment data shows substantial regional differences. The share of wage and salaried employment in the capital, Ulaanbaatar (67.9 percent), was more than twice as high as in the remote and rural Khangai region (23.7 percent), where the majority of workers were either own-account (38.3 percent) or contributing family workers (37.7 percent).

The substantial regional differentials in the status in employment of workers in Mongolia point toward important geographic disparities in economic development and employment opportunities. Generally, regions with large shares of self-employed and contributing family workers in particular are likely to suffer from poor development, little formal job growth, and higher poverty rates.

Screenshot 3.21: Table 15: Status in Employment by Region, Mongolia, 2009

	Table 15: Status in employment, by region					
	Mongolia LFS 2009					
	Wage and salaried workers	Employers	Own-account workers	Contributing family workers	Not classifiable	Total
Status in employment ('000s)						
West region	41.4	1.4	63.2	57.6	0.6	164.1
Khangai region	55.4	0.4	89.4	87.9	0.2	233.4
Central region	70.3	1.5	69.4	38.6	0.3	180.2
East region	19.5	0.2	31.1	15.2	0.1	66.1
Ulaanbaatar	196.9	7.9	77.3	7.4	0.6	290.0
Total	383.4	11.4	330.5	206.7	1.8	933.9
Share of status category in total employment (%)						
West region	25.2	0.8	38.5	35.1	0.4	100.0
Khangai region	23.7	0.2	38.3	37.7	0.1	100.0
Central region	39.0	0.8	38.5	21.4	0.2	100.0
East region	29.4	0.3	47.1	23.0	0.1	100.0
Ulaanbaatar	67.9	2.7	26.7	2.5	0.2	100.0
Total	41.1	1.2	35.4	22.1	0.2	100.0

Source: Mongolia Labour Force Survey 2009.

Table 16: Vulnerable Employment by Sex

To reduce poverty and enhance decent work in countries, policy makers and other stakeholders need to identify and monitor vulnerable groups in the labor market. The pressing question is: how can this be done in quantitative terms, while most dimensions are qualitative?

The vulnerable employment indicator is the sum of own-account workers and contributing family workers. Own-account workers and contributing family workers have a lower likelihood of having formal work arrangements, and are therefore more likely to lack elements associated with adequate social security and a voice at work (KILM [Key Indicators of the Labour Market] 3). Wage and salaried workers—as well as employers—are less likely to lack these elements, especially in developed economies.[4]

In 2010, Timor-Leste had a very large proportion of its employment concentrated outside of wage and salaried employment (table 14b, screenshot 3.20). More specifically, taking own-account and contributing family employment together, almost 7 out of 10 workers (69.6 percent of total employment) were in vulnerable employment. Women in particular seem less likely to have formal work arrangements and are therefore more likely to lack elements associated with decent employment. In 2010, the share of vulnerable employment in total female employment was

78.1 percent, which is 12.4 percentage points higher than the corresponding share of men (65.7 percent) (table 16, screenshot 3.22).

In contrast, data from Mongolia in 2008 and 2009 (table 16, screenshot 3.23) show 60.4 percent of men compared to 54.4 percent of working women in vulnerable employment. Further, analysis of LFS data for Mongolia reveals that during 2008 and 2009 the share of vulnerable employment increased by 4.4 percentage points. The causes behind this may include the sharp economic downturn after the collapse of international copper prices in 2008 and the overall unstable macroeconomic situation in the country. An increase in vulnerability was especially high for men (5.8 percentage points) when compared to women (2.9 percentage points).

Screenshot 3.22: Table 16: Vulnerable Employment by Sex, Timor-Leste, 2010

Table 16: Vulnerable employment, by sex	
	Timor-Leste, LFS 2010
Vulnerable employment ('000s)	
Male	113.4
Female	62.3
Both sexes	175.7
Share of vulnerable employment in total employment (%)	
Male	65.7
Female	78.1
Both sexes	69.6

Source: Timor-Leste Labour Force Survey 2010.

Screenshot 3.23: Table 16: Vulnerable Employment by Sex, Mongolia, 2008 and 2009

Table 16: Vulnerable employment, by sex			
	Mongolia LFS 2008	Mongolia LFS 2009	Change
Vulnerable employment ('000s)			
Male	254.4	294.1	39.7
Female	223.7	243.2	19.4
Both sexes	478.1	537.2	59.1
Share of vulnerable employment in total employment (%)			
Male	54.6	60.4	5.8
Female	51.6	54.4	2.9
Both sexes	53.1	57.5	4.4
Note: Changes shown between years Mongolia LFS 2008 and Mongolia LFS 2009			

Sources: Mongolia Labour Force Surveys 2008 and 2009.

Shifts in the proportions of status in employment groups and hence of vulnerable employment are usually associated with shifts in sectoral employment. For example, an increase in the share of wage and salaried workers in total employment often occurs alongside a shift from an agriculture-based economy to a more industrialized and services-based one, since vulnerable employment tends to be associated with a large agriculture sector (KILM 4). To examine whether there has been widespread progress toward nonvulnerable employment, it is advisable to examine the distribution of status in employment across and within the various sectors (KILM 4).

Table 17: Employment by Sector and Sex

Sectoral employment gives insights into the structure of employment (table 17, screenshot 3.24). It refers to employment according to the specific industries (1-digit categories according to the International Standard Industrial Classification of All Economic Activities[5] [ISIC]) where people work, such as agriculture, manufacturing, trade, or services. Sectoral employment estimates are shown for all persons employed, with the percentage of distributions

Screenshot 3.24: Table 17, Part 1: Employment by Sector and Sex, Mongolia, 2008 and 2009

	Table 17: Employment by sector and sex								
		Mongolia LFS 2008			Mongolia LFS 2009			Change		
		Male	Female	Both sexes	Male	Female	Both sexes	Male	Female	Both sexes
4	Employment by sector ('000s)									
5	Agriculture, forestry and fishing	195.3	170.0	365.2	200.6	173.1	373.7	5.3	3.1	8.4
6	Mining and quarrying	20.2	7.0	27.2	17.3	5.6	22.8	-3.0	-1.5	-4.4
7	Manufacturing	30.1	28.1	58.2	26.0	28.1	54.0	-4.1	0.0	-4.1
8	Electricity, gas, steam and air conditioning supply	9.4	4.9	14.3	9.7	2.8	12.6	0.3	-2.1	-1.8
9	Water supply; sewerage, waste management and remediation activities	2.2	2.3	4.6	4.0	2.1	6.1	1.7	-0.2	1.5
10	Construction	24.6	8.1	32.7	33.9	10.1	44.0	9.3	2.0	11.3
11	Wholesale and retail trade; repair of motor vehicles and motorcycles	36.3	58.5	94.7	45.4	67.7	113.0	9.1	9.2	18.3
12	Transportation and storage	44.0	10.0	54.0	49.5	10.5	59.9	5.5	0.4	5.9
13	Accommodation and food service activities	5.4	16.1	21.5	5.1	14.8	19.9	-0.3	-1.2	-1.5
14	Information and communication	6.3	5.1	11.3	6.0	4.9	10.9	-0.2	-0.2	-0.4
15	Financial and insurance activities	5.0	7.7	12.7	5.6	8.3	13.9	0.6	0.6	1.2
16	Real estate activities	0.3	0.4	0.7	0.3	0.1	0.4	0.0	-0.3	-0.3
17	Professional, scientific and technical activities	5.1	5.7	10.7	4.0	3.4	7.5	-1.0	-2.3	-3.3
18	Administrative and support service activities	4.2	3.2	7.4	5.3	4.0	9.3	1.1	0.8	1.9
19	Public administration and defence; compulsory social security	32.0	19.4	51.4	35.0	20.1	55.2	3.0	0.7	3.7
20	Education	22.8	48.5	71.3	19.2	50.1	69.3	-3.6	1.5	-2.1
21	Human health and social work activities	7.9	23.6	31.4	6.4	28.6	35.0	-1.5	5.1	3.6
22	Arts, entertainment and recreation	3.4	3.5	6.9	3.1	3.3	6.4	-0.3	-0.2	-0.5
23	Other service activities	9.1	9.6	18.7	8.2	7.2	15.4	-0.9	-2.3	-3.3
	Activities of households as employers; undifferentiated goods- and services-producing activities of households for	1.8	1.1	2.9	1.4	0.4	1.8	-0.4	-0.7	-1.1

Sources: Mongolia Labour Force Surveys 2008 and 2009.

Screenshot 3.25: Table 17, Part 2: Employment by Sector and Sex, Mongolia, 2008 and 2009

	Table 17: Employment by sector and sex								
		Mongolia LFS 2008			Mongolia LFS 2009			Change		
		Male	Female	Both sexes	Male	Female	Both sexes	Male	Female	Both sexes
29	Sector employment shares (%)									
30	Agriculture, forestry and fishing	41.9	39.2	40.6	41.2	38.7	40.0	-0.7	-0.4	-0.6
31	Mining and quarrying	4.3	1.6	3.0	3.5	1.2	2.4	-0.8	-0.4	-0.6
32	Manufacturing	6.5	6.5	6.5	5.3	6.3	5.8	-1.1	-0.2	-0.7
33	Electricity, gas, steam and air conditioning supply	2.0	1.1	1.6	2.0	0.6	1.3	0.0	-0.5	-0.2
34	Water supply; sewerage, waste management and remediation activities	0.5	0.5	0.5	0.8	0.5	0.7	0.3	-0.1	0.1
35	Construction	5.3	1.9	3.6	7.0	2.3	4.7	1.7	0.4	1.1
36	Wholesale and retail trade; repair of motor vehicles and motorcycles	7.8	13.5	10.5	9.3	15.2	12.1	1.5	1.7	1.6
37	Transportation and storage	9.4	2.3	6.0	10.2	2.3	6.4	0.7	0.0	0.4
38	Accommodation and food service activities	1.2	3.7	2.4	1.1	3.3	2.1	-0.1	-0.4	-0.3
39	Information and communication	1.3	1.2	1.3	1.2	1.1	1.2	-0.1	-0.1	-0.1
40	Financial and insurance activities	1.1	1.8	1.4	1.1	1.9	1.5	0.1	0.1	0.1
41	Real estate activities	0.1	0.1	0.1	0.1	0.0	0.0	0.0	-0.1	0.0
42	Professional, scientific and technical activities	1.1	1.3	1.2	0.8	0.8	0.8	-0.3	-0.5	-0.4
43	Administrative and support service activities	0.9	0.7	0.8	1.1	0.9	1.0	0.2	0.2	0.2
44	Public administration and defence; compulsory social security	6.9	4.5	5.7	7.2	4.5	5.9	0.3	0.0	0.2
45	Education	4.9	11.2	7.9	3.9	11.2	7.4	-0.9	0.0	-0.5
46	Human health and social work activities	1.7	5.4	3.5	1.3	6.4	3.7	-0.4	1.0	0.3
47	Arts, entertainment and recreation	0.7	0.8	0.8	0.6	0.7	0.7	-0.1	-0.1	-0.1
48	Other service activities	2.0	2.2	2.1	1.7	1.6	1.7	-0.3	-0.6	-0.4
49	Activities of households as employers; undifferentiated goods- and services-producing activities of households for own use	0.4	0.3	0.3	0.3	0.1	0.2	-0.1	-0.2	-0.1
50	Activities of extraterritorial organizations and bodies	0.1	0.3	0.2	0.3	0.3	0.3	0.1	0.1	0.1

Sources: Mongolia Labour Force Surveys 2008 and 2009.

of total employment in the lower part of the table. (Screenshots 3.24 and 3.25 present the first and second parts of table 17, respectively.)

Agriculture is the largest sector of Mongolia's employment (table 17, parts 1 and 2, screenshots 3.24 and 3.25, respectively). In 2009, 373,700 persons were employed in the sector (about 40 percent of total employment). Wholesale and retail trade (including motor vehicle repair), with around 12 percent of all people employed in 2009, was the next largest sector. This sector had grown since 2008, with 113,000 workers, a gain of 18,300 in just one year. The third largest sector in 2009 was the education sector, with 7.4 percent of total employment and 69,300 employed.

Table 18: Employment by Sector and Region

Analysis of the regional breakdown of employment in table 18 (screenshot 3.26) tries to help the understanding of the extent to which particular economic sectors attract larger shares of employment in one region as compared with another. The sectoral composition of the economy within

Screenshot 3.26: Table 18: Employment by Sector and Region, Mongolia, 2009

	Table 18: Employment by sector and region					
				Mongolia LFS 2009		
	West region	Khangai region	Central region	East region	Ulaanbaatar	Total
Employment by sector ('000s)						
Agriculture, forestry and fishing	98.0	147.3	81.2	40.4	6.8	373.7
Mining and quarrying	0.9	8.9	6.6	1.9	4.6	22.8
Manufacturing	3.8	8.8	8.3	1.3	31.9	54.0
Electricity, gas, steam and air conditioning supply	0.8	1.8	2.8	0.7	6.6	12.6
Water supply; sewerage, waste management and remediation activities	0.7	1.2	1.8	0.2	2.2	6.1
Construction	4.1	4.2	5.6	1.0	29.2	44.0
Wholesale and retail trade; repair of motor vehicles and motorcycles	15.7	17.7	17.9	4.5	57.2	113.0
Transportation and storage	4.2	6.1	13.4	0.9	35.3	59.9
Accommodation and food service activities	1.7	2.6	2.3	1.0	12.4	19.9
Information and communication	1.0	0.8	1.2	0.6	7.3	10.9
Financial and insurance activities	2.0	1.6	1.6	0.4	8.2	13.9
Real estate activities		0.1			0.3	0.4
Professional, scientific and technical activities	1.1	1.1	0.5	0.2	4.5	7.5
Administrative and support service activities	0.4	0.9	1.5	0.4	6.0	9.3
Public administration and defence; compulsory social security	7.9	8.0	13.0	4.3	22.0	55.2
Education	13.0	13.7	12.8	3.5	26.3	69.3
Human health and social work activities	5.7	5.5	5.5	3.4	14.9	35.0
Arts, entertainment and recreation	0.8	0.9	1.1	0.7	2.9	6.4
Other service activities	1.8	1.4	1.7	0.6	9.8	15.4
Activities of households as employers; undifferentiated goods- and services-producing activities of households for own use	0.1	0.4	1.0	0.1	0.3	1.8
Activities of extraterritorial organizations and bodies	0.6	0.4	0.4		1.3	2.8

Source: Mongolia Labour Force Survey 2009.

regions affects employment patterns in several ways. For example, sectors differ in rates of growth in production and demand, employment intensities, regulations and policies, capital intensity, and patterns of technological change. These factors influence employment in each sector differently.

In the case of Mongolia, regional differences in sectoral employment are highly visible in all key economic sectors, which can be partly explained by a sector's degree of specialization. For example, agriculture provides few jobs in urban Ulaanbataar although it is the main provider of jobs in rural areas of the country (table 18, screenshot 3.26).

A comparison of the sectoral employment composition along these lines can shed light on structural labor market disparities across regions in a country.

Table 19: Employment by Occupation and Sex

Occupations in table 19 (screenshot 3.27) are usually coded according to the 1-digit categories of the International Standard Classification of Occupations[6] (ISCO) or the National Standard Classification of Occupations (NSCO), a nationally adapted version of ISCO, where the major groups of occupations are used.

Screenshot 3.27: Table 19: Employment by Occupation and Sex, Greece, 2008

Table 19: Employment by occupation and sex			
	Greece LFS 2008		
	Male	Female	Both sexes
Employment by occupational category ('000s)			
Armed forces	50.6	5.1	55.7
Legislators, senior official and managers in public and private sector	343.0	134.8	477.8
Professionals	343.6	329.8	673.4
Technicians and associate professionals	196.0	192.5	388.5
Office clerks and related professions	210.3	313.2	523.6
Service workers and shop and market sales workers	290.6	361.4	651.9
Skilled agricultural, farming, forestry and fishery workers	290.6	203.2	493.8
Craft and related trades workers	606.6	48.0	654.6
Plant and machine operators and assemblers	302.3	28.5	330.8
Unskilled workers, hand workers and elementary occupations	141.8	167.5	309.3
Total	2,775.3	1,784.1	4,559.4
Occupation employment shares (%)			
Armed forces	1.8	0.3	1.2
Legislators, senior official and managers in public and private sector	12.4	7.6	10.5
Professionals	12.4	18.5	14.8
Technicians and associate professionals	7.1	10.8	8.5
Office clerks and related professions	7.6	17.6	11.5
Service workers and shop and market sales workers	10.5	20.3	14.3
Skilled agricultural, farming, forestry and fishery workers	10.5	11.4	10.8
Craft and related trades workers	21.9	2.7	14.4
Plant and machine operators and assemblers	10.9	1.6	7.3
Unskilled workers, hand workers and elementary occupations	5.1	9.4	6.8
Total	100.0	100.0	100.0

Source: Greece Labour Force Survey 2008.
Note: The data refer to the average of Q1 to Q4 of the quarterly LFS for 2008.

In 2008, employment in Greece was somewhat evenly spread among 10 different occupational groups (screenshot 3.27). Six out of 10 groups accounted for 76.3 percent of total employment, each of these groups ranging between 10.5 percent (legislators, senior officials, and managers) and 14.8 percent (professionals), while the remaining four occupational groups accounted for 23.8 percent of total employment, varying between 1.2 percent (armed forces) and 8.5 percent (technicians and associate professionals).

However, when looking at the distribution between men and women in Greece in 2008, the picture was more uneven (screenshot 3.27). Almost twice the proportion of men than women were in the higher occupational group of legislators, senior officials, and managers in the public and private sectors. Men were also overrepresented in the elementary occupational groups of craft and related trade workers and plant and machine operators and assemblers. To the contrary, far more women were in the occupational groups of technicians and associate professionals; office clerks and related professions; service workers and shop and market sales workers; and skilled agricultural, farming, forestry, and fishery workers. The data indicate a segregated labor market.

Table 20: Employment by Occupation and Region

In Mongolia, the distribution of occupational groups among regions in 2009 reflects pronounced regional divides. The geographic differences in sectoral employment are also reflected in the occupational distribution of workers (table 18, screen 3.26). In 2009, the largest share of workers in skilled agricultural and fishery jobs was employed in rural areas (table 20, screenshot 3.28).

Screenshot 3.28: Table 20: Employment by Occupation and Region, Mongolia, 2009

		West region	Khangai region	Central region	East region	Ulaanbaatar	Total
1	Table 20: Employment by occupation and region						
2	Mongolia LFS 2009						
3							
4	Employment by occupational category ('000s)						
5	Legislators, senior officials and managers	4.9	5.6	7.6	2.4	26.3	46.8
6	Professionals	13.7	17.6	18.0	4.8	63.1	117.2
7	Technicians and associate professionals	6.1	5.3	7.7	2.4	17.4	39.0
8	Clerks	1.6	2.6	3.3	0.9	8.6	17.1
9	Service workers and shop and market sales workers	18.8	20.8	19.9	5.7	56.3	121.5
10	Skilled agricultural and fishery workers	97.5	145.8	78.8	40.8	4.9	367.7
11	Craft and related trades workers	9.3	16.4	12.8	4.2	54.7	97.3
12	Plant and machine operators and assemblers	7.1	10.7	16.5	2.9	39.0	76.2
13	Elementary occupations	5.1	8.7	15.6	1.9	19.7	51.1
14							
15	Total	164.1	233.4	180.2	66.1	290.0	933.9
16							
17	Occupation employment shares (%)						
18	Legislators, senior officials and managers	3.0	2.4	4.2	3.7	9.1	5.0
19	Professionals	8.3	7.5	10.0	7.3	21.8	12.6
20	Technicians and associate professionals	3.7	2.3	4.3	3.7	6.0	4.2
21	Clerks	1.0	1.1	1.8	1.4	3.0	1.8
22	Service workers and shop and market sales workers	11.4	8.9	11.0	8.7	19.4	13.0
23	Skilled agricultural and fishery workers	59.4	62.5	43.7	61.7	1.7	39.4
24	Craft and related trades workers	5.6	7.0	7.1	6.3	18.9	10.4
25	Plant and machine operators and assemblers	4.3	4.6	9.1	4.4	13.4	8.2
26	Elementary occupations	3.1	3.7	8.7	2.9	6.8	5.5
27							
28	Total	100.0	100.0	100.0	100.0	100.0	100.0

Source: Mongolia Labour Force Survey 2009.

In contrast, the shares of legislators, senior officials, and managers (9.1 percent), professionals (21.8 percent), and service workers and shop and market sales workers (19.4 percent) were the highest in the capital, Ulaanbaatar. Regional disparities in occupational employment are usually also reflected in the wage or income distribution of workers.

Table 21a: Employment by Status and Sector

The cross-tabulation of employment by status and sector provides important insights regarding the extent of formal versus vulnerable employment across different industries (table 21a, screenshot 3.29).

For example, analysis of table 21a (screenshot 3.29) shows that out of the 2.9 million wage and salaried workers in Greece in 2008, the largest number (439,800) were employed in the sector comprising wholesale and

Screenshot 3.29: Table 21a, Part 1: Employment by Status and Sector, Greece, 2008

		Table 21a: Employment by status and sector			
			Greece LFS 2008		
		Employee	Employer	Own-account worker	Contributing family worker	Total
4	Employment ('000s)					
5	Agriculture, forestry and fishery	38.5	40.9	321.8	115.7	516.8
6	Mining and quarrying	16.0	0.6	0.4	0.3	17.3
7	Manufacturing	398.0	55.6	60.5	24.8	538.9
8	Electricity, gas, steam and air conditioning	34.0	0.4	0.3		34.7
9	Water supply; sewerage, waste management and remediation activities	29.4	0.2	0.7	0.2	30.5
10	Construction	276.5	49.0	61.7	8.0	395.1
11	Wholesale and retail trade; repair of motor vehicles and motocycles	439.8	105.3	217.6	65.3	828.0
12	Transportation and storage	152.2	10.4	47.7	3.1	213.3
13	Accommodation and food service activities	181.1	48.4	47.4	38.2	315.1
14	Information and communication	66.9	2.1	5.6	0.4	75.0
15	Financial and insurance services	106.5	1.7	9.7	0.3	118.3
16	Real estate management	1.5	1.8	4.9	0.6	8.8
17	Professional, scientific and technical	106.4	33.2	86.8	5.8	232.3
18	Administrative and support service activities	62.3	6.7	5.6	1.5	76.1
19	Public administration and defence; compulsory social security	377.5				377.5
20	Education	296.2	8.6	15.7	0.7	321.2
21	Human health and social work activities	196.1	6.8	29.4	0.6	232.9
22	Arts, entertainment and recreation	42.3	3.1	11.2	1.6	58.2
23	Other service activities	51.9	10.9	27.9	1.8	92.5
24	Activities of households as employers	70.3	0.1	5.0		75.3
25	Activities of extraterritorial organisations and bodies	1.6				1.6
26						
27	Total	2,944.8	385.8	960.0	268.9	4,559.4

Source: Greece Labour Force Survey 2008.
Note: The data refer to the average of Q1 to Q4 of the quarterly LFS for 2008. Empty spaces reflect missing values for the particular group.

retail trade and repair of motor vehicles and motorcycles. In absolute numbers, very few wage and salaried workers were employed in the agriculture, forestry, and fishery or real estate management sectors.

A look at the percentage distribution of the employment status by sector shows that in 2008 the majority of Greek workers in the agricultural sector were employed as own-account (62.3 percent) and contributing family workers (22.4 percent). This indicates that 84.7 percent of agricultural employment is in the two vulnerable employment status groups (table 21a, screenshot 3.30).

The high share of own-account workers in real estate management points toward the limited opportunities to find wage and salaried jobs in the sector. On the other hand, all the persons employed in the sector comprising public administration and defense and compulsory social security workers are employees (table 21a, screenshot 3.30).

Screenshot 3.30: Table 21a, Part 2: Employment by Status and Sector, Greece, 2008

1		Table 21a: Employment by status and sector			
2			Greece LFS 2008		
3		Employee	Employer	Own-account worker	Contributing family worker	Total
29 Shares in total employment (%)					
30 Agriculture, forestry and fishery	7.4	7.9	62.3	22.4	100.0
31 Mining and quarrying	92.4	3.7	2.4	1.5	100.0
32 Manufacturing	73.8	10.3	11.2	4.6	100.0
33 Electricity, gas, steam and air conditioning	98.0	1.2	0.8	0.0	100.0
34 Water supply; sewerage, waste management and remediation activities	96.5	0.5	2.4	0.5	100.0
35 Construction	70.0	12.4	15.6	2.0	100.0
36 Wholesale and retail trade; repair of motor vehicles and motocycles	53.1	12.7	26.3	7.9	100.0
37 Transportation and storage	71.3	4.9	22.3	1.4	100.0
38 Accommodation and food service activities	57.5	15.4	15.0	12.1	100.0
39 Information and communication	89.2	2.8	7.5	0.5	100.0
40 Financial and insurance services	90.0	1.4	8.2	0.3	100.0
41 Real estate management	16.8	19.9	56.0	7.2	100.0
42 Professional, scientific and technical	45.8	14.3	37.4	2.5	100.0
43 Administrative and support service activities	81.9	8.8	7.4	1.9	100.0
44 Public administration and defence; compulsory social security	100.0	0.0	0.0	0.0	100.0
45 Education	92.2	2.7	4.9	0.2	100.0
46 Human health and social work activities	84.2	2.9	12.6	0.3	100.0
47 Arts, entertainment and recreation	72.6	5.4	19.2	2.8	100.0
48 Other service activities	56.1	11.8	30.2	1.9	100.0
49 Activities of households as employers	93.3	0.1	6.6	0.0	100.0
50 Activities of extraterritorial organisations and bodies	100.0	0.0	0.0	0.0	100.0
51					
52 Total	64.6	8.5	21.1	5.9	100.0

Source: Greece Labour Force Survey 2008.
Note: The data refer to the average of Q1 to Q4 of the quarterly LFS for 2008.

Table 21b: Employment by Sex, Status, and Sector

Analysis of table 21b (screenshot 3.31) can help to explore gender-based inequalities in the employment structure of countries. For example, table 21b indicates that Greece in 2008 had a very large proportion of workers concentrated in wage and salaried employment when compared to Timor-Leste in 2010 (see screenshot 3.20, table 14b). More specifically, 2.9 million out of 4.6 million employed Greeks (64.6 percent of total employment) were employees in 2008.

Women in Greece are more likely to have formal wage and salaried arrangements than men (table 21b, part 2, screenshot 3.32). In 2008, the share of wage and salaried employment in total female employment was 69 percent, 7.2 percentage points higher than the share of men (61.8 percent). The largest differences in wage and salaried employment between male and female employees are observed in the professional, scientific, and technical sector (a difference of 22.1 percentage points in 2008), the transportation and storage sector (a difference of 20 percentage points in 2008), and the sector comprising wholesale and retail trade and repair of motor vehicles and motorcycles workers (a difference of 14.1 percentage points in 2008).

Screenshot 3.31: Table 21b, Part 1: Employment by Sex, Status, and Sector, Greece, 2008

Table 21b: Employment by sex, status and sector
Greece LFS 2008

	Male					Female				
	Employee	Employer	Own-account worker	Contributing family worker	Total	Employee	Employer	Own-account worker	Contributing family worker	Total
Employment ('000s)										
Agriculture, forestry and fishery	29.0	31.5	208.1	37.1	305.7	9.4	9.3	113.7	78.6	211.1
Mining and quarrying	14.3	0.5	0.4		15.3	1.6	0.1		0.3	2.0
Manufacturing	288.5	47.3	50.3	10.2	396.2	109.4	8.4	10.2	14.6	142.7
Electricity, gas, steam and air conditioning	25.7	0.4	0.3		26.4	8.3				8.3
Water supply; sewerage, waste management and remediation activities	24.0	0.2	0.5	0.1	24.7	5.5		0.2	0.1	5.8
Construction	270.2	48.0	61.0	6.8	386.0	6.3	1.0	0.6	1.1	9.0
Wholesale and retail trade, repair of motor vehicles and motocycles	223.7	81.8	148.2	21.3	475.0	216.1	23.5	69.4	44.0	353.0
Transportation and storage	124.7	9.6	46.3	1.7	182.2	27.5	0.8	1.4	1.4	31.1
Accommodation and food service activities	90.9	38.5	28.5	13.0	170.8	90.2	9.9	18.9	25.3	144.3
Information and communication	42.2	2.0	4.5	0.2	48.9	24.7	0.1	1.2	0.2	26.1
Financial and insurance services	50.5	1.5	5.9	0.1	58.1	56.0	0.3	3.8	0.2	60.2
Real estate management	0.8	0.8	3.2	0.6	5.4	0.7	0.9	1.7	0.0	3.4
Professional, scientific and technical	46.0	24.7	56.2	1.3	128.2	60.4	8.6	30.7	4.5	104.1
Administrative and support service activities	30.2	5.4	3.6	0.7	40.0	32.1	1.3	2.0	0.7	36.1
Public administration and defence; compulsory social security	236.5				236.5	141.0				141.0
Education	107.1	3.7	6.3	0.1	117.1	189.2	4.9	9.4	0.6	204.1
Human health and social work activities	60.0	4.4	14.8		79.2	136.0	2.4	14.6	0.6	153.6
Arts, entertainment and recreation	25.4	2.6	7.4	0.6	36.1	16.8	0.5	3.8	1.0	22.1
Other service activities	20.7	5.8	12.2	0.6	39.4	31.2	5.1	15.7	1.2	53.1
Activities of households as employers	2.7		0.1		2.8	67.5	0.1	4.9		72.5
Activities of extraterritorial organisations and bodies	1.2				1.2	0.5				0.5
Total	1,714.4	308.7	657.7	94.5	2,775.3	1,230.3	77.1	302.2	174.4	1,784.1

Source: Greece Labour Force Survey 2008.
Note: The data refer to the average of Q1 to Q4 of the quarterly LFS for 2008. Empty spaces reflect missing values for the particular group.

Screenshot 3.32: Table 21b, Part 2: Employment by Sex, Status, and Sector, Greece, 2008

			Table 21b: Employment by sex, status and sector							
					Greece LFS 2008					
			Male					Female		
	Employee	Employer	Own-account worker	Contributing family worker	Total	Employee	Employer	Own-account worker	Contributing family worker	Total
Shares in total employment (%)										
Agriculture, forestry and fishery	9.5	10.3	68.1	12.1	100.0	4.5	4.4	53.9	37.2	100.0
Mining and quarrying	93.9	3.5	2.7	0.0	100.0	81.3	5.3	0.0	13.4	100.0
Manufacturing	72.8	11.9	12.7	2.6	100.0	76.8	5.9	7.1	10.2	100.0
Electricity, gas, steam and air conditioning	97.4	1.5	1.1	0.0	100.0	100.0	0.0	0.0	0.0	100.0
Water supply; sewerage, waste management and remediation activities	97.1	0.7	2.0	0.2	100.0	94.0	0.0	4.3	1.7	100.0
Construction	70.0	12.4	15.8	1.8	100.0	69.8	10.9	6.8	12.5	100.0
Wholesale and retail trade; repair of motor vehicles and motocycles	47.1	17.2	31.2	4.5	100.0	61.2	6.7	19.7	12.5	100.0
Transportation and storage	68.4	5.3	25.4	0.9	100.0	88.4	2.6	4.5	4.4	100.0
Accommodation and food service activities	53.2	22.5	16.7	7.6	100.0	62.5	6.9	13.1	17.5	100.0
Information and communication	86.3	4.1	9.2	0.4	100.0	94.5	0.3	4.4	0.8	100.0
Financial and insurance services	87.0	2.5	10.2	0.3	100.0	92.9	0.4	6.3	0.3	100.0
Real estate management	14.4	15.0	59.2	11.4	100.0	20.6	27.8	50.9	0.7	100.0
Professional, scientific and technical	35.9	19.3	43.8	1.0	100.0	58.0	8.2	29.5	4.3	100.0
Administrative and support service activities	75.6	13.6	9.0	1.8	100.0	88.8	3.5	5.6	2.1	100.0
Public administration and defence; compulsory social security	100.0	0.0	0.0	0.0	100.0	100.0	0.0	0.0	0.0	100.0
Education	91.4	3.1	5.4	0.1	100.0	92.7	2.4	4.6	0.3	100.0
Human health and social work activities	75.8	5.6	18.6	0.0	100.0	88.5	1.6	9.5	0.4	100.0
Arts, entertainment and recreation	70.4	7.3	20.6	1.8	100.0	76.4	2.3	17.0	4.4	100.0
Other service activities	52.6	14.8	31.1	1.5	100.0	58.7	9.6	29.5	2.2	100.0
Activities of households as employers	95.8	0.0	4.2	0.0	100.0	93.2	0.1	6.7	0.0	100.0
Activities of extraterritorial organisations and bodies	100.0	0.0	0.0	0.0	100.0	100.0	0.0	0.0	0.0	100.0
Total	61.8	11.1	23.7	3.4	100.0	69.0	4.3	16.9	9.8	100.0

Source: Greece Labour Force Survey 2008.
Note: The data refer to the average of Q1 to Q4 of the quarterly LFS for 2008.

However, wage and salaried employment is *not necessarily* decent employment. Far too often wage and salaried employees work as irregular paid employees, with long hours and casual contract arrangements for low pay and without social protection.

Table 22a: Employment by Status and Occupation

Table 22a (screenshot 3.33) shows employment by status and occupation, which, among other things, can help users develop skills development programs and policies.

For example, in Greece the highest shares of wage and salaried workers are in the occupational groups of office clerks and related professions (94.8 percent in 2008) and unskilled workers, hand workers, and elementary occupations (92.1 percent). Just 12.6 percent of wage and salaried workers are in the occupational group of legislators, senior officials, and managers in the public and private sectors. In 2008, the majority of these highly skilled groups of people worked as employers (39.5 percent) and own-account workers (47.2 percent). In addition, 65 percent of skilled agricultural, farming, forestry, and fishery workers are employed as own-account workers.

Screenshot 3.33: Table 22a: Employment by Status and Occupation, Greece, 2008

Table 22a: Employment by status and occupation					
	Greece LFS 2008				
	Employee	Employer	Own-account worker	Contributing family worker	Total
Employment ('000s)					
Armed forces	55.7				55.7
Legislators, senior official and managers in public and private sector	60.1	188.6	225.3	3.7	477.8
Professionals	499.0	48.2	121.9	4.3	673.4
Technicians and associate professionals	328.2	12.9	43.3	4.1	388.5
Office clerks and related professions	496.6	4.2	5.6	17.2	523.6
Service workers and shop and market sales workers	505.4	11.9	48.0	86.6	651.9
Skilled agricultural, farming, forestry and fishery workers	19.0	38.9	321.0	114.9	493.8
Craft and related trades workers	444.3	67.4	118.7	24.2	654.6
Plant and machine operators and assemblers	251.7	10.9	61.5	6.7	330.8
Unskilled workers, hand workers and elementary occupations	284.7	2.8	14.6	7.1	309.3
Total	2,944.8	385.8	960.0	268.9	4,559.4
Shares in total employment (%)					
Armed forces	100.0	0.0	0.0	0.0	100.0
Legislators, senior official and managers in public and private sector	12.6	39.5	47.2	0.8	100.0
Professionals	74.1	7.2	18.1	0.6	100.0
Technicians and associate professionals	84.5	3.3	11.2	1.0	100.0
Office clerks and related professions	94.8	0.8	1.1	3.3	100.0
Service workers and shop and market sales workers	77.5	1.8	7.4	13.3	100.0
Skilled agricultural, farming, forestry and fishery workers	3.8	7.9	65.0	23.3	100.0
Craft and related trades workers	67.9	10.3	18.1	3.7	100.0
Plant and machine operators and assemblers	76.1	3.3	18.6	2.0	100.0
Unskilled workers, hand workers and elementary occupations	92.1	0.9	4.7	2.3	100.0
Total	64.6	8.5	21.1	5.9	100.0

Source: Greece Labour Force Survey 2008.
Note: The data refer to the average of Q1 to Q4 of the quarterly LFS for 2008. Empty spaces reflect missing values for the particular group.

Table 22b: Employment by Sex, Status, and Occupation

Looking at differences in employment by status and occupation by sex, table 22b (screenshot 3.34) shows a fairly equal distribution of male and female employment statuses among most occupational groups in Greece in 2008. However, the share of women in vulnerable employment (either own-account workers or contributing family workers) among skilled agricultural, farming, forestry, and fishery workers (94.3 percent) was noticeably higher than that for men (84.1 percent). Further, the share of women working as contributing family workers in the occupational group of service and shop and market sales workers was 8.1 percentage points higher than for men of the same group.

Screenshot 3.34: Table 22b: Employment by Sex, Status, and Occupation, Greece, 2008

Table 22b: Employment by sex, status and occupation

Greece LFS 2008

	Male					Female				
	Employee	Employer	Own-account worker	Contributing family worker	Total	Employee	Employer	Own-account worker	Contributing family worker	Total
Employment ('000s)										
Armed forces	50.6				50.6	5.1				5.1
Legislators, senior official and managers in public and private sector	42.5	151.7	146.9	1.8	343.0	17.6	37.0	78.3	1.9	134.8
Professionals	238.5	31.3	72.3	1.5	343.6	260.5	16.9	49.6	2.8	329.8
Technicians and associate professionals	154.5	10.7	29.3	1.4	196.0	173.7	2.2	14.0	2.6	192.5
Office clerks and related professions	201.0	2.2	2.8	4.3	210.3	295.6	1.9	2.8	12.9	313.2
Service workers and shop and market sales workers	237.1	6.1	21.9	25.4	290.6	268.3	5.7	26.1	61.2	361.4
Skilled agricultural, farming, forestry and fishery workers	16.5	29.8	207.6	36.6	290.6	2.5	9.1	113.4	78.3	203.2
Craft and related trades workers	415.4	63.7	110.2	17.3	606.6	28.9	3.7	8.5	6.9	48.0
Plant and machine operators and assemblers	227.3	10.4	59.9	4.6	302.3	24.4	0.5	1.6	2.1	28.5
Unskilled workers, hand workers and elementary occupations	131.0	2.6	6.7	1.5	141.8	153.7	0.2	7.9	5.7	167.5
Total	1,714.4	308.7	657.7	94.5	2,775.3	1,230.3	77.1	302.2	174.4	1,784.1
Shares in total employment (%)										
Armed forces	100.0	0.0	0.0	0.0	100.0	100.0	0.0	0.0	0.0	100.0
Legislators, senior official and managers in public and private sector	12.4	44.2	42.8	0.5	100.0	13.1	27.4	58.1	1.4	100.0
Professionals	69.4	9.1	21.0	0.4	100.0	79.0	5.1	15.0	0.9	100.0
Technicians and associate professionals	78.8	5.5	15.0	0.7	100.0	90.2	1.1	7.3	1.4	100.0
Office clerks and related professions	95.6	1.1	1.3	2.0	100.0	94.4	0.6	0.9	4.1	100.0
Service workers and shop and market sales workers	81.6	2.1	7.5	8.7	100.0	74.3	1.6	7.2	16.9	100.0
Skilled agricultural, farming, forestry and fishery workers	5.7	10.3	71.5	12.6	100.0	1.2	4.5	55.8	38.5	100.0
Craft and related trades workers	68.5	10.5	18.2	2.9	100.0	60.2	7.6	17.7	14.4	100.0
Plant and machine operators and assemblers	75.2	3.4	19.8	1.5	100.0	85.5	1.7	5.4	7.4	100.0
Unskilled workers, hand workers and elementary occupations	92.4	1.9	4.7	1.0	100.0	91.8	0.1	4.7	3.4	100.0
Total	61.8	11.1	23.7	3.4	100.0	69.0	4.3	16.9	9.8	100.0

Source: Greece Labour Force Survey 2008.
Note: The data refer to the average of Q1 to Q4 of the quarterly LFS for 2008. Empty spaces in the table reflect missing values for the particular group.

Table 23: Employment by Sector and Occupation

Information about sectors and occupations as presented in tables 23, 24a, and 24b (screenshots 3.35, 3.36, and 3.37, respectively) is essential to assist planners and individuals in making informed decisions about employment opportunities and human resource needs. For example, it informs employment services by helping individuals identify what type of jobs they would like to work in, the training they will need, and where they may find successful employment opportunities. For policy planners it can provide a good indicator of the drivers in the local economy and the changing nature of work, while pointing at arising job opportunities or, conversely, spotting where there is likely to be a surplus of labor and higher levels of unemployment. Analysis about occupations in certain sectors can also help to pinpoint jobs that are likely to be in higher demand elsewhere and that therefore might pose competitive challenges for accessing workers in the future.

For South Africa in Q3-2010, table 23 (screenshot 3.35) shows that 74.2 percent of people employed in the agriculture, hunting, forestry, and fishing sector had no more than elementary skills, while nearly 6 out of

Screenshot 3.35: Table 23: Employment by Sector and Occupation, South Africa, Q3-2010

	Legislators, senior officials and managers	Professionals	Technical and associate professionals	Clerks	Service workers and shop and market sales workers	Skilled agricultural and fishery workers	Craft and related trades workers	Plant and machine operators and assemblers	Elementary Occupation	Domestic workers	Not applicable	Total
Table 23: Employment by sector and occupation — South Africa LFs 3rd Quarter 2010												
Employment ('000s)												
Agriculture, hunting, forestry and fishing	25.3	3.2	6.8	12.4	4.2	65.3	9.9	41.3	484.2			652.6
Mining and quarrying	10.4	15.8	12.0	14.2	2.8		87.3	100.4	63.3			306.3
Manufacturing	144.8	52.8	158.7	137.2	43.5	7.3	444.6	484.7	266.4			1,740.0
Electricity, gas and water supply	10.3	10.0	14.9	14.8	3.0		13.7	18.6	14.7			100.0
Construction	107.0	17.1	47.0	31.5	8.3		628.3	36.4	209.7			1,085.4
Wholesale and retail trade	300.7	42.2	112.8	433.1	836.8	0.5	318.9	87.3	852.4			2,984.6
Transport, storage and communication	114.4	25.0	58.8	120.2	21.5		17.0	313.6	110.8			781.3
Financial intermediation, insurance, real estate and business services	197.1	238.8	230.2	286.3	372.1	2.7	54.7	30.5	238.9			1,651.2
Community, social and personal services	196.8	314.3	808.3	371.7	554.4	3.4	38.0	56.6	364.7			2,708.1
Private households				0.2	23.6			4.6	214.3	893.0		1,135.8
Other				1.1								1.1
Not applicable											0.0	0.0
Total	1,106.7	719.3	1,449.8	1,422.3	1,870.3	79.1	1,617.0	1,169.4	2,819.4	893.0	0.0	13,146.5
Shares in total employment (%)												
Agriculture, hunting, forestry and fishing	3.9	0.5	1.0	1.9	0.7	10.0	1.5	6.3	74.2	0.0	0.0	100.0
Mining and quarrying	3.4	5.2	3.9	4.6	0.9	0.0	28.5	32.8	20.7	0.0	0.0	100.0
Manufacturing	8.3	3.0	9.1	7.9	2.5	0.4	25.5	27.9	15.3	0.0	0.0	100.0
Electricity, gas and water supply	10.3	10.0	14.9	14.8	3.0	0.0	13.7	18.6	14.7	0.0	0.0	100.0
Construction	9.9	1.6	4.3	2.9	0.8	0.0	57.9	3.4	19.3	0.0	0.0	100.0
Wholesale and retail trade	10.1	1.4	3.8	14.5	28.0	0.0	10.7	2.9	28.6	0.0	0.0	100.0
Transport, storage and communication	14.6	3.2	7.5	15.4	2.8	0.0	2.2	40.1	14.2	0.0	0.0	100.0
Financial intermediation, insurance, real estate and business services	11.9	14.5	13.9	17.3	22.5	0.2	3.3	1.8	14.5	0.0	0.0	100.0
Community, social and personal services	7.3	11.6	29.8	13.7	20.5	0.1	1.4	2.1	13.5	0.0	0.0	100.0
Private households	0.0	0.0	0.0	0.0	2.1	0.0	0.0	0.0	18.9	78.6	0.0	100.0
Other	0.0	0.0	0.0	100.0	0.0	0.0	0.0	0.0	0.0	0.0	0.0	100.0
Not applicable	0.0	0.0	0.0	0.0	0.0	0.0	0.0	0.0	0.0	0.0	100.0	100.0
Total	2.2	1.4	2.9	2.8	3.7	0.2	3.2	2.3	5.6	1.8	73.7	100.0

Source: South Africa Labour Force Survey Q3-2010.
Note: Empty spaces reflect missing values for the particular group.

10 workers in the construction sector were craft and related trades workers. The majority of professionals in the country are in the community, social, and personal services sector and financial intermediation, insurance, real estate, and business services sector.

Table 24a: Employment by Broad Sector and Occupation

Table 24a (screenshot 3.36) presents the employed population by occupation and the share of each occupation in total employment by broad sector. The sectors of economic activity are aggregated according to ISIC Rev. 3, whereby "agriculture" includes sectors A–B, "industry" includes sectors C–F, and "services" include sectors G–Q.

The more condensed cross-tabulations of sectors by occupation can help users to study the types of occupations that dominate sectors of economic activity. However, to complement data from household surveys and to get a more accurate picture, it would be useful to have establishment survey data and information on vacancies and skills needs from other sources (e.g., compared and analyzed with the information in tables 24a and 24b, screenshots 3.36 and 3.37, respectively).

Screenshot 3.36: Table 24a: Employment by Broad Sector and Occupation, Greece, 2008

1	Table 24a: Employment by broad sector and occupation			
2		Greece LFS 2008		
3		Agriculture	Industry	Services	Total
4	**Employment by occupational category ('000s)**				
5	Armed forces			55.7	55.7
6	Legislators, senior official and managers in public and private sector	2.0	62.0	413.7	477.8
7	Professionals	1.6	38.4	633.4	673.4
8	Technicians and associate professionals	1.2	54.1	333.1	388.5
9	Office clerks and related professions	1.9	63.8	457.9	523.6
10	Service workers and shop and market sales workers	0.9	14.2	636.9	651.9
11	Skilled agricultural, farming, forestry and fishery workers	486.8	0.2	6.8	493.8
12	Craft and related trades workers	0.4	538.1	116.1	654.6
13	Plant and machine operators and assemblers	1.8	159.4	169.6	330.8
14	Unskilled workers, hand workers and elementary occupations	20.2	86.2	202.9	309.3
15					
16	Total	516.8	1,016.4	3,026.1	4,559.4
17					
18	**Occupation employment shares (%)**				
19	Armed forces	0.0	0.0	1.8	1.2
20	Legislators, senior official and managers in public and private sector	0.4	6.1	13.7	10.5
21	Professionals	0.3	3.8	20.9	14.8
22	Technicians and associate professionals	0.2	5.3	11.0	8.5
23	Office clerks and related professions	0.4	6.3	15.1	11.5
24	Service workers and shop and market sales workers	0.2	1.4	21.0	14.3
25	Skilled agricultural, farming, forestry and fishery workers	94.2	0.0	0.2	10.8
26	Craft and related trades workers	0.1	52.9	3.8	14.4
27	Plant and machine operators and assemblers	0.3	15.7	5.6	7.3
28	Unskilled workers, hand workers and elementary occupations	3.9	8.5	6.7	6.8
29					
30	Total	100.0	100.0	100.0	100.0

Source: Greece Labour Force Survey 2008.
Note: The data refer to the average of Q1 to Q4 of the quarterly LFS for 2008. Empty spaces reflect missing values for the particular group.

LFS data for Greece show that the services sector provided the majority of jobs in 2008. This sector employed approximately 3 million workers (66.4 percent of total employment) compared to 1 million workers in industry (22.3 percent of total employment) and 0.5 million in agriculture (11.3 percent of total employment) (screenshot 3.36).

The services sector was dominated by the occupational groups of professionals; office clerks and related professions; and service workers and shop and market sales workers. Together, these occupations accounted for more than half of the jobs available in the sector. In industry, more than half (52.9 percent in 2008) of all workers were engaged in craft and related trade occupations, while 94.2 percent of the agricultural workforce were employed in skilled agricultural, farming, forestry, and fishing occupations in 2008 (screenshot 3.36).

Table 24b: Employment by Broad Sector, Occupation, and Sex

Table 24b (screenshot 3.37) supports the analysis of gender-based differences across sectors and occupations. For example, the occupational structure of Greek men and women across broad sectors shows gender-based occupational and industrial segregation. Analysis of LFS data for 2008 reveals that in the services and industry sectors, the share of men holding positions as legislators, senior officials, and managers was significantly higher than that of women. In contrast, the shares of females in professional positions were much higher than for males in both services and industry sectors. Traditional gender segregation also exists in the industry sector, where men dominate the occupational groups of craft and related trade workers and plant and machine operators and assemblers.

Screenshot 3.37: Table 24b: Employment by Broad Sector, Occupation, and Sex, Greece, 2008

	Agriculture		Industry		Services		Total	
	Male	Female	Male	Female	Male	Female	Male	Female
Employment by occupational category ('000s)								
Armed forces					50.6	5.1	50.6	5.1
Legislators, senior official and managers in public and private sector	1.8	0.2	53.3	8.8	287.9	125.8	343.0	134.8
Professionals	0.6	0.9	26.1	12.3	316.8	316.6	343.6	329.8
Technicians and associate professionals	0.6	0.6	37.1	17.0	158.3	174.8	196.0	192.5
Office clerks and related professions	1.0	0.8	26.5	37.3	182.8	275.1	210.3	313.2
Service workers and shop and market sales workers	0.8	0.1	3.2	11.0	286.6	350.5	290.6	361.4
Skilled agricultural, farming, forestry and fishery workers	283.9	203.0	0.1	0.1	6.7	0.1	290.6	203.2
Craft and related trades workers	0.4		496.3	41.8	109.9	6.2	606.6	48.0
Plant and machine operators and assemblers	1.8		136.8	22.6	163.6	5.9	302.3	28.5
Unskilled workers, hand workers and elementary occupations	14.8	5.5	69.3	16.9	57.8	145.1	141.8	167.5
Total	305.7	211.1	848.6	167.8	1,621.0	1,405.1	2,775.3	1,784.1
Occupation employment shares (%)								
Armed forces	0.0	0.0	0.0	0.0	3.1	0.4	1.8	0.3
Legislators, senior official and managers in public and private sector	0.6	0.1	6.3	5.2	17.8	9.0	12.4	7.6
Professionals	0.2	0.4	3.1	7.3	19.5	22.5	12.4	18.5
Technicians and associate professionals	0.2	0.3	4.4	10.2	9.8	12.4	7.1	10.8
Office clerks and related professions	0.3	0.4	3.1	22.2	11.3	19.6	7.6	17.6
Service workers and shop and market sales workers	0.3	0.0	0.4	6.6	17.7	24.9	10.5	20.3
Skilled agricultural, farming, forestry and fishery workers	92.9	96.1	0.0	0.1	0.4	0.0	10.5	11.4
Craft and related trades workers	0.1	0.0	58.5	24.9	6.8	0.4	21.9	2.7
Plant and machine operators and assemblers	0.6	0.0	16.1	13.5	10.1	0.4	10.9	1.6
Unskilled workers, hand workers and elementary occupations	4.8	2.6	8.2	10.1	3.6	10.3	5.1	9.4
Total	100.0	100.0	100.0	100.0	100.0	100.0	100.0	100.0

Source: Greece Labour Force Survey 2008.
Note: The data refer to the average of Q1 to Q4 of the quarterly LFS for 2008. Empty spaces in the table reflect missing values for the particular group.

Table 25a: Employment by Type of Contract and Age Group

Precarious and vulnerable work is often caused by atypical employment contracts and can result in uncertain and unpredictable circumstances for workers, such as low wages, no social benefits, lack of rights, and overall job insecurity. Further, the lack of an employment relationship is fundamentally denying workers the possibility to exercise their rights and constitutes a key reason for the difficulties in extending collective bargaining coverage.

Thus, table 25a (screenshot 3.38) seeks to uncover job insecurities or nondecent employment arrangements. For example, in Greece, 88.5 percent of workers reported that their main job was permanent in 2008. The highest proportion of permanent, employed workers—more than 90 percent—were those ages 35 and older.

As shown in screenshot 3.38, the percentage share of young people (ages 15–24) was—at 70.8 percent in 2008—significantly lower than for adults (25 and older), in which all categories were 85 percent or above. In addition, 22.8 percent of young people with a temporary contract reported that their jobs were temporary because they were either trainees or apprentices (5.8 percent) or could not find a permanent job (17.0 percent),

Screenshot 3.38: Table 25a: Employment by Type of Contract and Age Group, Greece, 2008

	Permanent	Temporary, apprentice or trainee	Temporary, could not find a permanent job	Temporary, did not want a permanent job	Temporary, probationary period	Temporary, but no reason is given	Total
1				Table 25a: Employment by type of contract and age group			
2				Greece LFS 2008			
4 Employment ('000s)							
5 15-24	149.5	12.1	36.0	1.9	3.3	8.4	270.3
6 25-34	783.1	10.7	99.2	2.3	8.2	17.6	1,222.7
7 35-44	817.9	2.4	60.5	2.5	3.3	10.1	1,343.0
8 45-54	617.9	0.5	33.3	2.4	0.6	6.1	1,087.4
9 55-64	226.3	0.1	10.7	0.6	0.2	3.5	550.3
10 65+	12.7		0.4	0.3	0.0	0.3	85.7
11							
12 15+	2,607.3	25.8	240.1	9.9	15.6	46.0	4,559.4
13							
14 Shares in total employment (%)							
15 15-24	70.8	5.8	17.0	0.9	1.5	4.0	100.0
16 25-34	85.0	1.2	10.8	0.2	0.9	1.9	100.0
17 35-44	91.2	0.3	6.7	0.3	0.4	1.1	100.0
18 45-54	93.5	0.1	5.0	0.4	0.1	0.9	100.0
19 55-64	93.7	0.0	4.5	0.2	0.1	1.5	100.0
20 65+	92.2	0.0	3.2	1.9	0.2	2.4	100.0
21							
22 15+	88.5	0.9	8.2	0.3	0.5	1.6	100.0

Source: Greece Labour Force Survey 2008.
Note: The data refer to the average of Q1 to Q4 of the quarterly LFS for 2008. The empty space in the table reflects a missing value for the particular group.

suggesting a higher incidence of job insecurities for youth when compared to the rest of the employed in 2008.

The data suggest better strategies might be needed to improve and expand social protection programs for young people and tailor labor market reforms for their specific needs. Policy makers should also note that such social protection measures are not viewed as a cost to society but rather as an investment. Investing in young persons has significant positive impacts on human development and productivity (ILO 2013a).

Table 25b: Employment by Type of Contract, Sex, and Age Group

Undeniably, a key labor market trend over the past decades is the growth of insecurities in the world of work. However, men and women experience the trends differently. Therefore, analyses of table 25b (screenshot 3.39) can help to identify gender-specific challenges regarding job security, which can inform effective strategies to reduce and even eliminate precarious work conditions for all.

Screenshot 3.39 for South Africa in Q3-2010, for example, shows that noticeably more men (6.2 million) than women (4.8 million) had contractual arrangements with their employers, either as a written contract or a verbal agreement. Among those with a written contract, the share for women (42.7 percent) was noticeably lower than the share for men (57.3 percent).

Screenshot 3.39: Table 25b: Employment by Type of Contract, Sex, and Age Group, South Africa, Q3-2010

	Table 25b: Employment by type of contract, sex and age group							
	South Africa LFS 3rd Quarter 2010							
	Not applicable		A written contract		A verbal agreement		Total	
	Male	Female	Male	Female	Male	Female	Male	Female
Employment ('000s)								
15-24	81.0	45.9	456.3	356.3	231.3	123.9	768.6	526.2
25-34	321.0	212.3	1,719.7	1,267.0	483.8	361.6	2,524.6	1,840.9
35-44	365.2	243.0	1,412.5	1,070.6	289.0	327.0	2,066.8	1,640.7
45-54	292.5	201.9	937.2	697.2	158.8	213.3	1,388.5	1,112.4
55-64	160.7	115.4	390.9	275.5	73.1	90.2	624.7	481.2
65+	58.1	26.0	34.7	24.3	17.7	11.1	110.5	61.4
15+	1,278.6	844.7	4,951.3	3,690.9	1,253.8	1,127.1	7,483.8	5,662.7
Shares in total employment (%)								
15-24	49.2	50.8	56.2	43.8	65.1	34.9	50.3	49.7
25-34	41.0	59.0	57.6	42.4	57.2	42.8	48.4	51.6
35-44	40.4	59.6	56.9	43.1	46.9	53.1	47.9	52.1
45-54	40.1	59.9	57.3	42.7	42.7	57.3	46.9	53.1
55-64	41.6	58.4	58.7	41.3	44.8	55.2	45.6	54.4
65+	40.5	59.5	58.8	41.2	61.5	38.5	41.2	58.8
15+	44.0	56.0	57.3	42.7	52.7	47.3	47.9	52.1

Source: South Africa Labour Force Survey Q3-2010.

The difference between the shares of men and women with a written contract were more or less equally pronounced throughout all age groups. Gender imbalances also existed between workers with verbal agreements, particularly between young men and women ages 15–24. Out of 10 young workers with a verbal agreement, 6 were men and 4 were women. Thus, national policies and action plans that address job insecurities in the labor market while promoting decent work and productive employment should be gender sensitive, with a special focus on youth employment.

Table 26: Public and Private Wage Employment by Sex

One way analysts can disaggregate total wage employment is by distinguishing between public and private sector jobs. Public sector jobs are usually jobs with the government, whereas private sector jobs constitute employment with private companies (either for-profit or nonprofit).

Table 26 (screenshots 3.40 and 3.41, respectively) shows that overall, the share of public employment in wage and salaried employment in Timor-Leste was relatively high (56.1 percent in 2010) as compared with the share in South Africa (18.7 percent in Q3-2010).

In South Africa (screenshot 3.41), the share of female wage and salaried workers in public employment was 22.2 percent, or 6.3 percentage points higher than the share for men.

Screenshot 3.40: Table 26: Public and Private Wage Employment by Sex, Timor-Leste, 2010

Table 26: Public and private wage employment, by sex

Timor-Leste, LFS 2010

	Non public	Public	To al
Wage employment ('000s)			
Male	24.5	31.2	55.7
Female	6.9	9.0	15.9
Both sexes	31.4	40.2	71.6
Share in total wage employment (%)			
Male	44.0	56.0	100.0
Female	43.6	56.4	100.0
Both sexes	43.9	56.1	100.0

Source: Timor-Leste Labour Force Survey 2010.

Screenshot 3.41: Table 26: Public and Private Wage Employment by Sex, South Africa, Q3-2010

1	Table 26: Public and private wage employment, by sex		
2		South Africa 2010 3rd Quarter	
3		Non public	Public
4	Wage employment ('000s)		
5	Male	5,217.2	988.0
6	Female	3,747.8	1,070.2
7			
8	Both sexes	8,965.0	2,058.2
9			
10	Share of in total wage employment (%)		
11	Male	84.1	15.9
12	Female	77.8	22.2
13			
14	Both sexes	81.3	18.7

Source: South Africa Labour Force Survey Q3-2010.

Table 27: Employed Population with a Second Job, by Sex and Age Group

The incidence of persons having more than one job appears to have increased considerably in a number of countries in recent decades, particularly in the transition economies and in some industrialized economies where workers often have to take on an additional job or jobs to maintain their standard of living. It is also often a strategy by the self-employed to minimize the impact of economic downturns on their income (ILO 2004). Workers who have experienced wage arrears, were placed on involuntary leave, or are working less than full-time are all significantly more likely to take on second jobs.

Despite this global trend, according to the LFS data for Timor-Leste (screenshot 3.42), very few Timorese workers (2.4 percent of the employed population) had a secondary job. Also, more men than women were engaged in multiple jobs, especially those ages 35–44 (4.1 percent of the employed male population of that age range) or 65 and above (6.4 percent of employed Timorese of that age group). Yet low incidence of secondary jobs does not mean that the primary jobs of most Timorese were decent. Often workers are engaged in informal employment activities outside of their primary job to bolster household income.

Screenshot 3.42: Table 27: Employed Population with a Second Job by Sex and Age Group, Timor-Leste, 2010

Table 27: Employed population with a second job, by sex and age group Timor-Leste, LFS 2010	Male	Female	Both sexes
Employed population with a second job ('000s)			
15-24	0.2	0.0	0.2
25-34	1.2	0.2	1.4
35-44	2.2	0.1	2.3
45-54	0.8	0.1	0.9
55-64	0.6	0.0	0.7
65+	0.6	0.0	0.6
15+	5.7	0.5	6.1
Share of employed population with a second job in total employment (%)			
15-24	1.0	0.0	0.7
25-34	3.2	1.1	2.5
35-44	4.1	0.5	3.1
45-54	2.5	0.7	1.9
55-64	2.9	0.1	2.0
65+	6.4	0.0	4.6
15+	3.3	0.6	2.4

Source: Timor-Leste Labour Force Survey 2010.

Table 28: Employed Population with a Second Job by Sex and Status

Table 28 (screenshot 3.43) presents the distribution of Timorese who had a second job by their status in employment and disaggregated by sex. As discussed in the previous section, more Timorese men (5,700) than women (500) were engaged in multiple jobs in 2010. As screenshot 3.43 reveals, the majority of these Timorese men with a secondary job were engaged in wage and salaried work (4.8 percent of total male wage and salaried employed in 2010).

Table 29: Employment by Hours of Work per Week and by Sex

Statistics on employment by hours worked per week usually refer to information on employment by usual-hour bands[7] provided most commonly in household surveys that cover all persons in employment. In all cases, persons totally absent from work during the reference week are excluded (ILO 2015).

Screenshot 3.43: Table 28: Employed Population with a Second Job by Sex and Status, Timor-Leste, 2010

	Table 28: Employed population with a second job, by sex and status			
1				
2		Timor Leste, LFS 2010		
3		Male	Female	Both sexes
4	**Employed population with a second job ('000s)**			
5	Wage and salaried workers	2.7	0.1	2.8
6	Employers	0.1	0.0	0.1
7	Own-account workers	1.7	0.3	1.9
8	Contributing family workers	1.2	0.1	1.3
9	Not classifiable	0.0	0.0	0.0
10				
11	Total	5.7	0.5	6.1
12				
13	**Share of employed population with a second job in total employment (%)**			
14	Wage and salaried workers	4.8	0.8	3.9
15	Employers	2.9	0.0	2.0
16	Own-account workers	2.5	0.7	1.9
17	Contributing family workers	2.6	0.3	1.8
18	Not classifiable	0.0	0.0	0.0
19				
20	Total	3.3	0.6	2.4

Source: Timor-Leste Labour Force Survey 2010.

The standard workweek in many countries is 40 hours. However, *full time* is often defined as 35 hours or more, with people who work less than 35 hours often defined as part-time workers. At the other extreme, more than 48 hours are, by international standards, considered "excessive" for such reasons as the unfavorable effects on physical and mental health and the difficulties such long hours cause in balancing work and family life. Further, excessive working hours are often an indication of low hourly pay and are therefore reflected in low labor productivity when calculated by aggregate hours worked rather than by persons employed.

Table 29 (screenshot 3.44) classifies the number of employed women and men by the number of hours they worked per week. Labor force survey data for Timor-Leste reveal that men were more likely to have worked "excessive" hours than women (40.4 percent of men versus

Screenshot 3.44: Table 29: Employment by Hours of Work per Week and by Sex, Timor-Leste, 2010

Table 29: Employment by hours of work per week and sex

		Timor-Leste, LFS 2010	
	Male	Female	Both sexes
Employment by hours of work ('000s)			
<25	14.4	9.6	24.0
25-34	10.0	6.2	16.2
35-39	22.6	14.1	36.7
40-48	55.8	20.1	75.9
49-59	35.2	11.4	46.6
>=60	34.5	18.4	53.0
Total	172.6	79.8	252.4
Employment shares by hours of work (%)			
<25	8.3	12.1	9.5
25-34	5.8	7.7	6.4
35-39	13.1	17.6	14.5
40-48	32.3	25.2	30.1
49-59	20.4	14.3	18.4
>=60	20.0	23.1	21.0
Total	100.0	100.0	100.0

Source: Timor-Leste Labour Force Survey 2010.

37.4 percent of women) in 2010. Further, in 2010, approximately 16 percent of employed persons worked less than 35 hours a week.

Table 29 (screenshot 3.44) shows clearly that an estimated 8 out of 10 employed people in Timor-Leste worked 35 hours or more per week in 2010. Also, at least 39.4 percent of Timorese were working "excessive" hours (18.4 percent working between 49 and 59 hours and 21 percent working 60 or more hours).

Note that the estimates in screenshot 3.44 do not account for differences in employment status, experience, skills, occupation, and education that might impact the numbers of hours Timorese worked per week.

Table 30: Employment by Hours of Work per Week and by Age Group

Table 30 (screenshot 3.45) provides the absolute and percentage distribution of working hours of employed persons of an age cohort. In absolute terms, 99,600 out of the 252,400 employed Timorese were working "excessive" hours (49 hours or more) in 2010. About 22 percent of employed persons ages 25–34 and 45–54 worked 60 or more hours per week—the highest

Screenshot 3.45: Table 30: Employment by Hours of Work per Week and by Age Group, Timor-Leste, 2010

	<25	25-34	35-39	40-48	49-59	>=60	Total
Table 30: Employment by hours of work per week and age group Timor-Leste, LFS 2010							
Employment by hours of work ('000s)							
15-24	1.6	1.0	4.2	7.3	4.9	5.0	23.8
25-34	4.2	3.4	7.2	19.7	9.6	12.4	56.4
35-44	7.9	4.7	9.8	23.2	14.4	15.6	75.6
45-54	5.9	3.5	6.9	14.4	8.5	11.2	50.4
55-64	2.7	2.6	4.6	8.7	7.4	7.0	33.0
65+	1.9	1.1	3.9	2.6	1.9	1.7	13.2
15+	24.0	16.2	36.7	75.9	46.6	53.0	252.4
Employment shares by hours of work (%)							
15-24	6.5	4.1	17.7	30.5	20.4	20.8	100.0
25-34	7.4	6.0	12.8	35.0	16.9	22.0	100.0
35-44	10.4	6.2	13.0	30.7	19.0	20.7	100.0
45-54	11.7	6.9	13.6	28.5	16.9	22.2	100.0
55-64	8.1	7.9	13.9	26.5	22.3	21.3	100.0
65+	14.5	8.0	30.0	19.9	14.3	13.3	100.0
15+	9.5	6.4	14.5	30.1	18.4	21.0	100.0

Source: Timor-Leste Labour Force Survey 2010.

shares among the different age cohorts. The share of people working less than 25 hours was highest among employed people ages 65 and above.

Working time policies are government instruments that support men and women in reconciling work and family responsibilities, and they contribute significantly to achieving gender equality at work. Recent and modern forms of working time arrangements, such as flextime and telework, offer new opportunities and challenges for the employed.

Table 31: Employment by Hours of Work per Week and by Broad Economic Sector

Table 31 (screenshot 3.46) provides information on hours worked by broad economic sectors or industries. It can help policy makers gain insights into the productivity of work in economic sectors. For example, based on the calculations in screenshot 3.46, out of the 39.3 percent of Timorese who worked "excessive hours" (49 hours or more), the significant majority were employed in the agricultural sector, which reflects a large number of low-productivity jobs in this sector. Nearly half of all workers in the agricultural sector worked excessive hours. The table also indicates that almost half of the people who worked less than 35 hours were employed in the services sector.

Screenshot 3.46: Table 31: Employment by Hours of Work per Week and by Broad Economic Sector, Timor-Leste, 2010

Table 31: Employment by hours of work per week and broad economic sector				
	Timor-Leste, LFS 2010			
	Agriculture	Industry	Services	Total
Employment by hours of work ('000s)				
<25	8.5	2.6	13.1	24.2
25-34	7.5	0.9	7.7	16.1
35-39	26.0	1.8	9.1	37.0
40-48	25.5	11.7	38.1	75.9
49-59	31.7	3.5	11.4	46.6
>=60	28.6	2.8	21.0	52.6
Total	127.7	23.4	100.5	252.4
Employment shares by hours of work (%)				
<25	3.4	1.0	5.2	9.6
25-34	3.0	0.4	3.0	6.4
35-39	10.3	0.7	3.6	14.7
40-48	10.1	4.7	15.1	30.1
49-59	12.6	1.4	4.5	18.5
>=60	11.3	1.1	8.3	20.8
Total	50.6	9.3	39.8	100.0

Source: Timor-Leste Labour Force Survey 2010.

Table 32: Time-Related Underemployment by Sex and Age Group

Table 32 (screenshot 3.47) analyzes time-related underemployment. While unemployment figures often attract the most media attention among labor market indicators, economic instability is often reflected in other labor market indicators as well, such as shorter working hours, reduced incomes, and rising vulnerable employment. Particularly in low-income economies, few people can afford to be unemployed for any lengthy period of time.

As a result, statistics on time-related underemployment are crucial to complement figures on employment, unemployment, and economic inactivity. Overlooking the underemployment issue can lead to an incomplete picture of the extent of labor utilization. While not technically unemployed, persons who are time-related underemployed often compete for available hours of work in the labor market (ILO 2015).

Screenshot 3.47: Table 32: Time-Related Underemployment by Sex and Age Group, Greece, 2008

Table 32: Time-related underemployment, by sex and age group

	Greece LFS 2008		
	Male	Female	Both sexes
Underemployed ('000s)			
15-24	10.5	11.8	22.3
25-34	28.3	31.5	59.8
35-44	22.8	26.5	49.3
45-54	12.5	14.2	26.7
55-64	7.3	3.9	11.1
65+	0.3	0.5	0.8
15+	81.6	88.4	170.1
Underemployment as a share of labour force (%)			
15-24	5.3	7.9	6.4
25-34	3.6	5.4	4.4
35-44	2.8	4.4	3.5
45-54	1.8	3.1	2.3
55-64	1.9	2.0	2.0
65+	0.4	2.3	0.9
15+	2.8	4.4	3.4
Underemployment as a share of total employment (%)			
15-24	6.4	11.1	8.2
25-34	3.9	6.3	4.9
35-44	2.9	4.8	3.7
45-54	1.9	3.3	2.5
55-64	2.0	2.1	2.0
65+	0.4	2.3	0.9
15+	2.9	5.0	3.7

Source: Greece Labour Force Survey 2008.
Note: The data refer to the average of Q1 to Q4 of the quarterly LFS for 2008.

Screenshot 3.47 presents the number of time-related underemployed and their shares in the labor force and in total employment. Underemployment as a share of the labor force is a widely used measure to supplement unemployment rates, which allows for a more accurate picture of the magnitude of labor underutilization.

Selecting in the parameters a cutoff for time-related underemployment of 40 hours a week, analysis of table 32 (screenshot 3.47) for Greece shows that in 2008, young people ages 15–24 had the highest incidence of time-related underemployment (6.4 percent of the labor force and 8.2 percent of the employed youth population). Young women were almost twice as likely as young men to be among the time-related underemployed (7.9 percent of the female labor force and 11.1 percent of the employed versus 5.3 percent of the male labor force and 6.4 percent of employed males).

As shown in screenshot 3.47, labor underutilization of young people is a key issue in the Greek labor market, especially in the context of the large unemployment rates of young Greeks (22.1 percent in 2008). To maximize young people's potential in Greece, appropriate cross-cutting policies should be developed that support youth, such as enhancing the role of employment services in job matching, education, and training, and supporting business promotion and related services.

Table 33: Trade Union Density Rate by Sex and Age Group

Analysis of trade union density in countries indicates an important degree of social dialogue. The coverage of union membership by household surveys may be broad or narrow, depending on the inclusion of the self-employed, the unemployed, or the exclusion of certain groups. The rates in table 33 (screenshot 3.48) are calculated based on country-specific concepts.

In South Africa, trade union membership was measured for all those employed ages 15 and older. Example table 33 (screenshot 3.48) shows trade unions are a significant force in South Africa, with nearly 3.3 million members representing 29.6 percent of all wage and salaried employment in Q3-2010. The highest rates of trade union membership are found for men ages 45–54. In contrast, the lowest rates are observed for women ages 65 and above and young men ages 15–24.

Note that the right to organize is often limited to certain groups of workers, since in some countries, labor laws prevent civil servants from

Screenshot 3.48: Table 33: Trade Union Density Rate by Sex and Age Group, South Africa, Q3-2010

Table 33: Trade union density rate, by sex and age group			
South Africa LFS 3rd Quarter 2010			
	Male	Female	Both sexes
Union membership ('000s)			
15-24	85.6	70.4	156.0
25-34	566.8	384.1	950.9
35-44	622.0	428.5	1,050.5
45-54	486.5	297.2	783.7
55-64	197.0	112.8	309.8
65+	8.9	3.7	12.5
15+	1,966.7	1,296.7	3,263.4
Union membership as a share of wage and salaried employment (%)			
15-24	12.5	14.7	13.4
25-34	25.7	23.6	24.8
35-44	36.6	30.7	33.9
45-54	44.4	32.6	39.1
55-64	42.5	30.8	37.3
65+	16.9	10.3	14.2
15+	31.7	26.9	29.6

Source: South Africa Labour Force Survey Q3-2010.

organizing or limit their bargaining power. In most countries workers in agriculture or in the informal economy—a major part of the labor force—do not benefit from the right to organize (ILO 2011).

Table 34: Social Security Coverage by Sex and Age Group

Table 34 (screenshot 3.49) provides information on workers' social security coverage. According to ILO standards, social security covers nine principal categories: medical care, sickness, unemployment, old age, employment injury, family, maternity, invalidity, and survivors' benefits (ILO 1952).

Screenshot 3.49: Table 34: Social Security Coverage by Sex and Age Group, South Africa, Q3-2010

	Table 34: Social security coverage, by sex and age group			
1				
2		South Africa LFS 3rd Quarter 2010		
3		Male	Female	Both sexes
4	Employed population contributing to a social security scheme ('000s)			
5	15-24	417.2	326.8	743.9
6	25-34	1,682.0	1,232.2	2,914.2
7	35-44	1,396.5	1,064.6	2,461.1
8	45-54	940.9	707.5	1,648.4
9	55-64	386.2	280.2	666.4
10	65+	38.2	25.9	64.0
11				
12	15+	4,861.0	3,637.1	8,498.1
13				
14	Social security coverage rate (%)			
15	15-24	54.3	62.1	57.5
16	25-34	66.6	66.9	66.8
17	35-44	67.6	64.9	66.4
18	45-54	67.8	63.6	65.9
19	55-64	61.8	58.2	60.3
20	65+	34.5	42.1	37.2
21				
22	15+	65.0	64.2	64.6

Source: South Africa Labour Force Survey Q3-2010.

Available information for each category that determines social security in household surveys varies greatly among countries. Therefore, a proxy variable or index for social security coverage needs to be individually generated, based on the information available in the respective surveys, as part of the input file preparation for the ADePT-LMI module.

In South Africa (screenshot 3.49), the data demonstrate the number of employees who contributed to the national health or unemployment fund and received paid leave and sick leave benefits from their employers in Q3-2010. Analysis of the LFS data reveals that out of a total employed population of 13.1 million, around 8.5 million, or 64.6 percent, of employed men and women contributed to work-related social security schemes.

In contrast to this relatively low share, most African and South Asian countries are characterized by low levels of work-related social security coverage. Low coverage can also be an indication of a large informal economy (ILO 2014).

When analyzing the data, users must understand that many developing countries have contributory social insurance schemes for the formal sector that provide benefits based on statutory entitlements. These schemes are usually available only to workers in paid employment who have contributed for a certain period of time, and are often government-based for public servants.

The extension of social protection to a larger share of the labor force remains one of the core challenges in promoting decent work in many countries. For this reason, governments should seek to establish more comprehensive social protection programs. The South African government, for example, approaches health care, education, work-related benefits, and social assistance through cash grants and programs, which are part of a comprehensive response to address poverty. Contributory schemes and noncontributory social assistance programs in the form of cash transfers are meant to support the whole population. Without these programs, more than 50 percent of households in South Africa would fall below the minimum subsistence level (ILO 2010).

Nevertheless, contributory schemes in many developing countries are characterized by problems such as employer noncompliance, inappropriate statutory retirement age, early withdrawal of funds, noncoverage of migrant workers, inadequate benefit levels, and discrimination against women—issues that limit the schemes' effectiveness (ILO 2010).

Unemployment and Labor Underutilization Tables (Seven Tables)

The tables in this section help to uncover the extent and characteristics of the unemployed. Note that unemployment is a rather limited indicator with which to monitor the overall labor market situation. The indicator therefore should be used with other labor market indicators, such as the employment-to-population ratio, employment by status, sectoral employment data, and wage indicators.

Table 35: Unemployment and Unemployment Rate, by Sex and Age Group

Table 35 (screenshot 3.50) shows unemployment numbers and rates, which are a key indicator of labor underutilization—namely, individuals who are available for work and actively seeking jobs but remain jobless. Unemployment rates express the proportion of the total labor force that is not employed (since the labor force comprises the employed plus the unemployed). Defined by specific groups, such as by age, sex, region, or educational attainment (as discussed in the following sections), unemployment rates are also useful in identifying groups of workers most vulnerable to joblessness.

Screenshot 3.50: Table 35: Unemployment and Unemployment Rate by Sex and Age Group, Greece, 2008

	Table 35: Unemployment and unemployment rate, by sex and age group		
1			
2	Greece LFS 2008		
3	Male	Female	Both sexes
4 Unemployment ('000s)			
5 15-24	33.6	43.0	76.6
6 25-34	58.9	89.0	147.9
7 35-44	26.1	58.7	84.9
8 45-54	17.6	31.7	49.4
9 55-64	11.0	7.5	18.4
10 65+	0.7	0.0	0.7
11			
12 15+	147.9	230.0	377.9
13			
14 Unemployment rate (%)			
15 15-24	17.0	28.9	22.1
16 25-34	7.5	15.1	10.8
17 35-44	3.2	9.7	5.9
18 45-54	2.6	6.9	4.3
19 55-64	2.9	3.9	3.2
20 65+	1.1	0.2	0.8
21			
22 15+	5.1	11.4	7.7

Source: Greece Labour Force Survey 2008.
Note: The data refer to the average of Q1 to Q4 of the quarterly LFS for 2008.

However, unemployment rates say nothing about the economic resources of unemployed workers or their family members. The indicator's use is limited to serving as a measurement of the underutilization of labor and an indication of the failure to find work. When analyzing unemployment data one should also bear in mind that the unemployment rate does not tell if the type of unemployment is cyclical or structural, which is a critical issue for policy makers in formulating policy responses, since certain structural forms of unemployment cannot be addressed by boosting market demand only (ILO 2015).

In 2008, around 378,000 persons were unemployed in Greece, representing a rate of 7.7 percent (screenshot 3.50). Women comprised the largest proportion of the unemployed in 2008. Their unemployment rate of 11.4 percent was more than double the rate of 5.1 percent for men. The largest gender imbalances in unemployment occurred among youth and young adults (ages 15–34), who made up nearly 60 percent of the total unemployed.

Those in the prime working-age group (ages 35–54) comprised 36 percent of the unemployed in 2008. Unemployment among older Greek workers (ages 55 and above) was low. Thus, the ranks of the unemployed are dominated by young persons (screenshot 3.50).

Table 36: Unemployment and Unemployment Rate by Sex and Region

Table 36 (screenshot 3.51) allows for analyses of regional disparities in unemployment and unemployment rates. The example shows that in 2010, Timor-Leste had a very low incidence of unemployment when compared to Greece in 2008 (screenshot 3.50). A total of 9,800 Timorese in the labor force were unemployed in 2010, corresponding to an unemployment rate of 3.7 percent. However, regional disparities in unemployment rates were sharp, with the highest rates in the urban centers Dili (9.8 percent) and Aileu (7.6 percent) and the lowest rates in the coastal area of Oecusse[8] (0.4 percent). Thus, the national unemployment rate was heavily influenced by unemployment in a few urban and semi-urban areas.

Further, one can also notice large differences between male and female unemployment of Timorese, especially in the districts of Dili, where the unemployment rate for women was 6.1 percentage points higher than the rate for men, and Covalima, with a difference of 5.5 percentage points between the rates of men and women in 2010 (screenshot 3.51).

Screenshot 3.51: Table 36: Unemployment and Unemployment Rate by Sex and Region, Timor-Leste, 2010

Table 36: Unemployment and unemployment rate, by sex and region

Timor-Leste, LFS 2010

	Male	Female	Both sexes		Male	Female	Both sexes
Unemployment ('000s)				Unemployment rate (%)			
Ainaro	0.1	0.1	0.2	Ainaro	0.9	1.0	1.0
Aileu	0.7	0.2	0.8	Aileu	9.3	4.7	7.6
Baucau	0.1	0.1	0.2	Baucau	1.1	1.7	1.3
Bobonaro	0.0	0.2	0.2	Bobonaro	0.1	2.4	0.9
Covalima	0.3	0.3	0.6	Covalima	2.7	8.2	4.1
Dili	3.5	2.8	6.3	Dili	7.9	14.0	9.8
Ermera	0.0	0.3	0.3	Ermera	0.2	2.2	0.9
Liquica	0.3	0.2	0.4	Liquica	2.6	3.2	2.8
Lautem	0.1	0.0	0.1	Lautem	1.6	0.5	1.2
Manufahi	0.1	0.0	0.1	Manufahi	0.9	0.5	0.7
Manatuto	0.2	0.0	0.2	Manatuto	3.0	2.5	2.9
Oecusse	0.1	0.0	0.1	Oecusse	0.5	0.0	0.4
Viqueque	0.1	0.0	0.1	Viqueque	1.0	0.0	0.7
Total	5.6	4.2	9.8	Total	3.1	5.0	3.7

Source: Timor-Leste Labour Force Survey 2010.

Generally unemployment and unemployment rates are low in countries without the safety net of unemployment insurance and welfare benefits, since many individuals, although they might be supported by their families, cannot afford to be unemployed. Instead, they must make a living as best they can, often in the informal economy.

In countries with well-developed social protection schemes or when savings or other means of support are available, as the example of Greece in 2008 shows (screenshot 3.50), workers can better afford to take the time to find more desirable jobs. Therefore, the problem in Timor-Leste in 2010 (screenshot 3.51), as in many developing countries, is not so much unemployment but rather the lack of decent and productive work, which results in various forms of labor underutilization (e.g., underemployment, low income, and low productivity).

Table 37: Duration of Unemployment by Sex and Age Group

Policy makers designing policy interventions to improve the availability of decent and productive employment opportunities for people must also look at the duration of their job search. Lengthy job search periods might indicate gaps between the supply and demand of labor in the country. This mismatch could be the result of unemployed people simply not having the skills or work experience required for certain jobs. However, it could also be the result of people's expectations not being met by the jobs offered to them. The latter type of mismatch has a higher likelihood of occurring among the more educated young people who often come from a more affluent background and can afford to be unemployed.

Reducing the length of unemployment spells is a key element in many strategies to reduce overall unemployment. Long-duration unemployment—lasting one year or longer—is undesirable, especially in circumstances where unemployment results from difficulties in matching supply and demand because of demand deficiency. Further, governments and planners that manage unemployment benefits in countries must monitor the duration of unemployment by sex and age group.

Table 37 (screenshot 3.52) includes, by sex and age group, the absolute numbers of unemployment, the duration of unemployment, and the unemployment rates. For example, the data for Greece reflect that almost half of all unemployed Greeks were long-term unemployed (49.5 percent of all unemployed in 2008). The highest prevalence of long-term unemployment was found for men ages 65+. Their rate was 84.2 percent of total unemployment.

Table 38: Unemployed and Unemployment Rate by Educational Attainment, Sex, and Age Group

Educational qualifications are considered a good insurance against unemployment (evidence shows the lower the level of education, the higher likelihood of unemployment) unless fragile economic conditions, skills mismatches, or problems with the educational system hinder people to find a job. Knowing the educational structure of the unemployed gives further insight to the skills mismatch. Thus, table 38 (screenshot 3.53) presents the number of unemployed and the unemployment rate by level of educational attainment for population subgroups.

In Mongolia (screenshot 3.53), the largest shares of the 104,200 unemployed people had either secondary education (43.7 percent) or a university degree (16.0 percent of unemployed) in 2009. Overall, unemployment rates of youth (ages 15–24) were significantly higher than the rates for adults regardless of the educational level attained.

Screenshot 3.52: Table 37: Duration of Unemployment by Sex and Age Group, Greece, 2008

Table 37: Duration of unemployment, by sex and age group — Greece LFS 2008

	Will start now searching			Less than one month			1-2 months			3-5 months			6-11 months		
	Male	Female	Both sexes	Male	Female	Both sexes	Male	Female	Both sexes	Male	Female	Both sexes	Male	Female	Both sexes
Unemployment ('000s)															
15-24	0.3	0.4	0.7	2.1	3.1	5.2	6.3	6.3	12.6	6.1	6.9	13.0	7.6	8.9	16.4
25-34	0.5	0.8	1.3	4.1	4.6	8.7	10.6	10.2	20.8	8.7	11.4	20.1	9.6	14.4	24.0
35-44	0.2	0.6	0.7	1.3	2.3	3.6	4.1	6.8	10.9	3.6	7.6	11.2	4.4	6.5	10.9
45-54	0.1	0.2	0.3	1.2	1.0	2.2	3.4	4.4	7.7	3.7	3.9	7.6	2.0	3.4	5.4
55-64	0.0	0.0	0.0	0.5	0.5	1.0	1.3	1.0	2.3	1.2	0.7	1.9	1.3	0.7	2.0
65+							0.0	0.0	0.1			0.1	0.0	0.0	0.0
15+	1.1	2.0	3.1	9.2	11.5	20.7	25.7	28.6	54.4	23.5	30.5	54.0	24.9	34.0	58.9
Unemployment rate (%)															
15-24	0.0	0.0	0.0	0.1	0.2	0.1	0.2	0.3	0.3	0.2	0.3	0.3	0.3	0.4	0.3
25-34	0.0	0.0	0.0	0.1	0.2	0.2	0.4	0.5	0.4	0.3	0.6	0.4	0.3	0.7	0.5
35-44	0.0	0.0	0.0	0.0	0.1	0.1	0.1	0.3	0.2	0.1	0.4	0.2	0.1	0.3	0.2
45-54	0.0	0.0	0.0	0.0	0.0	0.0	0.1	0.2	0.2	0.1	0.2	0.2	0.1	0.2	0.1
55-64	0.0	0.0	0.0	0.0	0.0	0.0	0.0	0.1	0.0	0.0	0.0	0.0	0.0	0.0	0.0
65+							0.0	0.0	0.0			0.0	0.0	0.0	0.0
15+	0.0	0.1	0.1	0.3	0.6	0.4	0.9	1.4	1.1	0.8	1.5	1.1	0.9	1.7	1.2

	12-17 months			18-23 months			24-47 months			4 years or longer		
	Male	Female	Both sexes	Male	Female	Both sexes	Male	Female	Both sexes	Male	Female	Both sexes
Unemployment ('000s)												
15-24	5.2	7.7	12.9	2.1	4.0	6.1	2.6	3.9	6.6	1.2	1.8	3.0
25-34	7.7	12.2	19.9	4.2	7.5	11.7	6.2	13.1	19.3	7.3	14.8	22.0
35-44	3.5	7.3	10.8	1.8	4.5	6.3	3.5	8.6	12.1	3.7	14.7	18.4
45-54	1.6	2.7	4.3	1.0	2.3	3.3	1.8	4.6	6.4	2.9	9.3	12.2
55-64	0.7	0.3	1.0	0.7	0.8	1.5	2.5	0.8	3.3	2.7	2.6	5.3
65+	0.1		0.1	0.0		0.0	0.3		0.3	0.1		0.1
15+	18.8	30.2	49.0	9.9	19.0	29.0	16.9	31.0	47.9	17.9	43.1	61.0
Unemployment rate (%)												
15-24	0.2	0.4	0.3	0.1	0.2	0.1	0.1	0.2	0.1	0.0	0.1	0.1
25-34	0.3	0.6	0.4	0.1	0.4	0.2	0.2	0.7	0.4	0.2	0.7	0.4
35-44	0.1	0.4	0.2	0.1	0.2	0.1	0.1	0.4	0.2	0.1	0.7	0.4
45-54	0.1	0.1	0.1	0.0	0.1	0.1	0.1	0.2	0.1	0.1	0.5	0.2
55-64	0.0	0.0	0.0	0.0	0.0	0.0	0.1	0.0	0.1	0.1	0.1	0.1
65+	0.0		0.0	0.0		0.0	0.0		0.0	0.0		0.0
15+	0.6	1.5	1.0	0.3	0.9	0.6	0.6	1.5	1.0	0.6	2.1	1.2

Source: Greece Labour Force Survey 2008.
Note: The data refer to the average of Q1 to Q4 of the quarterly LFS for 2008. Empty spaces reflect missing values for the particular group.

Screenshot 3.53: Table 38: Unemployment and Unemployment Rate by Educational Attainment, Sex, and Age Group, Mongolia, 2009

Table 38: Unemployed and unemployment rate by educational attainment, sex and age group — Mongolia LFS 2009

	Male			Female			Both sexes		
	15-24	25+	15+	15-24	25+	15+	15-24	25+	15+
Unemployment ('000s)									
None	0.6	0.7	1.3	0.1	0.6	0.6	0.6	1.3	1.9
Primary	0.9	1.9	2.8	0.2	1.0	1.2	1.2	2.9	4.1
Basic	2.6	9.1	11.7	1.4	7.7	9.2	4.0	16.9	20.9
Secondary	5.2	17.1	22.3	5.0	18.1	23.1	10.2	35.2	45.5
Initial technical vocational diploma certificate	0.9	2.9	3.8	0.6	3.2	3.9	1.6	6.2	7.7
Technical vocational diploma certificate	0.2	2.4	2.7	0.6	3.2	3.8	0.8	5.7	6.5
University graduate	3.2	3.9	7.1	3.6	5.3	8.9	6.8	9.3	16.0
Master and above	0.0	0.3	0.3	0.0	0.4	0.4	0.0	0.7	0.7
Total	13.8	38.6	52.4	11.8	40.0	51.8	25.6	78.6	104.2
Unemployment rate (%)									
None	15.1	12.8	13.7	2.9	13.4	9.9	10.7	13.0	12.2
Primary	5.5	3.8	4.3	2.2	2.7	2.6	4.2	3.3	3.5
Basic	11.0	8.6	9.0	10.1	9.2	9.3	10.7	8.9	9.2
Secondary	19.1	12.2	13.3	20.6	14.8	15.8	19.8	13.4	14.5
Initial technical vocational diploma certificate	25.4	7.6	9.2	25.8	11.2	12.4	25.6	9.2	10.6
Technical vocational diploma certificate	10.7	5.6	5.8	17.8	5.0	5.6	14.9	5.3	5.7
University graduate	30.2	6.9	10.5	25.8	7.3	10.2	27.7	7.1	10.3
Master and above	0.0	5.5	5.4	0.0	7.0	6.7	0.0	6.3	6.1
Total	15.3	8.6	9.7	15.9	9.4	10.4	15.6	9.0	10.0

Source: Mongolia Labour Force Survey 2009.

Reasons for large shares of female unemployed with high levels of education can be manifold and would require a careful analysis to better understand. However, reasons are likely due to the lack of sufficient professional and high-level technical jobs for women in the country. Other reasons could be the lack of working experience, cultural values, and norms that hinder women in rising to managerial positions in economic sectors such as health, education, business services, and government that require higher education. At the same time, it must be noted that young men and women with high educational levels often come from a wealthier background, which means that they can afford to wait for the "right" job.

Table 39: Share of Youth in Total Unemployment and Share of Youth Unemployed in Youth Population by Sex and Region

Table 39 (screenshot 3.54) indicates the share of young people among the total unemployed and the extent to which the young suffer from unemployment. In Q3-2010, the share of unemployed South Africans ages 15–24 in the total unemployed population was 31 percent. There were no great differences between the sexes. Nevertheless, the young male share of 31.9 percent was slightly above the female rate of 30.1 percent for that year.

Looking at the regional distribution of the shares of youth among the unemployed, the picture was more or less the same regardless of the region (screenshot 3.54); about 2 or 3 out of 10 unemployed persons were ages 15–24. The highest share of 34.5 percent of youth among the unemployed is observed for the region KwaZulu-Natal. In general, high shares are critical since they are a powerful reflection of the significant representation of youth among the unemployed.

The shares of unemployed youth in the youth population, as presented in the lower part of table 39 (screenshot 3.54), are even more worrisome. More than half of the South African youth were unemployed. Young women suffered particularly from unemployment; their share outpaced the 47.9 percent of young men by 7.6 percentage points. The issue was especially pronounced in Mpumalanga, where the female share of unemployment in youth unemployment reached 63.8 percent in Q3-2010. Obviously, the majority of young people, and especially young women, face severe difficulties when entering the world of work.

Screenshot 3.54: Table 39: Share of Youth in Total Unemployment and Share of Youth Unemployment in Youth Population by Sex and Region, South Africa, Q3-2010

Table 39: Share of youth in total unemployment and share of youth unemployed in youth population, by sex and region			
	South Africa LFS 3rd Quarter 2010		
	Male	Female	Both sexes
Share of youth unemployed in total unemployment (%)			
Western Cape	31.0	37.5	34.2
Eastern Cape	36.0	29.7	32.8
Northern Cape	32.9	32.8	32.8
Free State	34.4	27.7	31.1
KwaZulu-Natal	35.2	33.8	34.5
North West	31.6	30.4	31.1
Gauteng	28.6	27.8	28.2
Mpumalanga	35.5	29.7	32.6
Limpopo	28.9	23.5	26.5
Total	31.9	30.1	31.0
Share of youth unemployed in youth population (%)			
Western Cape	45.2	51.7	48.4
Eastern Cape	51.3	57.9	54.2
Northern Cape	43.4	54.6	48.9
Free State	53.7	58.0	55.4
KwaZulu-Natal	39.1	44.8	41.7
North West	56.0	61.0	58.0
Gauteng	52.1	60.8	56.2
Mpumalanga	48.2	63.8	54.3
Limpopo	43.1	52.2	46.3
Total	47.9	55.5	51.3

Source: South Africa Labour Force Survey Q3-2010.

Spells of unemployment early in a young person's work life can have lasting negative effects on future earnings, productivity, and employment opportunities. Therefore, policy makers must try to understand the causes of youth unemployment in the broader macroeconomic context so they can create jobs for young workers and help them build the skills necessary to successfully enter the labor market.

Screenshot 3.55: Table 40: Ratio of Youth-to-Adult Unemployment Rate by Sex and Region, South Africa, Q3-2010

	Table 40: Ratio of youth-to-adult unemployment rate, by sex and region		
1			
2	South Africa LFS 3rd Quarter 2010		
3	Male	Female	Both sexes
4	**South African provinces**		
5 Western Cape	2.5	2.8	2.7
6 Eastern Cape	2.6	2.5	2.5
7 Northern Cape	2.5	2.2	2.4
8 Free State	2.5	2.1	2.3
9 KwaZulu-Natal	2.7	2.7	2.7
10 North West	2.6	2.5	2.6
11 Gauteng	2.9	2.3	2.6
12 Mpumalanga	2.4	2.4	2.4
13 Limpopo	2.0	2.4	2.2
14			
15 Total	2.6	2.4	2.5

Source: South Africa Labour Force Survey Q3-2010.

Table 40: Ratio of Youth-to-Adult Unemployment Rate by Sex and Region

Table 40 (screenshot 3.55) shows the ratio of the youth-to-adult unemployment rates, which is a useful way of examining youth unemployment. In South Africa, the ratio in most regions was about 2.5 to 1, that is, the youth rate has been two and a half times that of adults. The key message is that youth compared to adults have much greater difficulties in the South African labor market in securing employment (see box 3.1).

Table 41: Youth Not in Education, Employment, or Training (NEET) by Sex and Region

Many unemployed youth find it especially hard to find a job. Since youth unemployment rates alone do not provide an indication of the extent of deficiencies in labor market opportunities for young people and idleness among youth, a newer measure that assesses the number of youth who are not in education, employment, or training (NEET) has been introduced. Youth who are not engaged in one of these activities are seen to be most

Box 3.1: Why Are Youth Unemployment Rates Usually Higher than Adult Unemployment Rates?

In many countries, youth unemployment rates are usually higher than adult unemployment rates, leading to the important question: why? There are many likely explanations:

The last-in, first-out explanation. Youth are more vulnerable than adults in difficult economic times. They are likely to have less work experience than adults. Assuming that employers seek employees with past experience, a youth entering the labor force for the first time will be at a disadvantage and have a harder time finding employment as compared to an adult with a longer history of work experience. In times of surplus labor competing for a limited amount of jobs, the youth will be the "last in." Similarly, because young workers are likely to have less tenure than adult workers, less company funds are invested in them for training purposes, and they are less likely to have a long-term contract, they will be considered cheaper to let go during economic downturns. Thus, young workers will be the "first out."

The lack of job search expertise explanation. A young person often lacks both labor market information and job search experience. In many developing countries, a young person finds work only through informal placement methods—typically through family and friends. Beyond the word-of-mouth approach, they simply might not know how and where to look for work. Adults, in contrast, might find future work through references from previous employers or colleagues and are more likely to know the "right" people.

The "shopping around" explanation. Another possibility is that youth might take longer to "shop around" for the right job, meaning they might wait longer to find work that suits their requirements. This, however, implies that a support structure, such as the family, exists to support them economically while they search for work. In low-income countries, this support structure does not exist for the majority of young people. As a result, a young person simply cannot afford to be unemployed and is likely to take whatever work becomes available, regardless of working conditions or whether or not the job fits their education or skills base.

The lack of mobility explanation. Young people starting out in the labor force are unlikely to have the financial resources to relocate, nationally or internationally, in pursuit of work. Because many will continue to depend on household incomes, their job search threshold will be limited to the vicinity of the family home.

The measurement explanation. Inactivity among young people is increasing. Conversely, the youth labor force, and thus the denominator of the youth unemployment rate calculation, is shrinking in many parts of the world since more young people are enrolled in education, staying in the education system for longer periods of time, or dropping out of the labor force as discouraged workers. This means that if from year X to year Y, the youth labor force in year Y is less than that of year X

(continued)

> **Box 3.1: Why Are Youth Unemployment Rates Usually Higher than Adult Unemployment Rates?** *(continued)*
>
> (and assuming the absolute total of unemployed youth remained constant), the youth unemployment rate (as the number of youth unemployed/youth labor force) will be higher in year Y than in year X. There has not been a similar shrinkage of the adult labor force, which means that the gap between the youth and the adult unemployment rates would grow.
>
> The explanations given above—and there are likely to be even more—are a mixture of demand-side causes ("last in-first out" particularly) and supply-side causes ("shopping around," etc.). None of the explanations is likely to explain in full the difference between youth and adult unemployment rates. What is most likely is that the different factors work together—and do not underestimate the influence of the shrinking youth labor force on the measurement—to result in the proportion of unemployed youth in the youth labor force being significantly higher than the proportion of unemployed adults in the adult labor force.
>
> *Source:* ILO 2006 (box 2.1).

vulnerable, facing a difficult process of integration or reintegration into the labor force and at risk of remaining idle and becoming alienated from society. For every economy, the presence of discouraged workers represents a waste of human resources and of productive potential.

Analyses of table 41 (screenshot 3.56) for Mongolia show that around 101,000 young people were NEET in 2009, or 19.4 percent of the youth population. The rate was 0.7 percentage points higher than in 2008. The increase was mainly driven by higher NEET rates in Ulaanbaatar and the western region compared to the previous year.

Gender analysis of table 41 (screenshot 3.56) reveals that the NEET rate for young women in 2009 was 21.7 percent, or 4.6 percentage points higher than the corresponding rate for men, and an increase of 2.4 percentage points compared to the prior year. Female NEET rates increased in four out of five regions while male rates decreased in three regions, remained unchanged in one, and increased only in the western region by 2.7 percentage points, reflecting an increasing disconnection from the labor market among young women, especially in Ulaanbaatar.

A variety of reasons could explain why young Mongolians were not in education, employment nor training in 2008 and 2009. Some were unemployed. Some might have been caring for other family members; were sick or disabled; or simply did not want to work. Perhaps culturally driven beliefs and

Screenshot 3.56: Table 41: Youth Not in Education, Employment, or Training (NEET) by Sex and Region, Mongolia, 2008 and 2009

	Mongolia LFS 2008			Mongolia LFS 2009			Change		
	Male	Female	Both sexes	Male	Female	Both sexes	Male	Female	Both sexes
Youth NEET ('000s)									
West region	4.2	4.2	8.4	5.0	5.6	10.6	0.8	1.4	2.2
Khangai region	11.0	9.9	20.9	9.2	11.0	20.2	-1.8	1.1	-0.7
Central region	10.9	8.3	19.2	8.0	8.7	16.7	-2.9	0.4	-2.5
East region	4.9	5.7	10.7	5.3	3.5	8.8	0.4	-2.3	-1.8
Ulaanbaatar	15.9	20.7	36.6	16.6	28.2	44.8	0.7	7.5	8.3
Total	46.8	48.8	95.7	44.1	57.0	101.1	-2.7	8.1	5.4
Youth NEET share of youth population (%)									
West region	11.3	12.4	11.8	14.0	16.5	15.2	2.7	4.0	3.4
Khangai region	18.2	18.3	18.3	16.3	19.1	17.7	-2.0	0.8	-0.6
Central region	23.7	19.9	21.9	18.4	20.9	19.6	-5.3	1.0	-2.3
East region	25.5	27.9	26.7	24.3	18.5	21.6	-1.2	-9.3	-5.1
Ulaanbaatar	16.7	20.1	18.5	16.6	25.6	21.3	0.0	5.4	2.9
Total	18.2	19.3	18.7	17.1	21.7	19.4	-1.0	2.4	0.7

Table 41: Youth not in education, employment or training (NEET), by sex and region

Sources: Mongolia Labour Force Survey 2008 and 2009.

family pressures kept them idle. It is likely that some were discouraged after being unemployed for a long period of time, and believed that undertaking any kind of job search would be pointless. Others might not have sought work because they were—or thought they were—insufficiently educated or skilled, had no suitable local work, or simply did not know how to look for work effectively. This complex issue underscores the need for high-quality government employment services or private sector initiatives to facilitate recruitment.

Persons Outside the Labor Force (One Table)

Persons outside the labor force (formerly known as the "economically inactive") are of working age who are neither employed nor unemployed. They are people who do not actively participate in the labor market because they are unable to find or are unwilling to start a job. Inactivity rates can be very different for men and women for a wide range of factors. These include the economic climate, social and cultural norms, and legislation and education (ILO 2015).

Most commonly, persons of working age outside the labor force are students, women or men looking after the family or home, those unable to work because of long-term illness or disability, those with a short-term illness, and discouraged persons who have given up looking for a job. Clearly some of these groups have a greater tendency for future labor market participation than others; for instance, students are very likely to join the labor force in a relatively short period of time, whereas retired people are not. Thus, policy makers must analyze the inactivity information to find ways to integrate young people into the labor market after they finish their education or to encourage them to use their potential to actively contribute to the country's economy.

Table 42: Persons Outside the Labor Force by Reason and Sex

As discussed previously, there are numerous reasons why people are outside the labor force. Government programs and interventions to promote increased participation in labor markets require a solid understanding of the underlying causes of inactivity. Thus, table 42 (screenshot 3.57) provides the number and share of persons outside the labor force by reason for not being in the labor force and by sex.

Based on the 2008 LFS data for Greece, table 42 (screenshot 3.57) shows that 4.3 million of the working-age population (46.5 percent, or almost half) were outside the labor force in 2008. The inactivity rates for men (35.1 percent of the male working-age population) were much lower compared to women (57.4 percent of the female working-age population). Relatively higher inactivity rates for women are very common around the world and can be partially explained by the large numbers of women in their 20s and 30s leaving the labor force to attend to family responsibilities such as childbearing and childcare.

In Greece (screenshot 3.57), the main reason for male inactivity was retirement (23.4 percent of the total working-age population). In comparison, females were not outside of the labor force just because of retirement. Some women did not actively participate in the labor market because of family or personal reasons (11.4 percent of total working-age population), training or education (8.3 percent of total working-age population), and other unspecified motives (15.7 percent of total working-age population). "Unspecified" motives may indicate discouraged people, particularly youth, who are available for work but stopped searching because they believe they will not find any. Young men and women today face increasing uncertainty in their hopes of entering the labor market satisfactorily, and this uncertainty and disillusionment can, in turn, have damaging effects on individuals, communities, economies, and society at large. Knowing the costs of nonaction, many governments prioritize the issue of youth employment and attempt to develop appropriate policies and programs (ILO 2012b).

Screenshot 3.57: Table 42: Persons Outside the Labor Force by Reason and Sex, Greece, 2008

1	Table 42: Persons outside the labour force by reason and sex		
2			Greece LFS 2008
3		Male	Female	Both sexes
4	**Persons outside the labour force ('000s)**			
5	Has a job and not seeking for another job	0.0	0.0	0.0
6	Looking after children or incapacitated adults	0.4	108.4	108.8
7	Family or personal reasons	9.1	538.5	547.6
8	Training or education	375.4	392.9	768.3
9	Retirement	1,052.5	780.5	1,833.0
10	Own illness or disability to work	86.8	87.2	174.0
11	Believes that will not find a job or does not know where to apply for a job	3.5	11.6	15.1
12	Waiting recall to work (persons on lay-off)	0.1		0.1
13	Other	39.2	744.4	783.5
14	No reason given	5.0	39.2	44.2
15	ADePT : N/A	9.5	12.6	22.1
16				
17	Total	1,581.5	2,715.3	4,296.8
18				
19	**Persons outside the labour force as share of the working-age population (%)**			
20	Has a job and not seeking for another job	0.0	0.0	0.0
21	Looking after children or incapacitated adults	0.0	2.3	1.2
22	Family or personal reasons	0.2	11.4	5.9
23	Training or education	8.3	8.3	8.3
24	Retirement	23.4	16.5	19.9
25	Own illness or disability to work	1.9	1.8	1.9
26	Believes that will not find a job or does not know where to apply for a job	0.1	0.2	0.2
27	Waiting recall to work (persons on lay-off)	0.0		0.0
28	Other	0.9	15.7	8.5
29	No reason given	0.1	0.8	0.5
30	ADePT : N/A	0.2	0.3	0.2
31				
32	Total	35.1	57.4	46.5

Source: Greece Labour Force Survey 2008.
Note: The data refer to the average of Q1 to Q4 of the quarterly LFS for 2008. Empty spaces reflect missing values for the particular group.

Working Poverty Tables (Six Tables)

The ADePT output tables contribute to a better understanding of the linkages between poverty, employment, and decent work in countries. Also, working poor estimates are another way to identify deficits or progress toward MDG [Millennium Development Goal] Target 1b, *"full and productive employment and decent work for all,"* since opportunities for people to earn an income that enables them to live above the poverty threshold are a core element of decent work.

Working poor figures usually are derived from HIESs, since they are calculated by cross-tabulating household poverty status with individuals' employment status. In this respect, working poverty data complement traditional poverty data because they take into account countries' labor market characteristics, such as the size of the working-age population, the labor force participation rate, and the unemployment rate. By combining these labor market factors with poverty data, working poverty estimates give a clearer picture of the relationship between poverty and employment than that provided by standard poverty data alone. Evaluating these two components side by side also provides a more detailed view of the nature of poverty in countries, since employment and poverty are intertwined.

The ILO describes the working poor as the proportion of those employed living in a household whose members are estimated to be below the poverty line.[9] This benchmark may be the national poverty line or the US\$1.25 or US\$2.00 a day international poverty line. Relative measures can also be used, such as 50 percent of median per capita consumption (expenditures). The household is the unit of reference, and the definition simply links household poverty to the number of employed persons in the household, rather than individual pay to the person employed.

The working poverty indicator is one of the four indicators under MDG Target 1b to *"achieve full and productive employment and decent work for all, including women and young people,"* and this indicator is calculated as the proportion of the working poor in total employment.

Knowing the profile of the working poor is helpful for any targeted policy initiative to help workers escaping the poverty trap. However, the variation of factors must inform the entire policy process, and can most effectively assist policy makers in designing programs that seek to permanently alleviate poverty. Nevertheless, the following tables 43–48 (screenshots 3.58–3.63) provide valuable information that, when analyzed, can highlight which workers need special attention and how best to assist them.

Table 43: Working Poor and Share of Working Poor in Total Employment by Sex and Age Group

Table 43 (screenshot 3.58) presents the number and share of employed persons living in households below the identified poverty line by sex and

Screenshot 3.58: Table 43: Working Poor and Share of Working Poor in Total Employment by Sex and Age Group, Mongolia, 2008

	Table 43: Working poor and share of working poor in total employment, by sex and age group Mongolia 2008		
	Male	Female	Both sexes
Working poor ('000s)			
15-24	41.1	32.2	73.3
25+	135.1	126.9	262.0
Total	185.2	166.0	351.2
Share of working poor in total employment (%)			
15-24	40.0	40.0	40.0
25+	30.7	28.9	29.8
Total	33.0	31.0	32.0

Source: Mongolia Household Income and Expenditure Survey 2008.

age group. It applies the ILO definition of the working poor (see previous section) and uses data from the Mongolian HIES of 2008. The national poverty line developed by the National Statistics Office[10] is used to determine whether a household is poor or not.

Note that HIES estimates of employment are typically not as precise as measurements from an LFS. Most HIESs contain a less comprehensive set of employment questions than in an LFS; consequently, estimates derived from an HIES may result in a different estimate of the working poor than would be derived by an LFS. However, since most LFSs do not include information on household consumption, HIES data are generally required to produce tabulations of the working poor. The same remarks also apply for tables 44–48 (screenshots 3.59–3.63).

Table 43 (screenshot 3.58) indicates that 351,200 Mongolians, or 32.0 percent of the employed, were living below the nationally defined poverty line. Almost 4 out of 10 employed young people ages 15–24 were identified as working poor. The share of working poor men (33.0 percent) was 2 percentage points higher than the share of working poor women (31.0 percent).

Table 44: Working Poor and Share of Working Poor in Total Employment by Sex and Region

Analysis of regionally disaggregated working poor estimates for Mongolia in 2008, presented in table 44 (screenshot 3.59), reveals significant differences in working poverty between regions. The incidence of working poor was highest in Mongolia's highlands and western regions, at 43.2 and 42.6 percent of total employment, respectively. These shares are more than twice as high as the 16.5 percent in Ulaanbaatar. The findings highlight that working poverty is largely a phenomenon of rural and agricultural areas in Mongolia.

Table 45: Working Poor and Share of Working Poor in Total Employment, by Status in Employment and Sex

Examinations of table 45 (screenshot 3.60) indicate that own-account workers and contributing family workers have a disproportionately high incidence of working poverty, which is to be expected since they often lack contractual arrangements, steady incomes, and social protection,

Screenshot 3.59: Table 44: Working Poor and Share of Working Poor in Total Employment by Sex and Region, Mongolia, 2008

	Table 44: Working poor and share of working poor in total employment, by sex and region		
2	Mongolia HS 2008		
3	Male	Female	Both sexes
4	**Working poor ('000s)**		
5 West	43.6	39.6	83.3
6 Highlands	61.2	54.3	115.5
7 Central	34.3	31.0	65.3
8 East	18.4	17.5	35.9
9 UB	27.7	23.6	51.2
11 Total	185.2	166.0	351.2
13 **Share of working poor in total employment (%)**			
14 West	43.5	41.6	42.6
15 Highlands	44.3	42.0	43.2
16 Central	28.1	27.5	27.8
17 East	40.0	40.2	40.1
18 UB	17.8	15.2	16.5
20 Total	33.0	31.0	32.0

Source: Mongolia Household Income and Expenditure Survey 2008.
Note: UB = Ulaanbaatar.

Screenshot 3.60: Table 45: Working Poor and Share of Working Poor in Total Employment by Status in Employment and Sex, Mongolia, 2008

Table 45: Working poor and share of working poor in total employment, by status in employment and sex Mongolia HS 2008			
	Male	Female	Both sexes
Working poor ('000s)			
Wage and salaried workers	58.9	52.8	111.7
Employers			
Own-account workers	95.0	41.2	136.3
Contributing family workers	31.1	71.7	102.7
Not classifiable	0.3	0.3	0.6
ADePT : N/A			
Total	185.2	166.0	351.2
Share of working poor in total employment (%)			
Wage and salaried workers	25.7	21.5	23.6
Employers			
Own-account workers	36.4	35.4	36.1
Contributing family workers	43.3	41.3	41.9
Not classifiable	84.8	100.0	92.0
ADePT : N/A			
Total	33.0	31.0	32.0

Source: Mongolia Household Income and Expenditure Survey 2008.

leading to job insecurities. In Mongolia, own-account workers (136,300) and contributing family workers (102,700) in 2008 comprised 68.1 percent of all 351,200 working poor.

However, table 45 (screenshot 3.60) also shows that 111,700 wage and salaried workers could be defined as working poor, or 23.6 percent of total wage and salaried employment in 2008. Since more than 2 out of 10 wage and salaried workers in Mongolia were identified as working poor in 2008, it highlights the fact that not all wage and salaried jobs were necessarily decent jobs. Many wage and salaried workers appear to be affected by job insecurities, low average wages, and limited social protection.

Table 46: Working Poor and Share of Working Poor in Total Employment by Sector and Sex

The sectoral breakdown of the working poor population in Mongolia reveals interesting patterns (table 46, screenshot 3.61). More than 4 out of 10 agricultural workers were defined as working poor; around 35 percent of manufacturing workers were living below the poverty line; about 24 percent working in services as a whole were living below the poverty line. Working poverty rates stood at 34.2 percent in construction and at 24.8 percent in transport and communication.

Screenshot 3.61: Table 46: Working Poor and Share of Working Poor in Total Employment by Sector and Sex, Mongolia, 2002

Table 46: Working poor and share of working poor in total employment, by sector and sex							
				Mongolia HS 2002			
	Male	Female	Both sexes		Male	Female	Both sexes
Working poor ('000s)				**Share of working poor in total employment (%)**			
Agriculture	7.1	7.0	14.1	Agriculture	38.4	43.2	40.6
Mining and Quarrying	3.9	0.6	4.6	Mining and Quarrying	26.6	11.2	22.5
Manufacturing	5.4	6.8	12.2	Manufacturing	37.4	33.9	35.4
Electricity, water supply	2.8	1.0	3.8	Electricity, water supply	26.7	24.0	25.9
Construction	6.2	2.6	8.8	Construction	35.3	31.9	34.2
Wholesale and retail trade	5.8	11.0	16.9	Wholesale and retail trade	22.3	24.6	23.8
Hotels and restaurants	0.3	1.5	1.7	Hotels and restaurants	11.5	21.4	18.9
Transport and communication	8.6	2.7	11.3	Transport and communication	23.2	31.8	24.8
Financial	0.0	0.2	0.2	Financial	0.0	7.8	5.7
Business activity	4.3	4.5	8.8	Business activity	23.7	28.2	25.8
Public administration	7.7	3.9	11.6	Public administration	20.0	18.1	19.3
Education	4.5	9.6	14.1	Education	21.5	19.4	20.1
Health	1.5	6.9	8.4	Health	22.8	23.2	23.1
Service	4.5	4.6	9.0	Service	25.1	23.3	24.2
Other	3.9	1.9	5.8	Other	39.0	22.3	31.3
ADePT : N/A	87.4	82.3	169.7	ADePT : N/A	38.7	38.4	38.6
Total	153.8	147.1	300.9	Total	32.0	30.9	31.5

Source: Mongolia Household Income and Expenditure Survey 2002.
Note: The reference period for the labor force status is the previous year, as in the 2008 HIES.

Table 47: Working Poor and Share of Working Poor in Total Employment by Education Completed and Sex

Table 47 (screenshot 3.62) looks at the educational profile of the working poor to better understand the causes of working poverty and its relationship with education. This, in turn, can help analysts facilitate targeted policy interventions. There is a common belief among researchers that education is the cure for poverty. However, when factoring employment into the equation, this theory does not seem to always hold—especially if the labor market demand for people with high educational attainment is not in the labor markets or wages are below a minimum standard.

Analysis of table 47 (screenshot 3.62) for Mongolia reveals that the least educated are the most likely to be working poor: 55.5 percent of the employed population with less than primary education and 46.6 percent of the employed population with primary education were defined as working poor. In contrast, only 13.6 percent of the employed population with higher education were defined as working poor. Gender differences in the

Screenshot 3.62: Table 47: Working Poor and Share of Working Poor in Total Employment by Education Completed and Sex, Mongolia, 2008

	Male	Female	Both sexes
Table 47: Working poor and share of working poor in total employment, by education completed and sex Mongolia HS 2008			
Working poor ('000s)			
Less than primary	16.2	10.9	27.1
Primary (completed)	96.6	74.7	171.3
Secondary (completed)	52.4	54.3	106.7
Tertiary	19.7	25.9	45.7
Other	0.3	0.2	0.5
Total	185.2	166.0	351.2
Share of working poor in total employment (%)			
Less than primary	55.7	55.2	55.5
Primary (completed)	45.9	47.5	46.6
Secondary (completed)	30.1	33.4	31.7
Tertiary	13.7	13.5	13.6
Other	7.4	5.7	6.5
Total	33.0	31.0	32.0

Source: Mongolia Household Income and Expenditure Survey 2008.

educational profile of the working poor were marginal in 2008, reflecting that the situation is more or less the same for men and women.

Table 48: Working Poor by Hours per Week and by Sex

In developed and transitioning economies, workers are often poor because they are time-related underemployed, meaning they are working less than they desire although they are actively seeking more work. Underemployment often has large impacts on the household income since fewer working hours often means having less income. On the contrary, in developing countries, workers usually have to work long hours to ensure a minimum household income. Since most of the working poor are own-account or contributing family workers, without any social security or protection, they simply cannot afford to stop working.

Analysis of the working hours of the working poor in Mongolia in table 48 (screenshot 3.63) shows that 195,300, or 55.6 percent, of the working poor were working more than 48 hours a week in 2008. However, among the various groups of working hours, the highest incidence of working poverty was found in the category of 25–34 hours per week (39.3 percent).

Similar to the data in table 47 (screenshot 3.62), data in table 48 show no clear picture on gender differences in working poverty. Among employed women working 35–39 hours per week, 41.3 percent were

Screenshot 3.63: Table 48: Working Poor by Hours of Work per Week and by Sex, Mongolia, 2008

	Table 48: Working poor, by hours of work per week and sex Mongolia HS 2008		
		Male	Female	Both sexes
1				
2				
3		Male	Female	Both sexes
4	Working poor ('000s)			
5	<25	12.6	15.1	27.8
6	25-34	8.6	13.1	21.7
7	35-39	7.3	11.6	19.0
8	40-48	40.2	46.8	87.0
9	49-59	46.6	40.8	87.5
10	>=60	69.6	38.1	107.8
12	Total	185.2	166.0	351.2
14	Share of working poor in total employment (%)			
15	<25	36.3	35.2	35.7
16	25-34	37.6	40.6	39.3
17	35-39	34.8	41.3	38.5
18	40-48	25.3	24.9	25.1
19	49-59	38.2	36.2	37.2
20	>=60	34.5	29.3	32.5
22	Total	33.0	31.0	32.0

Source: Mongolia Household Income and Expenditure Survey 2008.

defined as poor while almost 35 percent of the employed men working the same hours were poor. In contrast, the working poverty rate for men working excessive hours (60 or more) was 5.2 percentage points higher than the rate for women.

Earnings Tables (Five Tables)

As presented in tables 49–52b (screenshots 3.64–3.68), data on earnings should ideally relate to average[11] gross earnings (wages or salary) per worker, expressed as monthly averages in the primary job. Earnings data, collected through household surveys, usually cover cash payments received from employers before deduction of taxes and social security contributions payable by workers. The data comprise remuneration for normal working hours, overtime pay, incentive pay, and earnings of piece workers; remuneration for time not worked (annual vacation, public holidays, sick leave, and other paid leave); and bonuses and gratuities for the primary and secondary jobs.[12]

Earnings do not include employers' contributions paid for their employees, such as social security and pension schemes, or benefits received by employees under these schemes. Earnings also exclude severance and termination pay.

In some cases household surveys provide information on earnings derived from work activities of employers and the self-employed. Earning tables of this section are nominal values (unadjusted to inflation), expressed in absolute numbers and in national currency. However, ADePT can also provide calculations on real earnings (adjusted to inflation) if such information is in the input file.

Overall analysis of earnings statistics is needed for planning economic and social development, establishing income and fiscal policies, fixing social security contributions and benefits, and regulating minimum wages and collective bargaining. Policy makers—as well as employers and trade unions—must pay close attention to earning trends. For example, they may want to compare earning levels to other available indicators (e.g., labor productivity, poverty thresholds, or prices of goods).[13]

Overall, policy implementation and institutional arrangements play a significant role in reducing wage inequalities between and within worker groups. However, wage imbalances have persisted in many countries—across dimensions such as gender, education, sectors, and occupation—which therefore require continuous policy and institutional adaptation. Enhancing the supply of skilled labor is often cited as an effective means to minimize wage inequalities.

Table 49: Earnings by Occupation and Sex

Earnings by occupation and sex can facilitate detection of gender inequalities in earnings and earning trends, when analyzed over time. Based on LFS data for Q3-2010 for South Africa, table 49 (screenshot 3.64) presents monthly earnings of employees in the primary job. It reveals that, overall, the better the level of skills, the better the monthly median earnings. Legislators, senior officials, and managers earned a monthly median of 10,500 South African rand (R) in 2010, professionals earned monthly median earnings of R 11,000, and technical and associate professionals received monthly median earnings of R 8,000. The earnings of these highly skilled occupations were significantly above those of other professions. Domestic workers, with monthly median earnings of R 1,000, and workers in elementary occupations, with monthly median earnings of R 1,516, had the lowest monthly median wages when compared with other occupational groups in Q3-2010.

Screenshot 3.64: Table 49: Wages or Earnings by Occupation and Sex, South Africa, Q3-2010

	Table 49: Wages/earnings by occupation and sex			
2		South Africa LFS 3rd Quarter 2010		
3		Male	Female	Both sexes
4	**Main occupation**			
5	Legislators, senior officials and managers	11,700.0	9,000.0	10,500.0
6	Professionals	12,000.0	9,700.0	11,000.0
7	Technical and associate professionals	8,000.0	7,900.0	8,000.0
8	Clerks	5,000.0	4,010.0	4,500.0
9	Service workers and shop and market sales workers	2,600.0	2,000.0	2,400.0
10	Skilled agricultural and fishery workers	6,000.0	3,000.0	5,000.0
11	Craft and related trades workers	3,000.0	1,733.0	2,946.0
12	Plant and machine operators and assemblers	3,033.0	1,755.0	2,946.0
13	Elementary Occupation	1,646.0	1,408.0	1,516.0
14	Domestic workers	1,000.0	1,000.0	1,000.0

Source: South Africa Labour Force Survey Q3-2010.
Note: Earnings are defined as monthly median earnings per employee in the primary job. The data cover wage earners of both sexes, without distinction as to age. Earnings are expressed in the national currency, South African rand (R). At the exchange rate from July 1, 2010, R 1.00 was equivalent to US$0.13.

In all occupational groups, men earned more than women, with the exception of domestic workers (male and female domestic workers received the same wages or earnings).

Table 50: Wages or Earnings by Sector and Sex

As shown for South Africa, table 50 (screenshot 3.65) allows for cross-sectional analyses of earning inequalities in countries. Employees in community, social, and personal services had the highest monthly median earnings of R 6,000 in Q3-2010. In contrast, workers in the agriculture, hunting, forestry, and fishing industry and those working for private households earned the lowest median earnings compared to other sectors, with median monthly earnings of R 1,300 and R 1,000, respectively.

Comparing male and female earnings in economic sectors in screenshot 3.65 highlights existing gender imbalances throughout all industries in Q3-2010. The largest earning differentials of men and women are in the electricity, gas, and water supply sector. Here, women earned a monthly median of R 9,000, which is significantly more than men in the sector (monthly median earnings of R 4,700); these data reflect a much

Screenshot 3.65: Table 50: Wages or Earnings by Sector and Sex, South Africa, Q3-2010

	Table 50: Wages/earnings by sector and sex		
	South Africa LFS 3rd Quarter 2010		
	Male	Female	Both sexes
Main industry			
Agriculture, hunting. forestry and fishing	1,300.0	1,200.0	1,300.0
Mining and quarrying	5,000.0	5,190.0	5,000.0
Manufacturing	3,900.0	2,166.0	3,200.0
Electricity, gas and water supply	4,700.0	9,000.0	5,900.0
Construction	2,600.0	1,729.0	2,600.0
Wholesale and retail trade	2,900.0	2,166.0	2,500.0
Transport, storage and communication	3,500.0	4,800.0	3,986.0
Financial intermediation, insurance, real estate and business services	3,640.0	5,000.0	4,000.0
Community, social and personal services	7,000.0	5,000.0	6,000.0
Private households	1,040.0	1,000.0	1,000.0
Other		16,000.0	16,000.0

Source: South Africa Labour Force Survey Q3-2010.
Note: Empty space reflects a missing value for the particular group. Earnings are defined as monthly median wages per employee in the primary job expressed as median earnings. The data cover wage earners of both sexes, without distinction as to age. Wages are expressed in the national currency, South African rand (R). At the exchange rate from July 1, 2010, R 1.00 was equivalent to US$0.13.

higher share of skilled female employees in these industries. On the contrary, monthly median earnings of men were significantly higher in the sectors of community, social, and personal services and in manufacturing.

Table 51: Wages or Earnings by Educational Attainment and Sex

As shown in the analysis of table 49 (screenshot 3.64), higher skill levels usually result in higher earnings. Table 51 (screenshot 3.66) focuses on earnings or wages across educational groups, allowing analysis of wage or earning differentials between men and women with the same educational background and between educational attainment levels.

Table 51 for Mongolia demonstrates the importance of educational attainment on wages. Overall, wages in Mongolia were fairly moderate and symmetrically distributed when compared to the earnings in South Africa (tables 49 and 50, screenshots 3.64 and 3.65, respectively), which is why ADePT calculated the mean (and not the median) of wages to reflect monthly average wages of Mongolian employees in the primary job.

Screenshot 3.66: Table 51: Wages or Earnings by Educational Attainment and Sex, Mongolia, 2008 and 2009

	Table 51: Wages/earnings by educational attainment and sex								
	Mongolia LFS 2008			Mongolia LFS 2009			Change		
	Male	Female	Both sexes	Male	Female	Both sexes	Male	Female	Both sexes
educational level									
None	108.6	249.3	143.9	128.2	76.3	121.9	19.6	-173.0	-22.0
Primary	126.2	168.8	134.2	127.5	129.2	127.8	1.2	-39.6	-6.4
Basic	137.9	121.6	133.6	162.5	141.5	157.3	24.6	19.9	23.6
Secondary	189.9	170.6	181.6	225.6	202.5	216.8	35.7	31.9	35.2
Initial technical/vocational diploma/certificate	197.2	167.2	184.6	226.3	197.3	215.4	29.1	30.1	30.8
Technical/vocational diploma/certificate	228.2	202.6	213.6	281.5	252.0	264.5	53.3	49.4	50.8
University graduate	257.0	227.6	240.9	348.6	285.8	313.6	91.5	58.2	72.7
Master and above	341.9	295.5	314.9	516.4	351.4	429.6	174.5	56.0	114.7

Sources: Mongolia Labour Force Surveys 2008 and 2009.
Note: Wages are defined as monthly average wages per employee in the primary job before deductions and expressed as average (mean) wages. The data cover wage earners of both sexes, without distinction as to age. Wages are expressed in thousands in the national currency, Mongolian tughrik (Tog). At the exchange rate from July 1, 2009, Tog 1.00 was equivalent to US$0.00070.

Analyses of table 51 (screenshot 3.66) show how wages of Mongolians gradually increased with better education. Employees with master's degrees and above earned 429,600 Mongolian tughrik (Tog) in 2009, on a monthly average, almost three times as much as employees with basic or even lower educational attainment.

As expected, monthly average wages for women were lower than for men, although the imbalances were far less pronounced when compared to South Africa (table 50, screenshot 3.65). Yet when looking at the wage trends, one notices increased gaps between monthly average earnings of men and women since earnings of women increased less than for men between 2008 and 2009 (screenshot 3.66).

Wage gaps between men and women in Mongolia widened the most for employees with less than basic education: monthly average wages for men increased and for women decreased. For employees with tertiary education, the monthly average wage increased much less for women when compared to men (screenshot 3.66). The widening gender gaps in wages raise concerns that gender inequalities may be rising, although gaps between wages of lowest and highest education attained reflect the increasing importance of good educational attainment to earn a decent income in Mongolia, especially for women.

Note that the comparison of monthly average wages between years might be misleading since the data in table 51 (screenshot 3.66) reflect nominal wages unadjusted to inflation. According to the International Monetary Fund (IMF), the average inflation in Mongolia was reported at a 10.0 percent change in 2009.[14] Thus increasing nominal wages might have been decreasing real wages in reality. However, it is legitimate to analyze gender wage gaps between different years, since the comparison is not between the values of monthly average wages but the gender wage gap between years.

Table 52a: Wages or Earnings by Educational Attainment and Occupation

Another perspective of the wages or earning distribution among employees is shown in analysis of table 52a (screenshot 3.67), which reflects wages or earnings by educational attainment and occupation. More precisely, table 52a can help to determine wage and earning gaps within occupational groups while considering the educational level of people in the group.

For example, screenshot 3.67 shows that the largest earning gaps in Mongolia are within the occupational groups of legislators, senior officials, and managers, and for technicians and associate professionals. The monthly average earnings in 2009 for people with the highest educational level were at least twice as high as for those with the lowest educational level. In contrast, educational attainment hardly had an impact on the earnings of craft and related trades workers. Employees of that occupational group earned more or less the same regardless of their educational level attained.

Screenshot 3.67: Table 52a: Wages or Earnings by Educational Attainment and Occupation, Mongolia, 2009

	Table 52a: Wages/earnings by educational attainment and occupation							
	Mongolia LFS 2009							
	None	Primary	Basic	Secondary	Initial technical/vocational diploma/certificate	Technical/vocational diploma/certificate	University graduate	Master and above
RECODE of ii53 (what was the main type of work, trade or profession								
Legislators, senior officials and managers	250.0	257.1	235.1	293.5	231.8	370.2	402.4	483.2
Professionals	202.2	240.0	207.3	238.5	273.3	274.1	304.8	376.2
Technicians and associate professionals		138.3	250.6	213.6	233.2	241.0	297.6	401.1
Clerks		144.9	173.8	198.4	201.1	243.3	230.0	
Service workers and shop and market sales workers	50.9	134.2	180.4	228.7	210.2	237.0	262.9	4,110.0
Skilled agricultural and fishery workers	120.4	122.6	127.1	144.9	125.8	176.2	161.3	147.9
Craft and related trades workers	315.0	130.3	197.7	228.1	234.5	292.1	330.9	327.5
Plant and machine operators and assemblers		143.0	210.6	252.3	256.5	238.8	312.2	
Elementary occupations	89.6	198.1	176.6	182.4	162.3	181.7	230.7	250.0

Source: Mongolia Labour Force Survey 2009.
Note: Empty spaces reflect missing values for the particular group. Wages are defined as monthly average wages per employee in the primary job before deductions and expressed as average (mean) wages. The data cover wage earners of both sexes, without distinction as to age. Wages are expressed in thousands in the national currency, Mongolian tughrik (Tog). At the exchange rate from July 1, 2009, Tog 1.00 was equivalent to US$0.00070.

Screenshot 3.68: Table 52b: Wages or Earnings by Educational Attainment, Occupation, and Sex, Mongolia, 2009

Table 52b: Wages/earnings by educational attainment, occupation and sex
Mongolia LFS 2009

	None		Primary		Basic		Secondary		Initial technical/vocational diploma/certificate		Technical/vocational diploma/certificate		University graduate		Master and above	
	Male	Female	Male	Female	Male	Female	Male	Female	Male	Female	Male	Female	Male	Female	Male	Female
Legislators, senior officials and managers	250.0	237.1			242.5	210.8	317.0	256.1	253.4	207.6	382.2	356.0	421.4	369.6	500.8	434.1
Professionals	202.2			240.0	249.2	196.4	281.1	219.2	419.3	242.4	301.7	264.1	338.7	284.9	456.2	343.0
Technicians and associate professionals				138.5	260.1	241.6	212.1	215.3	255.4	216.4	259.6	233.6	319.4	278.1	468.9	326.0
Clerks				144.9	177.0	160.0	228.9	182.7	172.2	205.0	247.0	241.7	228.9	230.3		
Service workers and shop and market sales workers	51.5	50.0	90.4	169.9	201.7	166.9	244.8	218.8	259.1	182.5	265.0	220.6	293.7	244.1	4,110.0	
Skilled agricultural and fishery workers	123.2	95.0	123.2	119.5	134.3	82.4	156.3	91.4	135.6	87.8	163.2	214.4	158.1	167.0	147.9	
Craft and related trades workers	315.0		113.1	182.5	207.3	170.7	239.1	208.0	237.2	228.6	319.6	252.1	350.7	297.6	360.7	240.0
Plant and machine operators and assemblers				143.0	210.6	211.1	252.3	252.7	260.1	209.9	240.6	223.4	318.3	295.4		
Elementary occupations	133.8	10.0	231.6	139.9	199.2	153.6	208.2	160.0	162.0	163.0	247.9	157.3	297.7	190.8	250.0	

Source: Mongolia Labour Force Survey 2009.
Note: Empty spaces reflect missing values for the particular group. Wages are defined as monthly average wages per employee in the primary job before deductions and expressed as average (mean) wages. The data cover wage earners of both sexes, without distinction as to age. Wages are expressed in thousands in the national currency, Mongolian tughrik (Tog). At the exchange rate from July 1, 2009, Tog 1.00 was equivalent to US$0.00070.

Table 52b: Earnings by Educational Attainment, Occupation, and Sex

Table 52b (screenshot 3.68) seeks to uncover gender-related wage imbalances within occupational groups while considering the educational levels of men and women. Often it is not just the educational attainment of people that drives the wage gaps in occupational groups, it is also the gender.

In Mongolia, for example, the largest gender wage gaps are observed between female and male professionals with a master's degree or above and between women and men with an initial technical vocational diploma or certificate (screenshot 3.68). Gender wage gaps were less visible for plant and machine operators and assemblers with basic and secondary education, since women and men earned more or less the same monthly average wage.

Final Remarks

In most countries, labor market data are collected but often are underutilized for analytical purposes and policy making. This is due to factors such as limited analytical capacity, weak institutional arrangements that hinder the exchange and coordination of LMI between various labor market stakeholders, and financial constraints. As a result, policy makers are hampered in their efforts to monitor labor markets and restricted in the use and applicability of more advanced analytical methods that can help inform development of appropriate, well-targeted labor market policies. The effectiveness of interventions hinges on the availability of high-quality statistics, in particular on time series data for labor market indicators.

The ADePT-LMI module was developed to help facilitate analysis of LMI. It provides analysts in national statistical offices and other government agencies—as well as researchers, academics, and members of the private sector and workers' organizations—with a tool to ease the process of interpreting and analyzing labor market data. While this new product will not replace a robust labor market information and analysis (LMIA) system to monitor labor markets in their broader macroeconomic context, it provides a powerful analytical tool to simplify the calculation of key labor market indicators that thereafter can be further used for LMIA and research and to strengthen the underlying LMIA system.

Notes

1. See European Commission, Eurostat, http://epp.eurostat.ec.europa.eu.
2. *LLL* is defined by the International Labour Organization (ILO) as "all learning activities undertaken throughout life for the development of competencies and qualifications," where *competencies* cover the knowledge, skills, and know-how applied and mastered in a specific context, and *qualifications* mean a formal expression of the vocational or professional abilities of a worker that is recognized at international, national, or sectoral levels. In 2005, ILO adopted a new instrument on human resources development with a strong focus on education, training, and LLL called "Recommendation 195" as part of an integrated set of policies for economic and employment growth: https://www.ilo.org/dyn/normlex/en/f?p=NO RMLEXPUB:12100:0::NO::P12100_INSTRUMENT_ID:312533.
3. Some kind of compensation might be given to the contributing family workers indirectly in the form of family income (ILO 2011).
4. As described in ILO (2013a, footnote 43): *"The vulnerable employment indicator has some limitations: (1) wage and salary employment is not synonymous with decent work, as workers may carry a high economic risk despite the fact that they are in wage employment; (2) the unemployed are not included in the indicator, though they are vulnerable; (3) a worker may be classified in one of the two vulnerable status groups but still not carry a high economic risk, especially in the developed economies."*

5. The International Standard Industrial Classification of All Economic Activities (ISIC) is a United Nations system for classifying economic data. The United Nations Statistics Division (UNSD 2012) describes it in the following terms: *"Wide use has been made of ISIC, both nationally and internationally, in classifying data according to type of economic activity in the fields of production, employment, gross domestic product and other statistical areas. ISIC is a basic tool for studying economic phenomena, fostering international comparability of data, providing guidance for the development of national classifications and for promoting the development of sound national statistical systems."*

6. ISCO is one of the main international classifications for which ILO is responsible. It belongs to the international family of economic and social classifications. ISCO is a tool for organizing jobs into a clearly defined set of groups according to the tasks and duties undertaken in the job. Its main aims are to provide (a) a basis for the international reporting, comparison, and exchange of statistical and administrative data about occupations; (b) a model for the development of national and regional classifications of occupations; and (c) a system that can be used directly in countries that have not developed their own national classifications. For further information see ISCO, http://www.ilo.org/public/english/bureau/stat/isco/index.htm.

7. ILO (2015, manuscript 7): *"The 'hours usually worked' per week identifies the most common weekly working schedule of a person in employment over a selected period. The internationally-agreed statistical definition of 'usual hours of work,' recently adopted, refers to the hours worked in any job during a typical short period such as one week, over a longer period of time, or more technically, as the modal value of the 'hours actually worked' per week over a longer observation period."*

8. Oecusse, East Timor, is a coastal exclave in the western part of the island of Timor. West Timor separates Oecusse from the rest of Timor-Leste, almost completely surrounding the exclave except to the north, where it faces the Savu Sea.

9. For more information on the ILO's estimates of the working poor, see Kapsos and Bourmpoula (2013). For more information on the World Bank's poverty estimates, see Chen and Ravallion (2004).

10. Mongolia determines the poverty line or minimum subsistence level based on the adult equivalent's consumption expenditure. The consumption expenditure of the population is estimated on the basis of the consumer basket. Although the estimation of poverty based on the

consumption expenditure cannot fully capture poverty, this is the most commonly practiced method.

11. Average wages can be expressed as mean or median wages. To know whether mean or median wages should be calculated with the help of ADePT software, users need to understand how the wage data are distributed in the input dataset. The mean is usually used if the data are symmetrically distributed on the contrary; the median is used if the data are distributed asymmetrically. Choosing an appropriate calculation method will lead to a more accurate reflection of an "average" value.

12. The definitions of *earnings* and *wage rates* as stated in the resolution adopted by the 12th International Conference of Labour Statisticians (1973) are given in ILO (1988).

13. The ILO *Global Wage Report* analyzes wage trends across different regions and discusses the role of wage policies.

14. See IMF eLibrary Data, http://data.imf.org/.

References

Chen, S., and M. Ravallion. 2004. *How Have the World's Poorest Fared Since the Early 1980s?* Washington, DC: World Bank.

Colombano, J., and L. Krkoska. 2006. *Does Enterprise-Level Training Compensate for Poor Country-Level Skills? Lessons from Transition Countries in Central and Eastern Europe.* London: European Bank for Reconstruction and Development.

Eurostat. 2010. *Regional Yearbook.* http://epp.eurostat.ec.europa.eu.

Hellenic Statistics Authority (ELSTAT), Government of Greece. 2010. *Labour Force Survey, 2010.* Athens. http://www.statistics.gr/en/statistics/-/publication/SJO01/-.

ILO (International Labour Organization). 1952. "ILO C102–Social Security (Minimum Standards) Convention, 1952 (No. 102)." Convention adopted Geneva, June 28. http://www.ilo.org/dyn/normlex/en/f?p=1000:12100:0::NO::P12100_ILO_CODE:C102.

———. 1988. *Current International Recommendations on Labour Statistics.* Geneva: ILO.

———. 2004. *Multiple Job-Holding.* Factsheet. Geneva: ILO. http://www.ilo.org/wcmsp5/groups/public/---ed_protect/---protrav/---travail/documents/publication/wcms_169672.pdf.

———. 2006. *Global Employment Trends for Youth, 2006*. Geneva: ILO. http://www.ilo.org/empelm/pubs/WCM_041929/lang--en/index.htm.

———. 2010. "Building a Social Protection Floor with the Global Jobs Pact." Background paper for the Second African Decent Work Symposium, Yaoundé, Cameroon, October 6–8. http://www.ilo.org/wcmsp5/groups/public/@ed_norm/@relconf/documents/meetingdocument/wcms_160210.pdf.

———. 2011. *Shaping Global Industrial Relations: The Impact of International Framework Agreements*. Geneva: ILO.

———. 2012a. *Global Employment Trends 2012: Preventing a Deeper Jobs Crisis*. Geneva: ILO. http://www.ilo.org/global/research/global-reports/global-employment-trends/WCMS_171571/lang--en/index.htm.

———. 2012b. *Global Employment Trends for Youth 2012*. Geneva: ILO. http://www.ilo.org/global/research/global-reports/youth/2012/lang--en/index.htm.

———. 2013a. *Global Employment Trends 2013: Recovering from a Second Jobs Dip*. Geneva: ILO. http://www.ilo.org/global/research/global-reports/global-employment-trends/2013/WCMS_202326/lang--en/index.htm.

———. 2013b. "Statistics of Work, Employment and Labour Underutilization." Resolution adopted by the 19th International Conference of Labour Statisticians, Geneva.

———. 2014. *Transitioning from the Informal to the Formal Economy*. Geneva: ILO. http://www.ilo.org/wcmsp5/groups/public/---ed_norm/---relconf/documents/meetingdocument/wcms_218128.pdf.

———. 2015. *Key Indicators of the Labour Market*. 9th ed. Geneva: ILO. http://www.ilo.org/global/statistics-and-databases/research-and-databases/kilm/lang--en/index.htm.

Kapsos, S., and E. Bourmpoula. 2013. "Employment and Economic Class in the Developing World." ILO Research Paper No. 6, International Labour Organization, Geneva. http://www.ilo.org/wcmsp5/groups/public/---dgreports/---inst/documents/publicationwcms_216451.pdf.

Mongolia Household Income and Expenditure Survey. 2002. National Statistical Office of Mongolia. http://web.nso.mn/nada/index.php/catalog.

Mongolia Household Income and Expenditure Survey. 2008. National Statistical Office of Mongolia. http://web.nso.mn/nada/index.php/catalog.

Mongolia Labour Force Survey. 2008. National Statistical Office of Mongolia. http://web.nso.mn/nada/index.php/catalog.

Mongolia Labour Force Survey. 2009. National Statistical Office of Mongolia. http://web.nso.mn/nada/index.php/catalog.

South Africa Quarterly Labour Force Survey. 2010. Statistics South Africa. http://www.statssa.gov.za/?page_id=737.

Timor-Leste Labour Force Survey. Report 2010. 2010. General Directorate of Statistics, Timor-Leste. http://www.statistics.gov.tl/leste-labour-force -survey-report-20-timor-10/.

UNSD (United Nations Statistics Division). 2012. *International Standard Industrial Classification of All Economic Activities (ISIC)*. New York. http://unstats.un.org/unsd/iiss/International-Standard-Industrial -Classification-of-all-Economic-Activities-ISIC.ashx.

World Bank. 2008. *Policy Note on Population Growth and Its Implications in Timor-Leste*. Dili: World Bank. http://siteresources.worldbank .org/INTTIMORLESTE/Data%20and%20Reference/21988255 /PopulationGrowth2008English.pdf.

Further Reading

ILO (International Labour Organization). 1990. *Surveys of Economically Active Population, Employment, Unemployment and Underemployment: An ILO Manual on Concepts and Methods*. Geneva: ILO.

———. 2008. *Global Employment Trends for Women, 2008*. Geneva: ILO.

———. 2009. *The Financial and Economic Crisis: A Decent Work Response*. Geneva: ILO.

———. 2009. *Global Job Crisis Observatory: Analytical and Statistical Information on the Impact and Policy Responses to the Jobs Crisis*. Geneva: ILO.

———. 2009. *Protecting People, Promoting Jobs: A Survey of Country Employment and Social Protection Policy Responses to the Global Economic Crisis*. Report to the G20 Leaders' Summit, Pittsburgh, September 24–25.

———. 2010. *Global Wage Report 2010/11: Wage Policies in Times of Crisis*. Geneva: ILO.

———. 2010. *Recovery and Growth with Decent Work*. Report of the Director-General, Geneva: ILO.

Schmidt, D., and D. Hassanien. 2011. "In Need of a Future: Causes and Consequences of High Youth Unemployment—The Case of North Africa." In *Youth for Democracy: Learning from Nonviolent Struggles around the*

World, edited by M. M. Harrison, 19–22. Copenhagen: Humanity in Action Denmark. http://www.humanityinaction.org/files/129-Antologifrdig .pdf.

Sparreboom, T., and A. Albee. 2011. *Towards Decent Work in Sub-Saharan Africa: Monitoring MDG Employment Indicators*. Geneva: ILO.

Sparreboom, T., and M. Powell. 2009. "Labour Market Information and Analysis for Skills Development." Employment Working Paper No. 27, International Labour Organization, Geneva.

UN (United Nations). 1997. *Handbook for Producing National Statistical Reports on Women and Men, Social Statistics and Indicators*. New York: UN.

Software User Guide

Introduction

The ADePT ILO Labor Market Indicators Module uses microlevel data from various types of household surveys, including the household income and expenditure survey (HIES), the living standards survey (LSS), and the labor force survey (LFS), and can generate up to 52 labor market tables.

Chapter 4 serves as a user guide for the module software. It provides information on how to construct variables from household survey microdata to prepare input files and variables required by the software to generate the desired output tables. The recommendations provided follow international guidelines and best practices.

Using the ADePT-LMI Module for Labor Market Information and Analysis

The production of output tables requires the following steps:

1. Study the original data files and questionnaires.
2. Prepare an input file.
3. Load the input file into ADePT and specify variables and parameters.
4. Choose table options and identify if-conditions.
5. Generate tables.

Understanding the Data

Before preparing the input file, users must understand the original source of the data file and its objectives to learn more about the quality of the available labor market statistics.

Survey questionnaires and datasets need to be carefully examined to see what labor market information (LMI) can be used for labor market information and analysis (LMIA) with the help of the ADePT-LMI module. It is also crucial to understand the underlying concepts, definitions, variable types, coding schemes, and metadata[1] corresponding to the labor market indicators from the survey datasets. A detailed understanding of the data will allow for correct preparation of the input file and variables. The tables generated with the help of the ADePT-LMI module are as meaningful (or meaningless) as the information fed into the software.

Data Sources

The key source for labor market data in many countries is the labor force survey (LFS). The LFS is a household sample survey designed to divide individuals of working age into three mutually exclusive groups: employed, unemployed, and outside the labor force. It collects detailed individual data on various key employment indicators to monitor the quantity and quality of work. In addition, the LFS is a major source of information on personal characteristics of the working-age population, including age, sex, marital status, educational attainment, and family characteristics. Usually the LFS is carried out frequently on an annual, quarterly, or monthly basis. LFS data for subprovincial labor markets or for more detailed disaggregation and analysis are often not available or not reliable due to relatively small labor force samples. Thus, the reliability of data needs to be ascertained before using the information for analysis.

The LSS and HIES are important tools in measuring and understanding poverty in developing countries. Typically, both the LSS and HIES sample households rather than individuals and thus provide household-level data files. The LSS is usually tailored for national accounts, and both the HIES and LSS study general income and expenditure patterns of households. Against this background they also often contain basic information regarding the employment situation of people living in the same household (mainly to find out how many members contribute financially to family income). These data allow the calculation of poverty lines, household-based poverty ratios, and headcounts for various target populations, but do not allow detailed analysis of the employment situation of individuals living in these households. This situation is simply because it is not the main objective of these surveys, and therefore labor market concepts and statistical methods differ from those generally used in an LFS.

Type of Data Files

Representative labor market data from household surveys are usually in system files created by and for specific software applications (e.g., Microsoft Excel, Stata, and SPSS). In most countries, the National Statistics Office has the official statistical data files.

LFS data usually are captured in one complete microdataset. HIES or LSS data, in contrast, are often stored in data files corresponding to the sections in the survey questionnaire. Thus, the user might have to reorganize or merge the relevant variables from different data files into one data file, whereby each row of the dataset should represent an observation (individual or household) and each column represents a variable (a characteristic of the household or individual). Users can use any software to prepare the input file (e.g., Excel or SAS). The ADePT-LMI module accepts a large number of diverse file formats.

Since it is difficult to explain the preparation of input files for each available statistical software program, the following sections use examples for the preparation of input files in Stata, a commonly used statistical software.

Household Survey Questionnaires

Household survey questionnaires vary enormously in content and length and are usually composed of several parts, often called modules. A module consists of one or more pages of questions that collect information on a particular subject, such as housing, employment, or health. For example, an LFS contains modules pertaining to different groups of employed, unemployed, and inactive. Each module contains several questions, sometimes only five or six, but other times as many as 50 or more. Questions relevant for use in the ADePT-LMI module should be carefully scrutinized.

Create Input File

To be able to generate tables, the user creates a rectangular input file based on labor market data obtained from the household surveys that one wants to analyze (screenshot 4.1). In a rectangular data file, columns represent variables and rows represent observations. Variables are commonly formatted as either numerical or string.[2]

Understanding Types of Input Variables

When preparing the input files, users must distinguish between four types of input variables accepted by the ADePT-LMI module.

- *Continuous variables.* In statistical terms, a variable is considered continuous if all values within a given range are possible. Continuous variables usually have numeric values, such as wage and earning information or the age of an individual.
- *Categorical variables.* Numeric or string variables are called categorical if they contain a small number of integer values. If a categorical string variable is loaded into the software, ADePT generates a numerical variable with categories corresponding to the distinct values in the string variable. An example of a field that requires a categorical variable is the "Sector of employment" field.

Screenshot 4.1: Example of a Rectangular Data File

	identif	q0006	hh_no	ind_id	q0102	sex	age	q0106	q0203	q0204	q0205
1	2194	7	6	7	SON / DAUGHTER	Female	6			NONE	NO
2	2194	7	6	1	HEAD	Male	44	MARRIED		NONE	NO
3	2194	7	6	4	SON / DAUGHTER	Male	15	NEVER MARRIED		NONE	NO
4	2194	7	6	6	SON / DAUGHTER	Male	9			NONE	NO
5	2194	7	6	3	SON / DAUGHTER	Male	12			NONE	NO
6	2194	7	6	2	WIFE / HUSBAND	Female	40	MARRIED		NONE	NO
7	2194	7	6	5	SON / DAUGHTER	Female	13	NEVER MARRIED		NONE	NO
8	188	7	5	3	SON / DAUGHTER	Female	21	NEVER MARRIED	2	COMPLETE SECONDARY	
9	188	7	5	2	WIFE / HUSBAND	Female	45	MARRIED		PRIMARY	NO
10	188	7	5	5	SON / DAUGHTER	Female	15	NEVER MARRIED	2	NONE	YES, WITH DIFFICULTY
11	188	7	5	1	HEAD	Male	48	MARRIED	2	PRIMARY	YES, WITH DIFFICULTY
12	188	7	5	6	SON / DAUGHTER	Male	12		2	NONE	YES, WITH DIFFICULTY
13	188	7	5	7	SON / DAUGHTER	Male	4				
14	188	7	5	4	SON / DAUGHTER	Male	17	NEVER MARRIED	2	SECONDARY	
15	2169	4	8	3	BROTHER / SISTER	Male	28	NEVER MARRIED	1	NONE	YES, WITH DIFFICULTY
16	2169	4	8	1	HEAD	Male	42	NEVER MARRIED		NONE	NO
17	2169	4	8	2	BROTHER / SISTER	Male	33	NEVER MARRIED	1	PRIMARY	YES, WITH DIFFICULTY
18	2169	4	8	4	BROTHER / SISTER	Female	18	NEVER MARRIED	1	NONE	NO
19	3432	4	5	3	SON / DAUGHTER	Female	31	NEVER MARRIED	2	NONE	NO
20	3432	4	5	2	SON / DAUGHTER	Female	42	NEVER MARRIED		SECONDARY	
21	3432	4	5	4	GRANDCHILD	Male	6		2	NONE	NO
22	3432	4	5	1	HEAD	Female	75	WIDOWED	1	PRIMARY	YES, WITH DIFFICULTY
23	7695	4	1	2	WIFE / HUSBAND	Female	48	MARRIED	1	PRIMARY	YES, EASILY

Source: Mongolia Labour Force Survey 2008.

- *Binary variables.* Binary variables have only two distinct values. The fields requiring binary variables accept a numerical binary variable or a logical expression (string). An example of a binary variable tab is the "Urban" field, where the value 1 represents "Urban" and any other value "Non-urban."
- *Other parameters.* These define household and population distributions. "Household ID," "Household weights," and "Poverty line" are examples of fields in this category.

Recoding of Variables

Some of the coding of variables in the household dataset might not be appropriate for the use of data in the ADePT-LMI module. Thus, users might need to recode variables to allow for LMIA based on international standards. Note that recoding variables shifts respondents into different categories and therefore will impact the output results.

It is recommended to recode a variable while generating a new variable rather than recoding existing variables to avoid irreparable modifications to the dataset. Also, new variables should immediately be renamed and relabeled since it is easy to forget the names and codes of the variables. Tables generated with ADePT software require labels. If the variables in the input files are not labeled, data in the tables will not be labeled either. Also, it is advised to run a cross-tabulation of the recoded variable against the original or "unrecoded" variable to verify that the coding has been done correctly. The following section gives comprehensive examples and Stata "do-files" that explain each step of recoding variables.

Identifying Variables for a Dataset and Preparing Dataset for ADePT-LMI Module

The type and number of variables in each dataset vary for each survey type. For example, information on welfare aggregates and poverty lines are usually available only in household surveys that measure household income, expenditure, or living standards of households. However, some countries conduct multiple-purpose household surveys that provide household and individual data corresponding to both welfare and labor market indicators. Nevertheless, labor market indicators meant to measure the labor force status of individuals in a household should ideally be derived from dedicated LFSs designed to collect LMI that when analyzed can guide labor, employment, and skills development policies. An LFS generally does not contain information on welfare aggregates and poverty lines. For analysis of such LFSs using ADePT, the variable fields "Welfare aggregate" and "Poverty line" can be left blank.

Tables 4.1–4.4 provide an overview of the variables and parameters that could theoretically be loaded into the ADePT-LMI module given the information available in the survey data. If the information is not available, most variable tabs can be left blank. However, there are some exceptions, such as "Household weights," that need to be provided as a precondition for the module to work.

The more variables loaded into the ADePT module, the more tables will be produced. Overall, the ADePT-LMI module distinguishes between four broad groups of information:

- Population and welfare variables
- Labor force variables
- Employment quality variables
- Parameters, including age brackets.

Population and Welfare Variables

The ADePT-LMI module presents six types of household-level variables, which are described in detail in table 4.1.

Household ID. Typically, household-level data files include variables that uniquely identify the surveyed household through a "household-id" (often called "household number") variable. Individual data files are likely to contain a variable that uniquely identifies the individual surveyed with a so-called "personal-id" (adding up to the total sample size of the survey). Both IDs can be loaded under the "Household ID" tab. If neither "household ID" nor "personal ID" is available in the dataset, the variable tab can be left blank.

Household Weights. To generate unbiased and representative estimates based on household survey data, the input file should include a variable with the survey weights. Each household in a survey represents a number of

Table 4.1: Type and Description of Household-Level Variables

Variable	Description
Household ID	Continuous variable with unique identification of interviewed households. If the survey data are stored in separate dataset modules, the *Household ID* variable is the only variable that can be used to merge one dataset module to another.
Household weights	Continuous variable with unique values for each household. Household surveys assign a specific household weight to every household. The weight gives each sample household a level of representation in the total household population. *Household weights* adjusts for differences in the probability of selecting a household in the household population. Household surveys generally have unequal probabilities of selecting households from different regions or from different subpopulations for which statistics are needed. As a result, weights need to be applied when producing tabulations to produce a proper representation. *Household weights* is also necessary when a sample design needs to correct for differential response rates.
Regions	Nominal variable with categories or regions in the dataset. Provinces or any other locally specific regional classification can be used for regional or geographic disaggregation with the help of the ADePT-LMI module.
Urban	Binary variable with value of 1 if the household is in an urban region and any other value if rural.
Welfare aggregate	Continuous variable containing values corresponding to the welfare aggregate used in the survey. The most common welfare aggregate is the monetary value of the monthly consumption per capita. Some datasets might also use income or asset-based wealth indices instead of consumption as the aggregate of welfare. The ADePT-LMI module works based on a range of welfare aggregates, including monetary measures (e.g., per capita consumption or household income) and nonmonetary values (e.g., an assets index, a basic needs index, or a welfare ratio [ratio of consumption to poverty line]).
Poverty line	Binary variable with value of 1 if the household is below the defined poverty threshold in the dataset and any other value if the household lives above the poverty line.

households in the population. The "weight" variable is typically the inverse of the probability of selection of that household (or group of households, for clustered sampling). To make inferences about the total population, the user should supply the correct statistical household weights, or expansion factors. Most of the microfiles obtained from national statistical offices contain a particular survey weight. Whichever weight is appropriate for the data analysis of the particular dataset can be loaded to the ADePT-LMI module.

ADePT always expects household weights irrespective of whether the data refer to household- or individual-level data.

Regions. To allow disaggregation of labor market data by geographical area, each household dataset usually includes "geographic region" variables. These do not necessarily need to be specified regions; they could also be provinces, districts, or areas that follow the institutional or political setup in countries. It is up to the data analyst to choose which geographical variable the ADePT-LMI module will apply when generating the tables.

Urban. Analyses of urban versus rural labor market development are vital for policy makers, especially in developing or transition economies. Thus, household datasets commonly provide a variable that distinguishes between rural and urban areas. Sometimes country or household surveys differentiate between agricultural areas and nonagricultural areas. Such information could also be uploaded in the user interface, under the "Urban" variable tag, if desired for analytical purpose. The *Urban* variable should ideally be binary; it will have the value 1 if the household is in an urban area.

Welfare Aggregate. An HIES or LSS provides information on the welfare distribution of households. Aggregates can vary significantly across countries. Therefore, the ADePT-LMI module can process a broad range of welfare aggregates. These include monetary welfare indicators, such as the per capita consumption, or income and nonmonetary welfare indicators, such as an assets index, a basic needs index, or a welfare ratio (ratio of consumption to poverty line). Whatever welfare information is relevant in the country and was used for the calculation of the national poverty line can be fed into the "Welfare" tab.

Note that welfare-related information is not available in individual files, such as LFS files, due to the nature or objective of the survey.

Also, the user should not upload a variable for deciles or quintiles under the "Welfare aggregate" tab, since deciles or quintiles will be generated internally by the ADePT-LMI module from the welfare aggregate specified by the user.

Poverty Line. Poverty lines are usually calculated based on the HIES or LSS. They are cutoff points separating the poor from the nonpoor and can be monetary (e.g., a certain consumption level) or nonmonetary (e.g., a certain literacy level). Often multiple poverty lines are applied in countries to distinguish between various dimensions of the phenomenon.

Before loading a "poverty line" variable into the ADePT-LMI module, users should know the appropriate poverty line for working poverty calculation and analysis. Usually, statistical standards and guidelines for poverty analysis are set by the National Statistics Office (NSO) in respective countries. Users can usually obtain from the NSO the Stata "do-file" or instructions on how to calculate the various poverty lines based on the survey data. The ADePT-LMI module can be fed with any type of poverty line under the "Poverty line" variable tab.

Individual-Level Variables

Each household dataset usually contains unique characteristics of individuals living in the household. The ADePT-LMI module runs ideally if there is individual information on age, gender, educational attainment, and enrollment. Information on all these characteristics is vital for understanding and analyzing labor markets since it allows more in-depth analysis of specific groups of individuals. See table 4.2 for a list of individual-level variables and their descriptions.

Age. The "age" variable (continuous) is normally available in each household survey dataset reflecting the individual age of persons living in a household. The relevant variable in a data file that captures age should be renamed *Age* if comparative analysis will be done with the help of the ADePT. In other words, all data files that users would like to compare need to contain the same variable names and value labels for the information uploaded (screenshot 4.2).

Table 4.2: Individual-Level Variables

Variable	Description
Age	Continuous numeric variable representing person's age in years.
Gender	Binary variable with value of 1 if person is male and any other value if female.
Education completed	Nominal variable with as many categories as the educational classification scheme applied in the survey. Ideally it follows the UNESCO International Standard Classification of Education (ISCED).
Enrolled in education	Binary variable with the value of 1 if person is enrolled in education and any other value if not enrolled.

Screenshot 4.2: Uploaded Data Files Containing the Same Variable and Value Labels

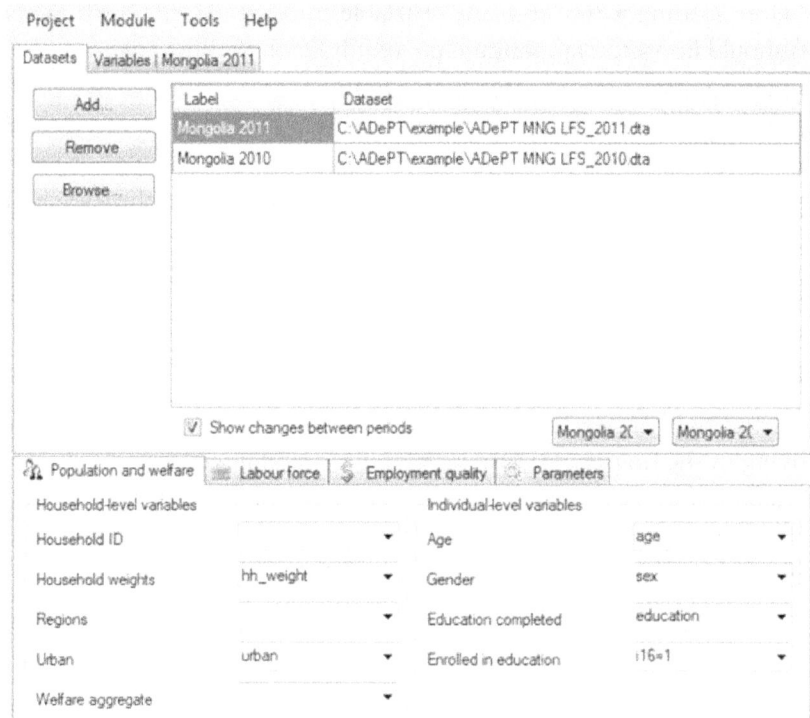

Gender. The "Gender" tab requires a variable, either numeric or string, that reflects the sex of the individual in the household. In most cases it will be a clear distinction between male and female. However, in some countries, such as Nepal, it might include a third gender (National Judicial Academy 2008). As with the variable *Age*, the same variable and value labels are needed if more than one dataset is uploaded to ADePT to allow for comparison of data between years and countries.

Education Completed. It is fairly common that members of the household will be asked about their level of formal education attained. Thus, the user needs to search for the relevant variable in the dataset. Although it is recommended to apply the International Standard Classification of Education (ISCED)[3] in household surveys, many countries apply a national classification scheme of educational attainment.

In some countries the level of formal education is even combined with the technical vocational training scheme. Thus, recoding of the variable might be necessary to reduce the number of categories or to separate the information on educational attainment from technical or vocational training. Having too many educational categories will create very complex ADePT tables that will be difficult to analyze. Thus, it is recommended to have no more than six education categories for this input variable.

Enrolled in Education. Information required under the variable tab "Enrolled in education" in the ADePT-LMI module does not need to be enrollment information at a given level of educational attainment. To measure the relative weight of education in terms of enrollment, all that is needed is a variable that provides information on who attended education or training and who did not, at a particular point in time. Educational enrollment information might or might not be available in household surveys. If enrollment information is available, it might be a stand-alone variable. However, at times it can be found with educational attainment information in the same variable. Thus, recoding of the variable is recommended (to generate two separate variables for educational attainment and enrollment) unless the values can be clearly distinguished.

The "enrollment" variable in the input file is often a binary variable with the value 1 for enrolled in education and any other value for not enrolled. (See box 4.1.)

Labor Force Variables

The ADePT-LMI module presents 16 different types of labor force variables, which are described in detail in table 4.3.

Employment, Unemployment, and Inactivity. As highlighted in chapter 2, the working-age population can be divided into the labor force (the employed and unemployed) and the persons outside the labor force. Note that all three categories add up to the total working-age population to allow the ADePT-LMI module to produce tables correctly and to allow for correct analysis. For the ADePT input dataset, these variables can be represented by variable categories or by binary variables, and they can be coded by more than one question from the original survey dataset.

Box 4.1: Example of Recoding the "Educational Attainment" Variable in Stata

Categories in the original *Education* variable:

1. None

2. Primary

3. Secondary

4. Complete Secondary

5. Vocational

6. Degree or higher education diploma

7. Bachelor

8. Other.

The recoding of the variable included:
Renaming of group "None" into "less than primary" (value 1)
Merging "Primary" and "Secondary" into the group "Primary (completed)" (value 2)
Merging "Complete Secondary" and "Vocational" into the group "Secondary (completed)" (value 3)
Merging "Degree or higher education diploma" and "Bachelor" into the group "Tertiary" (value 4)
Recoding "Other" (value 8) into "Other" (value 5)

Recoding in Stata do-file
recode q0204 (1=1)(2/3=2) (4/5=3) (6/7=4) (8=5), gen(education)
la def education 1 "Less than primary" 2 "Primary (completed)" 3 "Secondary (completed)" 4 "Tertiary" 5 "Other"
la val education education

Table 4.3: Categorical Labor Force Variables

Variable	Description
Employed	Value of a categorical variable measuring economic activity. The variable usually needs to be created in the input dataset.
Unemployed	Value of a categorical variable measuring economic activity. The variable usually needs to be created in the input dataset.
Outside the labor force	Value of a categorical variable measuring economic activity. The variable usually needs to be created in the input dataset.
Reasons for inactivity	Categorical variable that indicates reasons for economic inactivity in the country.

(continued)

Table 4.3: Categorical Labor Force Variables *(continued)*

Variable	Description
Duration of unemployment	Categorical variable usually based on a country-specific classification scheme. It is advised to recode the variable to also reflect the category "one year or longer" if it is not in the dataset.
Status in employment	Categorical variable that should ideally follow the ICSE. Some countries use their own classification scheme, which should be recoded. (See chapter 2, "Labor Force Framework," on labor market concepts and definitions.)
Occupation	Categorical variable with as many categories as the occupational classification (1-digit) scheme applied in the survey.
Sector	Categorical variable with as many categories as the industrial classification (1-digit) scheme applied in the survey.
Broad sector	Aggregated categorical sector variable with three categories: agriculture, industry, and services.
Public sector employment	Binary variable with value 1 if a person is employed in the public sector and any other value if employed in the private sector.
Wage employment	Value of a categorical variable, indicating wage and salaried employment.
Own-account workers	Value of a categorical variable, indicating own-account workers.
Contributing family workers	Value of a categorical variable, indicating the contributing family workers.
Secondary job	Binary variable with the value of 1 if the person has a secondary job and any other value if the person has no secondary job.
Status in employment in SJ (secondary job)	Categorical variable that should follow the ICSE. Some countries use their own classification scheme, which should be recoded. (See chapter 2, "Labor Force Framework," on labor market concepts and definitions.)
Trade union membership	A binary variable with value of 1 if the employee is a member of a trade union and any other value if not a member of a trade union.

Note: ICSE = International Classification of Status in Employment.

Unfortunately, it is very rare that household survey data files contain ready-made variables for all three groups of the working-age population. It is more common that the information is spread over separate sections and is retained in multiple questions and answers. Thus, it is highly recommended to create a variable with three mutually exclusive categories for the employed, unemployed, and inactive working-age population. (See figure 4.1.)

The core for generating a "labor force status" variable is a proper understanding of the labor force framework and concepts applied in the survey (see box 4.2; see chapter 2).

Figure 4.1: Identification of the Labor Force Status of the Working-Age Population: Simplified Diagram

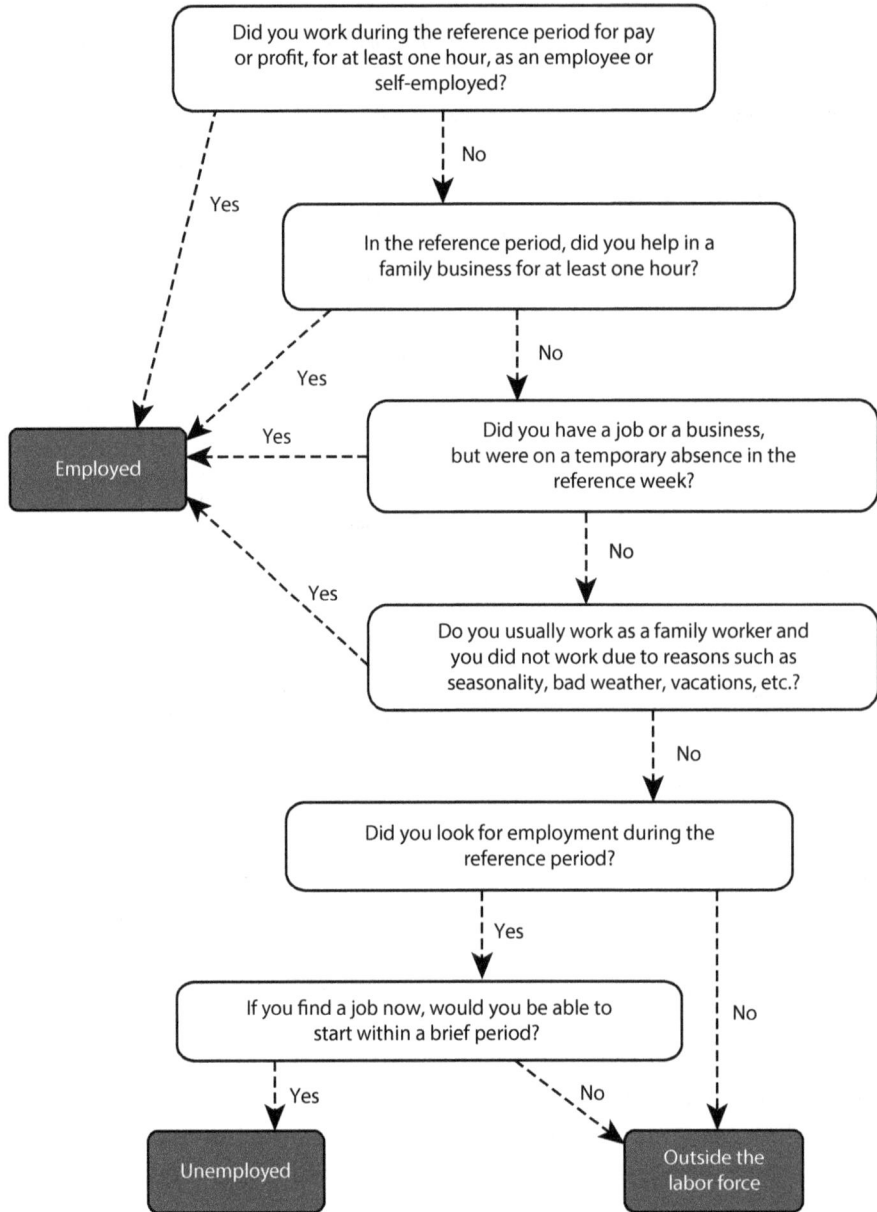

Did you work during the reference period for pay or profit, for at least one hour, as an employee or self-employed?

No

Yes

In the reference period, did you help in a family business for at least one hour?

No

Yes

Yes

Employed

Did you have a job or a business, but were on a temporary absence in the reference week?

No

Yes

Do you usually work as a family worker and you did not work due to reasons such as seasonality, bad weather, vacations, etc.?

No

Did you look for employment during the reference period?

Yes

No

If you find a job now, would you be able to start within a brief period?

Yes

No

No

Unemployed

Outside the labor force

Box 4.2: Example of Recoding and Generating a "Labour Force Status" Variable in Stata

Generate a variable with the value one for employment
gen lf_status=1 if age>=15 & (Hours of work >=1 | did not work but had a job==1)

Replace the variable value two if unemployed
replace lf_status=2 if age>=15 & lf_status~=1 & available==1 & seeking==1

Replace the variable value three if neither employed or unemployed
replace lf_status=3 if wpop==1 & lf_status~=1 & lf_status~=2

Label variable and values
la var lf_status "Labour force status"
la def lfstatus 1 "Employed" 2 "Unemployed" 3 "Not in labour force"
la val lf_status lfstatus

Step 1. The employed often can be most easily identified. If the questionnaire contains a question asking: *"Did you work during the reference period for pay, profit, or in a family enterprise for at least one hour?"* all people who answered with "yes" can be defined as employed. One can also assume that people who answered the question, *"Are you self-employed and did not work due to reasons such as seasonality, bad weather, labour dispute such as strike, etc.?"* or, *"Do you usually work as family worker and did no work due to reasons, such as seasonality, bad weather, vacations, etc.?"* are employed. Another way of identifying the employed is to search for the variable that collected the information on "hours of work." Working-age people who answered the question with a value that exceeded one hour of work per week can generally be identified as employed.

Step 2. Identification of the unemployed is usually more complicated. However, the ADePT-LMI module can be fed with any unemployment information regardless of the concept applied. By international standards, people are classified as unemployed if they are not working but are available for work and actively searching for work during the reference period.

National definitions of *unemployment* often differ from the recommended international standard definition in terms of, for instance, applied age limits, reference periods, criteria for seeking work, treatment of persons temporarily laid off, and persons seeking work for the first time.

Step 3. Identify all people of working age who were neither employed nor unemployed during the survey reference week, as inactive.

Reasons for Inactivity. Reasons for inactivity can be manifold and usually vary among countries. Thus, the categories and values of the "reasons for inactivity" variable will differ. However, the ADePT-LMI module accepts any type of categorical variable to be loaded under the "Reasons for inactivity" tab. To simplify analysis, users should limit the categories to a maximum of 10.

Duration of Unemployment. The duration of unemployment is usually captured in a categorical variable. The categories are likely to differ between countries and surveys. The ADePT-LMI module works with any type of categorical variable loaded under the variable tab. To allow for analysis of long-term unemployment, it is recommended to include a variable in the input file that contains the category "one year or longer." Usually original variables that capture "duration of unemployment" can be easily recoded to include such a group. Example categories to capture the duration of unemployment are the following:

- Less than 1 month
- 1 to 2 months
- Up to 6 months
- 7 to 11 months
- One year or longer.

Status in Employment. In most household survey data files there is already a variable for "employment status," though the categories corresponding to the value fields might differ significantly from the international standards corresponding to status in employment, as spelled out in the International Classification of Status in Employment (ICSE) (ILO 1993) (see chapter 2). In such cases it is recommended to generate a new "status in employment" variable by recoding and renaming the existing categories. (See box 4.3.)

Note that the purpose of international classification schemes for statistics is not to supersede national classifications. The former should be seen more as a framework for the international comparison of national statistics.

Box 4.3: Example of Recoding and Generating an "Employment Status" Variable in Stata

Recoding of employment status variable
Categories in the original status variable:

1. Paid employee on contract

2. Paid employee under civil law

3. Employers

4. Members of cooperatives

5. Own-account workers

6. Unpaid family workers

7. Other.

The recoding of the original status variable:
Merging group "Paid employee on contract" and "Paid employee under civil law" into the category "Wage and salaried workers" (value 1)
Recoding Employers from value 3 to value 2
Merging "Members of cooperatives" and "Own-account workers" into "own-account workers" (value 3)
Recoding and renaming the group "Unpaid family workers" into "Contributing family workers" (value 4)
Recoding and renaming the group of "Other" into "Not classifiable" (value 5)

Recoding in Stata do-file
recode status (1/2=1)(3=2)(4/5=3)(6=4)(7=5), gen(emp_status)
#delimit;
la def emp_status

1. "Wage and salaried workers"

2. "Employers"

3. "Own-account workers"

4. "Contributing family workers"

5. "Not classifiable";

#delimit cr
la val emp_status emp_status

Most countries, especially those that have to develop classifications for the first time or revise existing schemes, use international standards as the basis for development.

ADePT works best with a categorical variable that contains the following categories for status in employment: "Wage and salaried workers," "Employers," "Own-account workers," "Contributing family workers," and "Not classifiable."

Occupation. Information on the occupation of individuals is commonly collected in household surveys, regardless of the survey type. It generally refers to total employment, although in some cases it can relate to salaried employment. Statistics by detailed occupational groups can refer to different occupational classifications. Most countries use a national adaptation of an international classification (ISCO-68 or ISCO-88), but many developed nations use a national classification. Occupational data are usually presented in 3- to 4-digit formats.

Although the ADePT-LMI module can handle any detailed occupational category (as long as it is a categorical variable), users are advised to go as detailed as 1-digit occupations to produce meaningful and easy-to-read tables. Thus, a new occupational variable needs to be generated for the input file by aggregating 3- to 4-digit information on occupations. This is not always an easy task since in many datasets occupations do not have corresponding titles, just codes. Therefore, users must obtain the applied coding scheme from the national statistics office before creating a new 1-digit occupation variable. The number of 1-digit groups will be different for ISCO-68, ISCO-88, and ISCO-08. Users must label the values of the new *Occupation* variable. ADePT will use the information when generating the tables. (See box 4.4.)

Sector. Similar to the "occupation" variable in surveys, the "sector" variable uploaded into ADePT is recommended to be a 1-digit variable. Sector information generally refers to economic activities of the employed, but sometimes also to just salaried employment.

Statistics of economic activity can correspond to various industrial classification schemes. Most countries use a country-specific version of the International Standard Industrial Classification of All Economic Activities (ISIC Revisions 2, 3, or 4) (UN 2008). More recent sector data are often available in a 3- to 4-digit format. Although the ADePT-LMI

Box 4.4: Example of a "Do-File" on How to Recode 3-Digit National Occupational Classification Codes into 1-Digit Occupations

*** Recode occupation variable***
Recode occupation (111/141=1)(211/246=2)(311/348=3)(411/422=4)(511/549=5) (611/621=6)(711/744=7)(811/833=8)(911/999=9), gen(occupation_1_digit)
#delimit;
la def occupation_1_digit

1. "Legislators, senior officials and managers"

2. "Professionals"

3. "Technicians and associate professionals"

4. "Clerks"

5. "Service workers and shop and market sales workers"

6. "Skilled agricultural and fishery workers"

7. "Craft and related trades workers"

8. "Plant and machine operators and assemblers"

9. "Elementary occupations";

#delimit cr
la val occupation_1_digit occupation_1_digit

module can handle any detailed sectoral category (as long as it is a categorical variable), it is advisable to create a new "sector" variable by aggregating 3- to 4-digit information on industries to produce meaningful and easy-to-read tables. (See box 4.5.)

Since industries or sectors often do not have corresponding titles but, rather, numeric codes in the datasets, users need to obtain the applied coding scheme for the industrial classification from the national statistics office and follow the official aggregation scheme when generating a 1-digit "sector" variable. The number of 1-digit groups will be different for ISIC Revisions 2, 3, and 4. (See box 4.6.)

Broad Sector. Typically in surveys, the "broad sector" variable divides employment into three groupings of economic activity: agriculture, industry, and services. In the majority of cases a ready-made "broad sector" variable will not be available in the dataset. Thus, a *Broad sector* input variable needs to be generated to be loaded to the ADePT-LMI module.

Box 4.5: Example of a "Do-File" on How to Recode 2-Digit Industrial Classification Codes into 1-Digit Sectors

*** Recode employment sector variable (ISIC Rev.4)***
#delimit ;
recode sector (1/3=1)(5/9=2)(10/33=3)(35=4)(36/39=5) (41/43=6) (45/47=7)
(49/53=8) (55/56=9) (58/63=10) (64/66=11) (68=12) (69/75=13) (77/82=14)
(84=15) (85=16) (86/88=17) (90/93=18) (94/96=19) (97/98=20) (99=21),
gen(sector_1digit);
la def sector_1digit

1. "Agriculture, forestry and fishing"

2. "Mining and quarrying"

3. "Manufacturing"

4. "Electricity, gas, steam and air conditioning supply"

5. "Water supply; sewerage, waste management and remediation activities"

6. "Construction"

7. "Wholesale and retail trade; repair of motor vehicles and motorcycles"

8. "Transportation and storage"

9. "Accommodation and food service activities"

10. "Information and communication"

11. "Financial and insurance activities"

12. "Real estate activities"

13. "Professional, scientific and technical activities"

14. "Administrative and support service activities"

15. "Public administration and defence; compulsory social security"

16. "Education"

17. "Human health and social work activities"

18. "Arts, entertainment and recreation"

19. "Other service activities"

20. "Activities of households as employers; undifferentiated goods- and services-producing activities of households for own use"

21. "Activities of extraterritorial organizations and bodies";

#delimit cr
la val sector_1digit sector_1digit

Box 4.6: International Standard Industrial Classification of All Economic Activities

Revision 2, 1968, Major Divisions

0. Activities not adequately defined

1. Agriculture, hunting, forestry and fishing

2. Mining and quarrying

3. Manufacturing

4. Electricity, gas and water

5. Construction

6. Wholesale and retail trade and restaurants and hotels

7. Transport, storage and communication

8. Financing, insurance, real estate and business services

9. Community, social and personal services

Revision 3, 1990, Tabulation Categories 1

A. Agriculture, hunting and forestry

B. Fishing

C. Mining and quarrying

D. Manufacturing

E. Electricity, gas and water supply

F. Construction

G. Wholesale and retail trade; repair of motor vehicles, motorcycles and personal and household goods

H. Hotels and restaurants

I. Transport, storage and communications

J. Financial intermediation

K. Real estate, renting and business activities

L. Public administration and defence; compulsory social security

M. Education

N. Health and social work

(continued)

Box 4.6: International Standard Industrial Classification of All Economic Activities *(continued)*

O. Other community, social and personal services activities

P. Private households with employed persons

Q. Extra-territorial organizations and bodies

X. Not classifiable by economic activity

Revision 4, 2008, Tabulation Categories

A. Agriculture, forestry and fishing

B. Mining and quarrying

C. Manufacturing

D. Electricity, gas, steam and air conditioning supply

E. Water supply; sewerage, waste management and remediation activities

F. Construction

G. Wholesale and retail trade; repair of motor vehicles and motorcycles

H. Transportation and storage

I. Accommodation and food service activities

J. Information and communication

K. Financial and insurance activities

L. Real estate activities

M. Professional, scientific and technical activities

N. Administrative and support service activities

O. Public administration and defence; compulsory social security

P. Education

Q. Human health and social work activities

R. Arts, entertainment and recreation

S. Other service activities

T. Activities of households as employers; undifferentiated goods- and services-producing activities of households for own use

U. Activities of extraterritorial organizations and bodies

Note: Full details on the latest revision and links to crosswalks between previous revisions are available at http://unstats.un.org/unsd/cr/registry/isic-4.asp.

Box 4.7: Example of a "Do-File" on How to Recode 2-Digit Industrial Classification Codes into 1-Digit Sectors

```
*** Recode employment sector variable***
recode sector (1/3=1) (5/43=2) (45/99=3), gen(sector_broad)
#delimit ;
la def sector_broad
```

1. "Agriculture"

2. "Industry"

3. "Services";

```
#delimit cr
la val sector_broad sector_broad
```

There are two ways of generating a *Broad sector* variable: (a) recoding the original "sector" variable available in the dataset, or (b) recoding the newly created 1-digit sector variable. Both ways should lead to the same results. (See box 4.7.)

Public Sector Employment. Public sector employment information is often not captured in a stand-alone variable in household datasets, but rather is captured in another variable. For instance, it might be found under a "private sector employment" variable or in a variable that breaks down employment by type of business. Also, public sector information is very seldom available as a binary variable with the value 1 for public employment and any other value for nonpublic employment. Thus, recoding into a new variable is often required.

The following example shows the categories of a "type of business" variable. Categories 1 and 2 indicate public sector employment. Box 4.8 shows how a *"Public sector"* binary variable was generated for categories 1 and 2.

1. National/provincial/local government
2. Government-controlled business
3. A private enterprise
4. Nonprofit organization
5. Private household
6. Do not know.

Box 4.8: Example of a "Do-File" to Generate a "Public Sector" Variable

```
*** Generate public sector variable ***
recode BUSINESSTYPE (1/2=1) (3/6=2), gen(public_sector)
#delimit ;
la def public_sector
```

1. "public"

2. "non-public"

```
#delimit cr
la val public_sector public_sector
```

Wage Employment. The variable tab "Wage employment" accepts the loading of binary or categorical variables with distinct values. During the process of generating an "employment status" variable a "value 1," representing "wage employment and salaried employment," was created. The variable *Employment status* needs to be loaded into the tab specifying the value representing "Wage employment."

Another possibility would be to load the status variable originally available in the dataset (before recoding) and specify the value that represents wage and salaried employment. It needs to be mentioned that the value labels in the relevant ADePT tables will be the same as the ones used in the input variable. In other words, if the user loads the original variable with "wage employment" covered under "paid employment," the label "Paid employment" will also be used when generating the tables.

"Wage employment" needs be defined as a separate value in the ADePT interface to allow calculations of the trade union density rate in ADePT table 33 (screenshot 3.48 in chapter 3).

Own-Account Workers. The variable tab "Own-account workers" accepts the upload of binary or categorical variables with distinct values. During the process of generating an "employment status" variable, a "value 3" representing "Own-account worker" was created that can be loaded into the tab, specifying its value (screenshot 4.3).

Contributing Family Workers. As with the variable fields for "Wage and salaried workers" and "Own-account workers," the previously created

Screenshot 4.3: Specifying Values of the "Employment Status" Variable

🐾 Population and welfare	🏭 Labour force	$ Employment quality	🔍 Parameters

Employed	If_statusNSO=1 ▼	Broad sector	▼
Unemployed	If_statusNSO=2 ▼	Public sector employment	▼
Economically inactive	If_statusNSO=3 ▼	Wage employment	emp_status=1 ▼
Reason for inactivity	▼	Own-account workers	emp_status=3 ▼
Duration of unemployment	▼	Contributing family workers	emp_status=4 ▼

"employment status" variable should be loaded while entering the value corresponding to "Contributing family workers."

Secondary Jobs. Secondary employment describes any additional employment that an employed person is engaged in outside of the first or primary job. It can include working for another employer, running a business, providing paid consultancy services, or being involved in a family business.

Increasingly, household surveys collect employment indicators for the primary, secondary, and sometimes even tertiary job separately.

The variable can be identified by survey questions similar to, "During the reference period, did you have any secondary job from which you or your household obtain any income in cash or in kind?"

Variables that reflect the number of employed with a secondary job are usually binary with the value 1 for those who have another job outside of their primary work.

Status in Employment in Secondary Job. Some household surveys collect information on the employment status in the primary and secondary (sometimes even tertiary) job. The preparation of the variable *Status in employment in SJ* ("secondary job") follows the same classifications and preparation process as outlined in the section "Status in employment."

The *Status in employment* in the "Secondary job" tab runs when fed with a binary or categorical variable.

Trade Union Membership. A number of household surveys, mainly LFSs in transitioning or developed countries, include a variable that captures trade union membership.

"Trade union membership" is usually a binary variable with the value 1 designating trade union membership. When the variable is loaded into the ADePT-LMI module, the software will calculate trade union density rates. However, users need to consider the significant differences across countries and surveys in the definition of *trade unions* and *trade union membership*. Thus, data are often of limited comparability.

Employment Quality Variables

The ADePT-LMI module presents five types of employment quality variables, which are described in detail in table 4.4.

Contract Type. Information on the contract type is usually available only for wage and salaried workers, since self-employed and contributing family workers are unlikely to have proper contractual arrangements. The information in a "contract" variable is likely to vary significantly between countries and across household surveys. Some surveys focus more on the length of a contractual arrangement (temporary, full-time, part-time, etc.); others focus more on the type of the contract agreement (verbal or written, by piece rate, etc.). The ADePT software can be fed with any type of categorical "contract type" variable that users would like to analyze. However, if comparisons between survey years are desired, users need to apply the same categories for each survey. This, in turn, might require recoding of the variable.

Table 4.4: Variables for Information about Employment Quality

Variable	Description
Type of contract	Categorical variable that applies country-specific categories that will be adopted for analysis with the ADePT-LMI module.
Earnings	Continuous variable. Data on earnings in household surveys should ideally be in the form of continuous values. However, a number of surveys, especially in developed countries, provide categorical earning values that currently cannot be analyzed with the help of ADePT. One way around it, although less precise, would be the transformation of categorical values into continuous values through recoding of the relevant earning variable.
	Earnings information in surveys should ideally relate to average gross earnings (wages or salary) per worker, expressed as monthly averages in the primary job.
Hours	Continuous variable reflecting the total numbers of hours worked during the workweek. Ideally, users should analyze the usual hours worked in the primary job during the standard workweek.
Willing to work more hours	Usually a binary variable with value of 1 if the person is willing to work more hours and any other value if not.
Contributions to social security	A binary variable that needs to be created based on the information available in the survey.

Earnings. The "Earnings" tab accepts any type of earnings-related statistics in household surveys as long as the variable uploaded is numeric and continuous. This could be data related to the wage and salary of employees or earnings on a monthly, weekly, daily, or hourly basis, depending on the analytical needs and available data. Data on earnings are often collected for the primary and secondary jobs separately. In such cases, one might need to create a "total earnings" variable that reflects earnings of all employed in the primary and secondary job.

The ADePT-LMI module does not currently allow for analysis of categorical wage and earnings data. Thus, variables that provide categorical wage and earnings information cannot be used.

Hours. Generally, household surveys, especially LFSs, contain continuous variables that give information on the hours worked. Very often information on the working hours is collected separately for each day of the week and independently for the primary and secondary jobs.

Household data files may include "hour" variables that correspond to such concepts as "actual hours worked" or "usual hours worked." The ADePT-LMI module can run with any "hour" input variable, so it is up to the data analyst to choose the applicable working time variable and concept. However, according to international standards as spelled out in chapter 2, it is recommended to analyze "usual hours worked."

As with the "earnings" variable, ADePT currently does not allow for analysis of categorical working time information.

Willing to Work More Hours. Most LFS datasets include a binary variable that captures employed people who are willing to work more hours.

In some surveys, the information might be available as a categorical variable that reflects the general willingness of survey respondents to work more, either in the form of more work or more working hours. Either variable type can be loaded into the ADePT-LMI module while specifying the value that captures the willingness to work more hours.

Without the provision of this information, ADePT will not be able to generate estimates of workers who are considered "time-related underemployed," meaning they are working below a specified number of hours (often the cutoff is "less than 30 hours") and are willing to work additional hours.

Contributions to Social Security. Reliable statistics on contributions to social security are an important precondition for assessing the extent of and trends in social protection. ILO standards on social security provide for different types of social security coverage under different economic systems and stages of development. Thus the social security data available in household surveys vary significantly between countries.

According to the ILO, minimum standards of social security cover nine categories: medical care, sickness, unemployment, old age, employment injury, family, maternity, invalidity, and survivors' benefits (ILO 1952). However, very few household surveys collect information on all nine categories. Variables that capture social security coverage in household surveys are commonly binary with the value 1 if the persons are covered under a specific category and any other value if not.

The ADePT-LMI module offers two ways for generating estimates on social security coverage:

- Users load available data for each category of social security coverage separately (e.g., users change the table name in the produced spreadsheet to specify the category entered).
- Users load a "proxy" input variable for social security coverage based on the national indicators designed to capture social security coverage.

Box 4.9 shows how users can create a proxy variable in the input file.

Parameters for Hours, Earnings, and Age Brackets

The ADePT-LMI module introduces six parameters, including age brackets, which are described in detail in table 4.5.

Minimum Weekly Hours Parameter. The number of hours in the parameter tab define the cutoff points for time-related underemployment estimates shown in table 32 (screenshot 3.47 in chapter 3). The standard cutoff point for the minimum weekly hours is usually 30 hours per week. However, in some countries the cutoff point might equal a number representing the defined threshold for a full-time week. Thus, the user should study the methodological guide before setting the minimum weekly hours to match national statistical concepts.

Box 4.9: Example of a "Do-File" to Generate a Social Security Coverage "Proxy" Variable

The example household dataset provided three binary variables for the following:

1. Sick leave coverage (SICK)

2. Pension coverage (PENSION)

3. Medical coverage (MEDICAL).

If an employed person was covered under any of the categories it was classified as having social security coverage.
*** Generate a proxy "social security coverage" variable ***
gen Socsec=1 if age>=15 & (SICK==1 | PENSION==1 | MEDICAL==1)
replace Socsec=0 if age>=15 & Socsec~=1
la var Socsec "Social Security"
la def Socsec 1 "yes" 2 "no"
la val Socsec Socsec

Table 4.5: Overview of Hours, Earnings, and Age Bracket Parameters

Parameter	Description
Minimum weekly hours	Users must specify by country the minimum weekly working hours to allow the calculation of time-related underemployment estimates according to national circumstances.
Earnings measurement	Median and mean
	Users can choose whether the software calculates the mean or median of the earnings uploaded to the software. Calculating the mean of earnings is the same as obtaining their average. In a median measurement, the earnings are arranged from lowest to highest: 60, 80, 85, 90, and 100. The middle number is the median. The type of measure applied depends on the earnings distribution.
Age Brackets	
Minimum age	Users must specify the minimum age limit for defining the working-age population according to national circumstances such as the compulsory schooling age, minimum age for admission to employment, and extent of child labor.
Working-age minimum	The minimum working age is often defined as 15. However, in some countries it might be less or more depending on the national standards.
Working-age maximum	Some countries use a maximum age limit for defining the working-age population.
Youth age maximum	The maximum age for youth is often defined as 24 although in some countries it can be less or more depending on the monitoring needs.

Earnings Measurement Parameter. Depending on the earnings distribution in the dataset, the user should decide which statistical method to apply when calculating earnings tables in the ADePT-LMI module. The major difference between *median* and *mean* is the capacity of the median to eliminate mean-altering outliers in the dataset.

Earning averages configured by a mean are typically higher than the actual average earnings because of a small number of people whose earnings may exceed the average earnings in the field (for example, a millionaire who earns 1,000 times more than an average person). Sometimes, however, mean earnings could point in the opposite direction because the dataset might include a large number of employed people—mainly in part-time or temporary jobs—who earn minimal amounts (for example, US$100 per month).

Thus, median earning averages are often more appropriate since outliers have far less influence, and are generally more accurate when dealing with average earning estimations.

However, users should carefully examine available earnings distribution in the original dataset before choosing the appropriate earning measure.

Minimum Age Parameter. Setting the minimum age parameter correctly in the ADePT-LMI module is essential for ensuring accurate tables. Various types of household surveys usually apply different minimum age parameters. For example, a household LSS often collects information on all members of the household, thus defining the minimum age as 0+. An LFS, in turn, often has a higher lower age boundary, for instance ages 6 and older, if seeking to determine child labor.

The ADePT-LMI module's minimum age parameter should be set as the minimum age used in the survey. Minimum age information can usually be obtained from methodological documentation of the household survey.

Working-Age Minimum Parameter. The economically active and inactive population concepts applied in household surveys make reference to persons "above a specified age" to define the working-age population. Each country specifies the minimum age limit for defining the working-age population according to its national laws and practices (e.g., enforced schooling age, minimum age for admission to employment, and extent of child labor). These circumstances vary significantly among countries. Thus, the user of the ADePT-LMI module should set the working-age minimum parameter based on the national minimum working-age standards.

Working-Age Maximum Parameter. Some countries, especially developed countries, use a maximum age limit for defining the working-age population. If users would like to run an analysis for a specific age group (e.g., ages 20–40), they can set the minimum and maximum age parameters to produce tables for the specific age groups.

Youth Age Maximum Parameter. The maximum age of youth targeted in national policies and programs targeting youth varies greatly. In many countries the standard age for youth is ages 15–24. However, to allow for informing special youth programs and policies that target a particular age group, the youth maximum age might be as high as 29 or even 34. Thus, users must set the youth age maximum parameter according to analytical needs and national circumstances.

Treating Missing Values

Missing values in Stata and SPSS data files are usually coded with numbers that are larger than the largest allowable number for the data type (e.g., the values 9, 97, 98, 99, 997, etc.). The ADePT-LMI module will recognize these codes and treat them accordingly.

However, in a number of datasets, these universally used codes are not applied. Instead missing values are captured in variable categories that might be named "Refusal," "Do not know" (see screenshot 4.4, code 26), or "Not applicable," and coded with real or realistic values. If this is the case, users must recode these categories or values so the ADePT-LMI module recognizes them as missing values.

The ADePT-LMI module does not remove any observation from the loaded dataset if any of the assigned variables contain missing values. Instead, ADePT ignores observations with missing values, excluding them from the tabulations.

Screenshot 4.4: Hidden Missing Values in a Variable

```
definition
         0    No schooling
         1    Grade R/O
         2    Grade 1/sub A
         3    Grade 2/sub B
         4    Grade 3/standard 1
         5    Grade 4/standard 2
         6    Grade 5/standard 3
         7    Grade 6/standard 4
         8    Grade 7/standard 5
         9    Grade 8/standard 6/Form 1
        10    Grade 9/standard 7/Form 2
        11    Grade 10/standard 8/Form 3
        12    Grade 11/standard 9/Form 4
        13    Grade 12/standard 10/Form 5/Matric
        14    NTC I
        15    NTC II
        16    NTC III
        17    Certificate with less than Grade 12/Std 10
        18    Diploma with less than Grade 12/Std 10
        19    Certificate with Grade 12/Std 10
        20    Diploma with Grade 12/Std 10
        21    Bachelors Degree
        22    Bachelors Degree and Diploma
        23    Honours Degree
        24    Higher Degree (Masters, Doctorate)
        25    Other
        26    Do not know

variables:  Q17EDUCATION
```

Load Input File into ADePT

After having prepared the input file, users can load it into the ADePT-LMI module. The process requires the following five steps:

1. Read the input file into the ADePT-LMI module.
2. Assign the variables from the input file to the relevant fields.
3. Select the tables you want to generate.
4. Specify the options that affect the information in the tables.
5. Press **Generate** button.

ADePT can process a wide variety of system files (e.g., Excel, Stata, and SPSS). To load a dataset into ADePT, click "Add" in the main form quadrant and select the dataset you want to load in the "Open dataset" dialog box. The status bar then shows the following about the selected dataset: (a) the full path, (b) the number of variables and observations, and (c) the size.

Specify a label for the dataset. This label will be used in tables and graphs to identify results generated from different datasets. In the **"Label"** column, type the default label name for the dataset. It is recommended to label the dataset using the country name, survey type, and year of the survey (e.g., "Mongolia 2011") (screenshot 4.5).

When many survey datasets are loaded into the module, ADePT can calculate differences between surveys and will be able to calculate annualized rates of changes for the statistics it generates. However, if more than one dataset is loaded to the module, all datasets must contain either only individual observations or only household observations, *not both*. Also, users must make sure the input variables loaded into ADePT have the same names and value labels across the input datasets to allow ADePT to work correctly.

To remove a dataset: Click the dataset, then click the **Remove** button.

The ADePT-LMI module does not alter original datasets. It will always work with copies of the original datasets.

The loaded datasets, called "input files," can be the original datasets that include the newly created input variables or files that contain only the relevant input variables for the ADePT-LMI module.

Screenshot 4.5: Loading an Input File to the ADePT-LMI Module

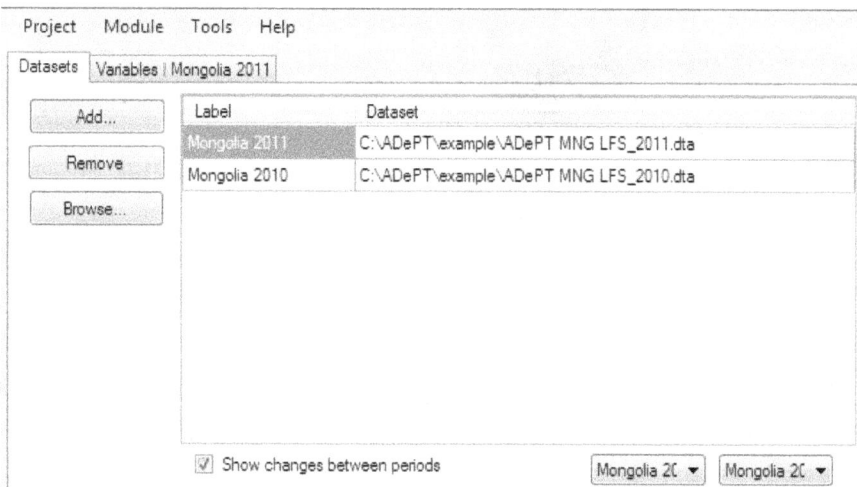

Assign the Variables from the Input File to the Relevant Fields

After loading the data file, the user must tell the module what variables and values in the datasets correspond to the fields required to produce the output. The user needs to select variables manually in the loaded dataset or drag them from the variable list (screenshot 4.6) into the relevant variable tabs. Another option is to choose the variable from the drop-down list while clicking on the relevant variable (screenshot 4.7).

Users can enter any variable name from the loaded dataset. Nevertheless, as mentioned earlier, variables need to be named consistently if multiple datasets are loaded. In other words, if *Age* is specified as the age indicator in one dataset, that wording should be used as the age indicator in all loaded datasets, not another name such as *ii6* or *AGE*.

Screenshot 4.6: Assigning Variables of the Input File to Variable Fields by Dragging

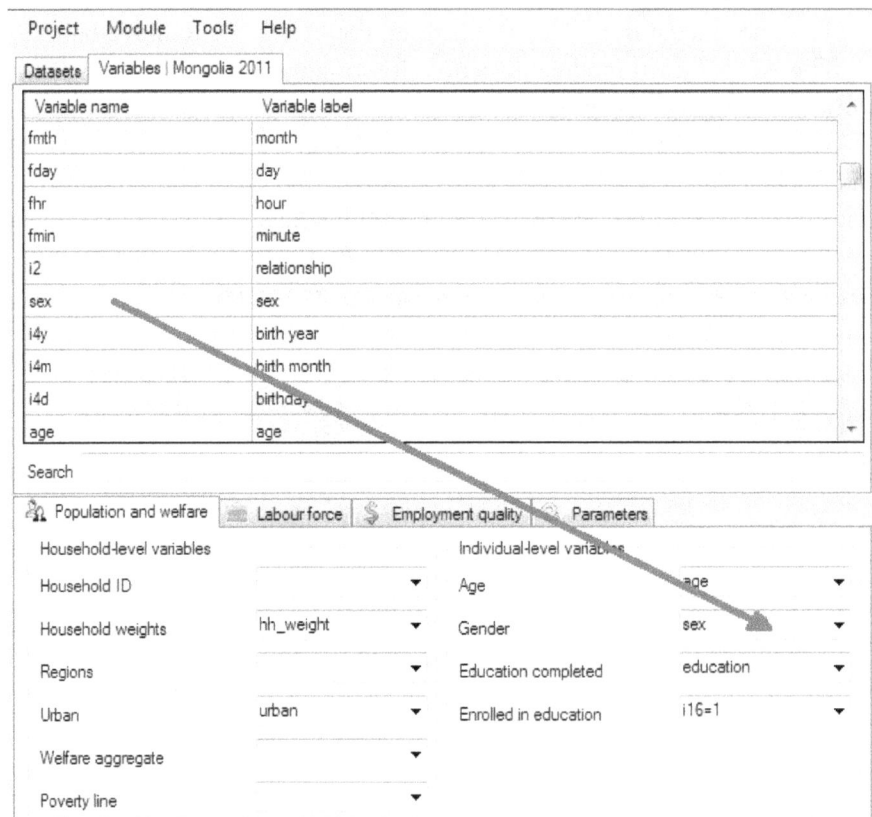

Screenshot 4.7: Assigning Variables of the Input File to Variable Fields by Choosing from the Drop-Down List

Screenshot 4.8: Report of Variable Check

The ADePT-LMI module automatically checks the variables entered manually into the tags and reports to the user if the variable entered is missing in any of the loaded datasets. If so, a red exclamation mark will appear beside the variable tab.

When uploading numerous datasets, ADePT does not report if the value labels of the variables are the same or different, but the user will notice in the produced tables (screenshot 4.8).

In addition to loading variables, users need to enter expressions to specify values of input variables. In screenshot 4.9, for example, the expression "lf_statusNSO=1" is entered in the input variable field *Employed*.

Screenshot 4.9: Using Expression to Specify Values of Input Variables

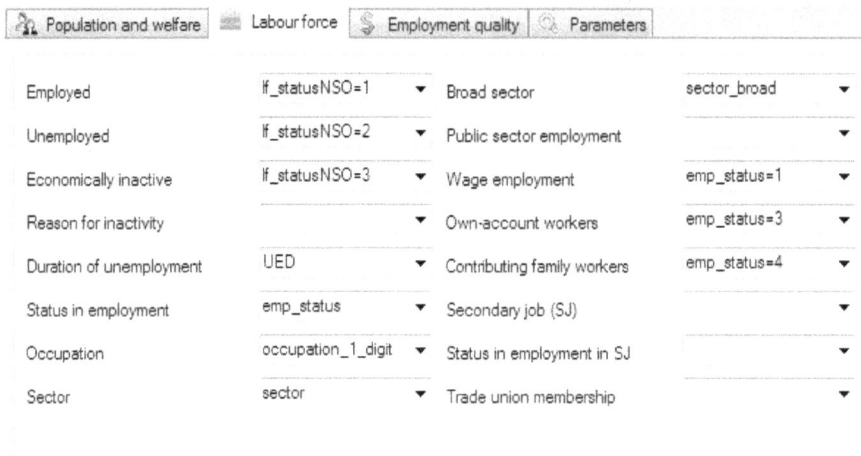

Population and welfare	Labour force	Employment quality	Parameters

Employed	If_statusNSO=1 ▼	Broad sector	sector_broad ▼
Unemployed	If_statusNSO=2 ▼	Public sector employment	▼
Economically inactive	If_statusNSO=3 ▼	Wage employment	emp_status=1 ▼
Reason for inactivity	▼	Own-account workers	emp_status=3 ▼
Duration of unemployment	UED ▼	Contributing family workers	emp_status=4 ▼
Status in employment	emp_status ▼	Secondary job (SJ)	▼
Occupation	occupation_1_digit ▼	Status in employment in SJ	▼
Sector	sector ▼	Trade union membership	▼

The operators shown in table 4.6 can be used in input variable expressions.

Table 4.6: Operators for Input Variable Expressions

Operator	Description
+ – * /	Mathematical operators
= ==	Equality check operators
^	Power (e.g., x^2 is x squared)
AND && &	Logical *and* operators (case-insensitive)
OR || |	Logical *or* operators (case-insensitive)

Choose Tables and Specify Table Option

This section explains how, once all the variables from the input files have been assigned to the relevant field, users can start to choose tables to generate and specify options.

Choosing Tables

Each table or graph requires particular variables and some parameters to be specified. For example, table 8b (screenshot 3.13 in chapter 3), which shows the distribution of the labor force by educational attainment, sex, and age group, requires five variables to be specified: *Household weights,*

Labour force status, *Education completed*, *Gender*, and *Age*. If one of these variables is not specified, the table cannot be created.

Table statistics are shown above the table tree. For example, screenshot 4.10 shows (a) 63 possible tables and graphs; (b) 31 feasible tables (i.e., that ADePT can generate based on the available variables); and (c) 7 selected tables and graphs.

To select a table, click on the small field next to the table name.

Users can select table options to produce, for each table, standard errors and frequencies (screenshot 4.11). This action is necessary if users want to formulate and test statistical hypotheses. Standard errors or frequencies will be produced by simply activating the equivalent fields (located below the list of tables) before generating tables.

Tables with frequencies show the unweighted number of observations used in the calculation of a particular cell in a table. No significant additional time is needed to calculate frequencies.

Screenshot 4.10: Selecting Tables

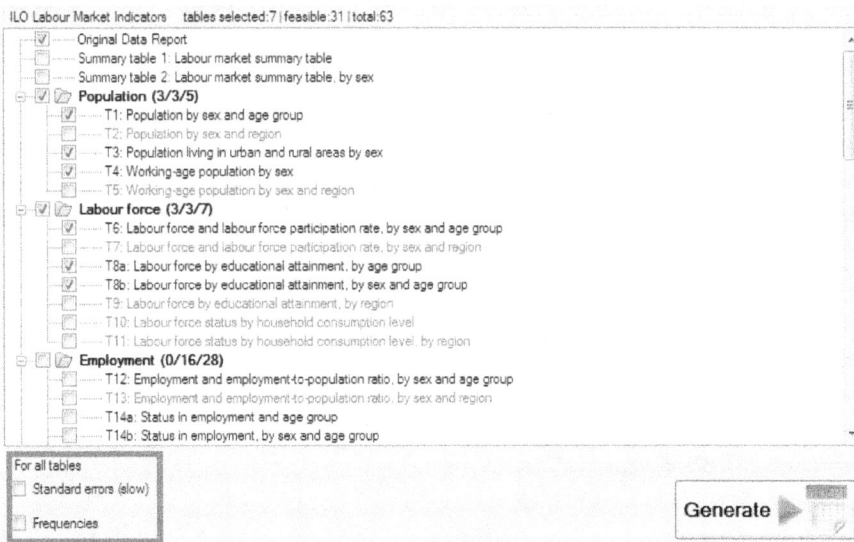

Screenshot 4.11: Standard Error and Frequency Tables

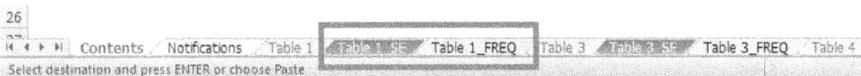

Results of a table's standard error and frequency calculations are in separate worksheets, labeled "SE" and "FREQ," within the output report.

Users can produce a set of separate tables presenting the standard errors or frequencies by ticking the equivalent fields below the list of tables.

Set "If-Condition" Tabs for Individual Tables

Users can set restrictions on observations in individual tables using "if-condition" tabs (screenshot 4.12). In the list of tables, click on the name of a selected table. This displays the table description and "if-condition" tab. Users can now enter the filter expression, for example, "urban=1" or "sex=1."

When clicking the **Set** button or pressing **Enter,** the if-condition will be applied to the chosen table. The if-condition field turns orange when the user is entering an expression, and remains orange until the **Set** button is clicked. Note that the chosen if-conditions are *not saved* in the ADePT project file. They always need to be set again before generating the ADePT tables.

The purpose of if-conditions is to include observations from a population's subgroup. The inclusion condition is formulated as a Boolean expression, a function of the variables existing in the dataset.[4] Each particular observation is included in the analysis if it satisfies the inclusion condition (the Boolean expression evaluates to value true). In many cases, the if-conditions are quite simple.

Users can use any valid Stata expression to form if-conditions. In addition, if-conditions can include any variables from the loaded input datasets, not only those that can be specified in the ADePT variable tabs. Nevertheless, users have to ensure the validity and consistency of the variables used for the formulation of if-conditions, since ADePT cannot conduct checks on them.

Screenshot 4.12: Setting If-Conditions

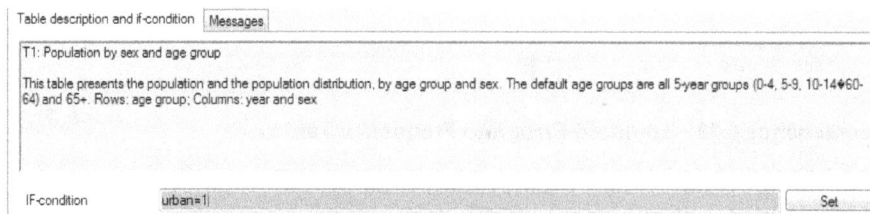

| Table description and if-condition | Messages |

T1: Population by sex and age group

This table presents the population and the population distribution, by age group and sex. The default age groups are all 5-year groups (0-4, 5-9, 10-14♦60-64) and 65+. Rows: age group; Columns: year and sex

| IF-condition | urban=1| | | Set |

Consider the following examples of if-condition expressions (table 4.7):

Table 4.7: Expression for If-Conditions

If-condition	Interpretation
urban=1	Only those observations having the value of variable **Urban** equal to 1 will be included in the analysis.
region==5	Only observations from the **region** with code **5** are included in the analysis.
age>=16	Only those individuals who are ages 16 or older are included in the analysis.

If-condition	Interpretation
(urban=1) & (region!=1)	Include observations from all urban locations; exclude the first region (e.g., the country capital).

Users that are familiar with Stata will note that there is no need to type the word **if** before if-conditions and that **==** can be used interchangeably with **=**.

Users can specify narrower groups by restricting several dimensions simultaneously, as in the following example: users click the item in the "tables and graphs" list, select the text in the if-condition field, and press delete.

Generate Tables

Once all desired tables are selected, and table option and if-conditions defined (optional), users simply hit the **Generate** button to run the software and create an Excel worksheet with all output results.

Save Projects

After specifying datasets, assigning input variables, and specifying other parameters and options, users can save the configurations for future use (screenshot 4.13). This will save considerable time when returning to work with datasets and ensures that the work in selecting and defining variables and parameters has been saved.

To save a project:

- "Project" > "Save Project" > "Save Project As (enter project name)."
- In the "Save Project As" dialog field, select a location for the project, then click the **Save** button.

Screenshot 4.13: ADePT-LMI Labor Module Projects

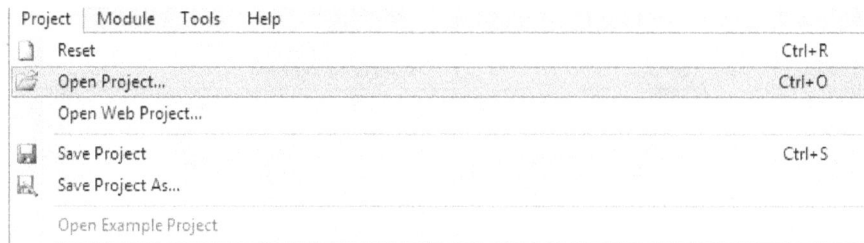

Project	Module	Tools	Help	
🗋 Reset				Ctrl+R
🗁 Open Project...				Ctrl+O
Open Web Project...				
🖫 Save Project				Ctrl+S
🖫 Save Project As...				
Open Example Project				

To open a saved project:

"Project" > "Open Project" > (browse project file to be loaded).

In the **Open** dialog, locate and select the project, then click the **Open** button.

To start a new project:

Project > Reset. This will clear all loaded information in the ADePT-LMI module.

Notes

1. Metadata can be described as controlling data that provide information on the way the data were produced and their scope, coverage, meaning, and limitations. Too often there are no or just vague metadata to available LMI. Without such basic information on the data, there is very little value of the information for meaningful and correct LMI and analysis. This issue accounts even more for employment trend analysis.

2. A numerical variable is needed when users wish to manipulate the data mathematically. Examples would be age, income, and job satisfaction rating. A string variable is needed when users wish to treat the data entries like words. Examples would be names, cities, case identifiers, and race. Many times variables that could be considered string are coded as numeric. For example, data for the variable "sex" might be coded "1" for "male" and "2" for "female" instead of using a string variable that would require letters (e.g., "male" and "female"). This has two benefits. First, numerical entries are easier and quicker to enter. Second, manipulation of numerical data with statistical software is generally much easier than using string variables.

3. The ISCED belongs to the United Nations International Family of Economic and Social Classifications, which are applied in statistics worldwide with the purpose of assembling, compiling, and analyzing cross-nationally comparable data. ISCED is the reference classification for organizing education programs and related qualifications by education levels and fields. ISCED is a product of international agreement and adopted formally by the General Conference of UNESCO Member States. For further information on the ISCED see http://www.uis.unesco .org/Education/Documents/isced-2011-en.pdf.

4. A Boolean expression is an expression in a programming language that produces a Boolean value when evaluated, that is, one of true or false.

References

ILO (International Labour Organization). 1952. "ILO C102–Social Security (Minimum Standards) Convention, 1952 (No. 102)." Convention adopted Geneva, June 28. http://www.ilo.org/dyn/normlex /en/f?p=1000:12100:0::NO::P12100_ILO_CODE:C102.

———. 1993. "Resolution Concerning the International Classification of Status in Employment." Resolution adopted by the 15th International Conference of Labour Statisticians. Geneva, January. http://www.ilo .org/global/statistics-and-databases/standards-and-guidelines/resolutions -adopted-by-international-conferences-of-labour-statisticians/WCMS _087562/lang--en/index.htm.

———. 2008. International Standard Classification of Occupations (ISCO-08). http://www.ilo.org/public/english/bureau/stat/isco/isco08/index.htm.

Mongolia Labour Force Survey. 2008. National Statistical Office of Mongolia. http://web.nso.mn/nada/index.php/catalog.

———. 2010. National Statistical Office of Mongolia. http://www.en.nso .mn/index.php.

———. 2011. National Statistical Office of Mongolia. http://www.en.nso .mn/index.php.

National Judicial Academy. 2008. "Decision of the Supreme Court on the Rights of Lesbian, Gay, Bisexual, Transsexual and Intersex (LGBTI) People." Nepal. http://www.gaylawnet.com/laws/cases/PantvNepal.pdf%20and%20 http://www.humandignitytrust.org/uploaded/Library/Case_Law/%20Sunil _Babu_Pant_and_others_v_Nepal_Government_and_others.pdf.

Further Reading

Eurostat. 2012. *Regional Yearbook.* http://ec.europa.eu/eurostat/publications/regional-yearbook.

ILO (International Labour Organization). ILOSTAT Database. Geneva: ILO. http://www.ilo.org/ilostat.

———. 1990. *Surveys of Economically Active Population, Employment, Unemployment and Underemployment: An ILO Manual on Concepts and Methods.* Geneva: ILO.

———. 2004. *Multiple Job-Holding.* Factsheet. Geneva: ILO. http://www.ilo.org/wcmsp5/groups/public/---ed_protect/---protrav/---travail/documents/publication/wcms_169672.pdf.

———. 2013. "Statistics of Work, Employment and Labour Underutilization." Resolution adopted by the 19th International Conference of Labour Statisticians, Geneva.

———. 2015. *Key Indicators of the Labour Market.* 9th ed. Geneva: ILO.

Kapsos, S. 2004. *Estimating Growth Requirements for Reducing Working Poverty: Can the World Halve Working Poverty by 2015?* Geneva: International Labour Organization.

Mongolia Household Income and Expenditure Survey. 2008. National Statistical Office of Mongolia. http://web.nso.mn/nada/index.php/catalog.

Mongolia Labour Force Survey. 2008. National Statistical Office of Mongolia. http://web.nso.mn/nada/index.php/catalog.

South Africa Quarterly Labour Force Survey. 2010. Statistics South Africa. http://www.statssa.gov.za/?page_id=737.

UN (United Nations). 1997. *Handbook for Producing National Statistical Reports on Women and Men, Social Statistics and Indicators.* New York: UN.

———. 2008. International Standard Industrial Classification of All Economic Activities, Revision 4. http://unstats.un.org/unsd/cr/registry/isic-4.asp.

UNESCO (United Nations Educational, Scientific, and Cultural Organization). 2011. *International Standard Classification of Education: ISCED 2011.* Montreal: UNESCO Institute for Statistics. http://www.uis.unesco.org/Education/Documents/isced-2011-en.pdf.

Chapter 5

Getting Started with ADePT

Introduction

This chapter provides basic information about installing and using ADePT. The instructions here are sufficient to perform a simple analysis. For more information:

- Detailed instructions for using ADePT are in the *ADePT User's Guide*, which you can download from www.worldbank.org/adept ▶ **Documentation**.
- Video tutorials are available at www.worldbank.org/adept ▶ **Video Tutorials**.
- ADePT provides online help via the **Help** ▶ **Contents** command.
- For help with using an ADePT module, see appropriate chapters in this book, or in another book in the Streamlined Analysis with ADePT Software series.
- Module-specific instructions, and example datasets, projects, and reports, are available at www.worldbank.org/adept ▶ **Modules**.
- Example datasets and projects are installed with ADePT. They are in the *example* subfolder in the ADePT program folder. Use the examples with the instructions in this chapter to familiarize yourself with ADePT operations.
- Windows, buttons, tabs, dialogs, and other features you see onscreen are shown in **bold**. For example, the **Save As** dialog has a **Save** button and a **Cancel** button.
- Keystrokes are shown in SMALL CAPS. For example, you may be instructed to press the ENTER key.
- Menu commands use a shorthand notation. **Project** ▶ **Exit**, for example, means "open the **Project** menu and click the **Exit** command."

Installing ADePT

This section provides basic information about the system requirements and the installation of ADePT.

System Requirements

- PC running Microsoft Windows XP (SP1 or later), Windows Vista, Windows Server 2003 and later, or Windows 7. ADePT runs in 32- and 64-bit environments.
- .NET 2.0 or later (included with recent Windows installations), and all updates and patches.
- 80MB disk space to install, plus space for temporary dataset copies.
- At least 512MB RAM.
- At least 1024 x 768 screen resolution.
- At least one printer driver must be installed (even if no computer is connected).
- Microsoft Excel for Windows (XP or later), Microsoft Excel Viewer or a compatible spreadsheet program for viewing reports generated by ADePT.
- A Web browser and Internet access are needed to download ADePT. Internet access is needed for program updates and to load Web-based datasets into ADePT. Otherwise, ADePT runs without needing Internet access.

Installation

1. Download the ADePT installer by clicking the **ADePT Downloads** button at www.worldbank.org/adept.
2. Launch the installer and follow the onscreen instructions.

ADePT automatically launches after installation.

Launching ADePT

1. Click the ADePT icon in the Windows **Start** menu.
2. In the **Select ADePT Module** window, double-click the name of the module you want to use. To open the LMI module, double-click on **ILO Labour Market Indicators**.

3. You now see the ADePT main window. (The example below shows ADePT configured with the ILO module. The lower left and upper right panels will be different when another module is loaded.)

- *To switch to another module after launching ADePT:*

a. **Module ▶ Select Module...**
b. In the **Select ADePT Module** window, double-click the name of the module you want to use.

Overview of the Analysis Procedure

There are four general steps in performing an analysis:

1. Specify one or more datasets that you want to analyze.
2. Map dataset variables to ADePT analysis inputs.
3. Select tables or graphs.
4. Generate the report.

Here is where you perform each step in the ADePT main window:

1. Click **Add** button to load dataset. Enter dataset year in **Label** column.

3. Select tables or graphs to be included in report.

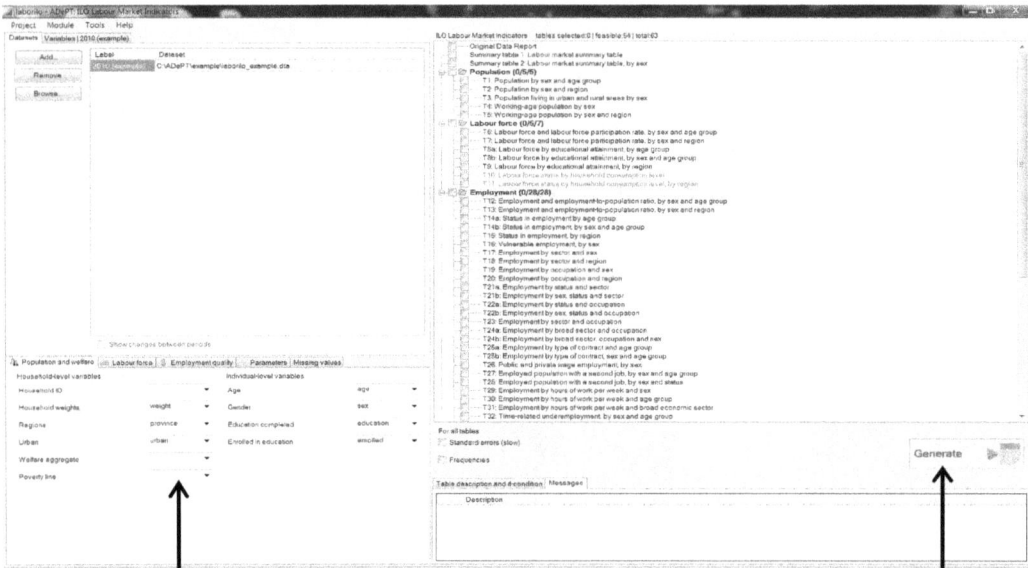

2. Map dataset variables to input variables by selecting dataset variables in drop-down lists.

4. Click **Generate** button.

The next sections in this chapter provide detailed instructions for the four steps.

Specify Datasets

Your first task in performing an analysis is to specify one or more datasets. ADePT can process data in Stata (*.dta*), SPSS (*.sav*), and tab delimited text (*.txt*) formats.

Operations in this section take place in the upper left corner of the ADePT main window.

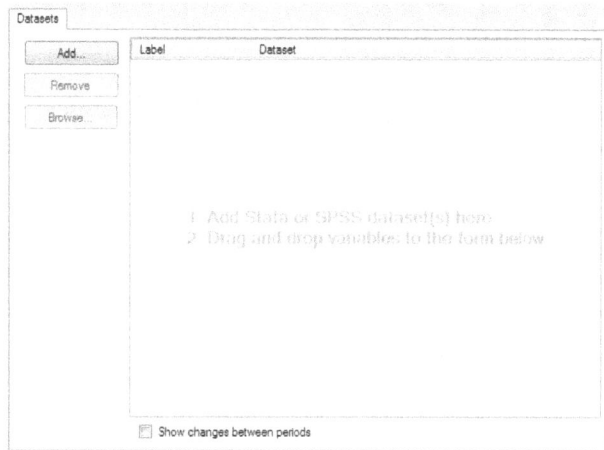

1. Click the **Add...** button.
2. In the **Open** dataset dialog, locate and click the dataset you want to analyze, then click the **Open** button. The dataset is now listed in the **Datasets** tab.

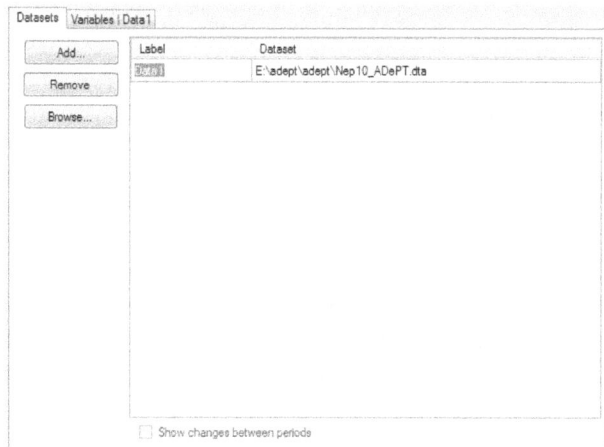

Tip: While learning to use ADePT, you may want to experiment with example data. You can find sample datasets in the *ADePT\Example* folder.

3. Specify a label for the dataset:
    a. In the **Label** column, select the default label.
    b. Type a label for the dataset. **Tip:** Label the dataset using the year the survey was conducted (for example, 2002). When labels are years, ADePT can calculate differences between surveys.
    c. Press ENTER.

4. Optional: Repeat steps 1 to 3 to specify each additional dataset.
    Note: If more than one dataset is specified, the datasets must contain only individual observations or household observations, but not both.

    • *To remove a dataset:* Click the dataset, then click the **Remove** button.

One dataset has been specified in this example.

Note: ADePT does not alter original datasets in any way. It always works with copies of datasets.

5. At the top of the **Datasets** tab:
    • Select **Individual-level** if the datasets contain one observation for each household member.
    • Select **Household-level** if the datasets contain one observation for each household.

6. By default, the **Show changes between periods** option is activated.
    • If you want ADePT to calculate changes between two periods, select the periods to the right of the option. The left period must be earlier than the right period, as shown here:

    • If you don't want ADePT to calculate changes between periods, deactivate the **Show changes between periods** option.

Map Variables

ADePT needs to know which variables in the dataset(s) correspond to the inputs to its calculations. You must manually map dataset variables to input variables.

Operations described in this section take place in the left side of the ADePT main window. These examples show the LMI module loaded into ADePT, but the process is similar for the other modules.

There are two methods for mapping variables:

- Method 1: In the lower input **Variables** tab, open the variable's list, then click the corresponding dataset variable, as shown here for the **Urban** variable.

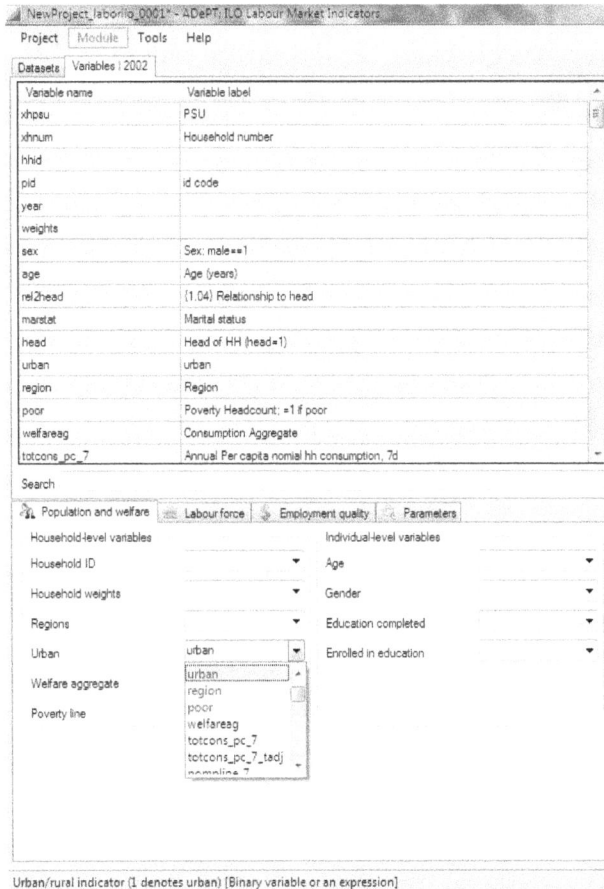

- Method 2: In the upper dataset **Variables** tab, drag the variable name and drop it in the corresponding field in the lower input **Variables** tab.

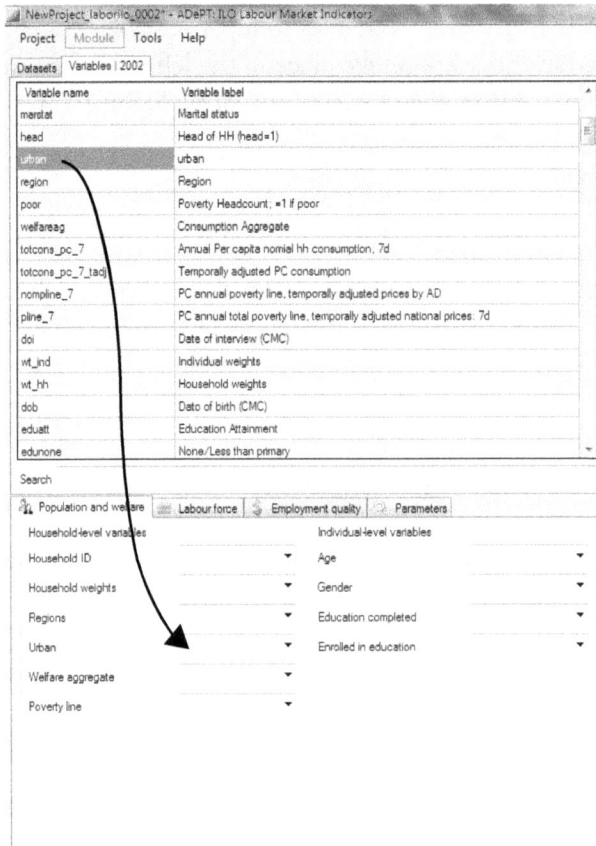

Note: You can also type dataset variable names in the input variable fields. The above methods are preferred, however, since typing may introduce spelling errors. A spelling error is indicated by the red exclamation point next to the input variable field.

- *To remove a mapping:* Select the variable name in the input variable field, then press DELETE.

Some modules have multiple input variable tabs. The ILO module, for example, organizes variables in three tabs.

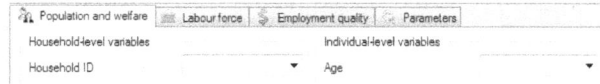

In some input variable fields you can specify multiple dataset variables. *Household ID*, for example, may not be unique within a dataset because the same ID was assigned to a household in another region. In such cases you can map multiple dataset variables to one input variable.

In this example, the **id** dataset variable has been mapped to the **Household ID** input variable.

The italic variable name indicates that this input variable field accepts multiple dataset variables. The **region** dataset variable can now be mapped to **Household ID** using either of the two methods described earlier.

ADePT uses this mapping to create its own internal *Household ID* variable to uniquely identify each household.

> **Tip:** Open the example project (**Project ▶ Open Example Project**) to see the result of mapping dataset variables to input variables.

Select Tables and Graphs

After mapping variables, you are ready to select the tables or graphs you want ADePT to generate.

Operations described in this section take place in the right side of the ADePT main window.

In the upper right (outputs) panel, select the tables or graphs you want to generate.

Note: If a name is gray, it cannot be selected. These tables and graphs cannot be generated because required variables have not been specified.

- *To see a description of a table or graph:* Click the name. Its description is displayed in the **Table description and if-condition** tab in the lower right corner of the ADePT window.

Generate the Report

1. Click the **Generate** button.

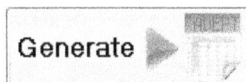

- *To stop calculating:* Click the **Stop** button.

2. Examine items in the **Messages** tab. ADePT lists potential problems in this tab.

ADePT can identify three kinds of problems:

- **Notification** provides information that may be of interest to you. Notifications do not affect the content of reports generated by ADePT.
- **Warning** indicates a suspicious situation in the data. Warnings are issued when ADePT cannot determine whether it is an impossible situation. Examples include violation of parameters, presence of potential outliers in the data, inconsistent data, and inconsistent category definitions. ADePT reports are not affected by warnings.
- **Error** prevents use of a variable in the analysis. For example, a variable may not exist in a dataset (in this case, ADePT continues its calculations as if the variable weren't specified). If ADePT can match the problem to a particular variable field, that field is highlighted in the input **Variables** tab.

3. As needed, correct problems, then generate the report again.

    Note: Notifications, warnings, and errors can negatively affect the results ADePT produces. Carefully review messages, and correct critical problems, before drawing conclusions from tables and graphs.

Examine the Output

When its analysis is complete, ADePT automatically opens the results as a spreadsheet in Excel or Excel Viewer. The results are organized in multiple worksheets:

- **Contents** worksheet lists all the other worksheets, including titles for tables or graphs.
- **Notifications** worksheet lists errors, warnings, and notifications ADePT identified during its analysis. This worksheet may be more useful than the **Messages** tab in the ADePT main window because the problems are organized by dataset.
- **Table** worksheets display tables generated by ADePT.

Tip: ADePT formats table data with a reasonable number of decimal places. Click in a cell to see the data with full resolution in the formula bar.

- **Figure** worksheets display graphs generated by ADePT.

Working with Variables

This section provides details about how you can work with variables in ADePT.

Viewing Basic Information about a Dataset's Variables

1. In the **Datasets** tab, click the dataset you want to examine.
2. Click the **Variables** tab.

Datasets	Variables	2002	
Variable name	**Variable label**
age	Age (years)
rel2head	{1.04} Relationship to head
marstat	Marital status
head	Head of HH (head=1)
urban	urban
region	Region
poor	Poverty Headcount; =1 if poor
welfareag	Consumption Aggregate
totcons_pc_7	Annual Per capita nomial hh consumption, 7d
totcons_pc_7_tadj	Temporally adjusted PC consumption
nompline_7	PC annual poverty line, temporally adjusted prices by AD
pline_7	PC annual total poverty line, temporally adjusted national prices: 7d
doi	Date of interview (CMC)
wt_ind	Individual weights
wt_hh	Household weights
dob	Dato of birth (CMC)
eduatt	Education Attainment
edunone	None/Less than primary
eduprim	Primary completed
edusec	Secondary completed
edupsec	Post secondary completed

Search

- *To search for a variable:* In the **Search** field, type a few characters in the variable name or variable label.
- *To view statistics for a variable:* Double-click the variable name or variable label. This opens the **MultiDataset Statistics** window for that variable.

Viewing a Dataset's Data and Variable Details

1. In the **Datasets** tab, click the dataset you want to examine.
2. Click the **Browse...** button. This opens the **ADePT Data Browser**.

The **Data Browser** lists observations in rows and organizes variables in columns.

- *To see underlying data:* Click the **Hide Value Labels** button.
- *To see value labels:* Click the **Show Value Labels** button.
- *To view a variable's statistics:*
  a. Click in the variable's column.
  b. Click the **Show Statistics...** button.
- *To view detailed information about the dataset's variables:* Click the **Variable View** tab in the bottom left of the **Data Browser**.

	Show	Name	Type	Width	Decimals	Label	Values Schema	Values
1	✓	xhpsu	Numeric	8	0	PSU		
2	✓	xhnum	Numeric	8	0	Household number		
3	✓	hhid*	Numeric	10	0			
4	✓	pid	Numeric	8	0	id code		
5	✓	year	Numeric	9	0			
6	✓	weights	Numeric	9	0			
7	✓	sex	Numeric	8	0	Sex, male==1	V01_02	{1,"Male"; 2,"Female"}
8	✓	age	Numeric	8	0	Age (years)		
9	✓	rel2head	Numeric	27	0	(1.04) Relationship to head	V01_04	{1,"Head"; 2,"Husband/wife"; 3,"Sor
10	✓	marstat	Numeric	13	0	Marital status	marstat	{1,"Never_married"; 2,"Married"; 3,"F
11	✓	head	Numeric	9	0	Head of HH (head=1)		
12	✓	urban	Numeric	8	0	urban	urban	{1,"urban"; 2,"rural"}
13	✓	region	Numeric	11	0	Region	region	{1,"Eastern"; 2,"Centeral"; 3,"Wester
14	✓	poor	Numeric	9	0	Poverty Headcount: =1 if poor	poor	{1,"Poor"; 2,"Non-poor"}
15	✓	welfareag	Numeric	9	0	Consumption Aggregate		
16	✓	totcons_pc_7	Numeric	10	0	Annual Per capita nomial hh consumption, 7d		
17	✓	totcons_pc_7_tadj	Numeric	10	0	Temporally adjusted PC consumption		
18	✓	nompline_7	Numeric	9	0	PC annual poverty line, temporally adjusted prices by AD		
19	✓	pline_7	Numeric	9	0	PC annual total poverty line, temporally adjusted national prices: 7d		
20	✓	doi	Numeric	9	0	Date of interview (CMC)		
21	✓	wt_ind	Numeric	9	0	Individual weights		
22	✓	wt_hh	Numeric	9	0	Household weights		
23	✓	dob	Numeric	9	0	Date of birth (CMC)		
24	✓	eduatt	Numeric	18	0	Education Attainment	eduatt	{0,"No_education"; 1,"Primary_comp
25	✓	edunone	Numeric	9	0	None/Less than primary		
26	✓	eduprim	Numeric	9	0	Primary completed		
27	✓	edusec	Numeric	9	0	Secondary completed		
28	✓	edupsec	Numeric	9	0	Post-secondary completed		
29	✓	literacy	Numeric	10	0	Reads_&_Writes	literacy	{0,"Illiterate"; 1,"Literate"}
30	✓	enrlprim	Numeric	9	0	Primary enrollment		
31	✓	enrlsec	Numeric	9	0	Secondary enrollment		

- *To hide or show variable columns in the **Data View** tab:* In the **Variable View** tab, click the checkbox next to the variable name.

  Tip: The *ADePT User's Guide* describes other functions available in the **Data Browser**.

Generating Variables

You can create new variables based on variables present in a dataset. This might be useful for simulating the effects of changes in parameters on various economic outcomes. For example, in the Poverty module you can model the impact of income transfers to some population groups based on poverty and inequality.

1. In the **Datasets** tab in the main window, click the dataset that you want to modify.
2. Click the **Variables | [dataset label]** tab.

3. Right-click in the table, then click **Add or replace variable...** in the pop-up menu.
4. In the **Generate/Replace Variable** dialog:
   a. In the **Expression** field, define the new variable using the following syntax:

      <new_variable_name> = <expression> [if <filter_expression>]

      where

<new_variable_name>	is a unique name not already in the dataset(s).
<expression>	calculates new data for the variable (see "Variable Expressions" section, later in this chapter).
<filter_expression>	(optional) filters observations that take account in the calculation. (See the "Variable Expressions" section later in the chapter for more information about expressions.)

   b. Optional: Activate the **Apply to all datasets** option.
      Note: If you loaded multiple datasets, but don't generate the new variable for all datasets, you will not be able to use the new variable in calculations. However, you may want to generate a new variable differently for each dataset in the project.
   c. Click the **Generate** button.
5. In the **Information** dialog, click the **OK** button.

The new variable will be listed in the **Variables | [dataset name]** tab, and in the **Data Browser**. If the variable was generated for all loaded datasets, it will appear in the drop-down lists in the input **Variables** tab.

When you save a project, variable expressions are saved with the project, and the variables are regenerated when you open that project. Generating new variables does not change original datasets.

Replacing Variables

You can replace an existing numeric variable by following the instructions in "Generating numeric dataset variables," but in the **Generate/Replace Variable** dialog (step 4a in the previous subsection), specify an existing variable name instead of a new variable name.

As with generated variables, these expressions are saved with a project and the variables are regenerated when you open the project. Replacing variables does not change original datasets.

Variable Expressions

The following operators can be used in expressions:

Operator				Description
+	**–**	*****	**/**	Basic mathematical operators
abs	**sign**			
=	**==**			Equality check operators
^	**pow**	**sqrt**		Exponent (e.g., **x^2** is x squared), power (e.g., **pow(4,2)** is 42 = 16) and square root
round	**truncate**			Shortening operators
min	**max**			Range operators
ceiling	**floor**			

Variable expressions can include constants, and strings can be used for variables that are of type string.

Expression examples:

Expression	Description
x = 1	Sets all variable x observations to 1
x = y + z	Sets variable x observations to y observation plus z observation
x = y = 1	Sets variable x observations to 1 (true) if y is 1, otherwise sets to 0 (false)
x = 23 if z == .	Sets variable x observations to 23 if z is missing (.), otherwise sets to .
x = Log(y) if z = 1	Sets variable x observations to log of y observation if z is 1, otherwise sets to .
s = "test"	Sets all variable x observations to the string "test"

Another example: To simulate the impact on poverty of a 10 percent increase in incomes of households with more than four members, replace the existing *Income* variable using this expression:

$$\text{income} = \text{income} * 1.1 \text{ if hhsize} > 4.$$

Deleting Variables

You can remove variables from the working copy of a dataset that ADePT uses for its calculations. This operation does not change the original dataset. Native, generated, and replaced variables can all be deleted.

1. In the dataset **Variables** tab, right-click in the row containing the variable you want to delete, then click **Drop Variable [variable name]** in the pop-up menu.
2. In the **Confirmation** dialog, click the **Yes** button.

Setting Parameters

Some modules have a **Parameters** tab next to the input **Variables** tab. In the **Parameters** tab you can set ranges, weightings, and other module-specific factors that ADePT will apply during its processing. A **Parameters** tab may also have input variable fields for mapping dataset variables, as shown by the open list that follows.

The mechanics for setting parameters are straightforward: activate options, set values, and select items in drop-down lists. The analytical reasons for setting parameters can be found elsewhere in this book, or in the appropriate book in the Streamlined Analysis with ADePT Software series.

Working with Projects

After specifying datasets and mapping variables, you can save the configuration for future use. A saved project stores links to datasets, variable names, and other information related to analysis inputs. Projects do not retain table and graph selections, corresponding if-conditions, and frequencies and standard errors choices, since these are related to analysis outputs.

- *To save a project:*
  a. **Project ▶ Save Project** or **Project ▶ Save As...**
  b. In the **Save As** dialog, select a location and name for the project, then click the **Save** button.

- *To open a saved project:*
  a. **Project ▶ Open Project...**
  b. In the **Open** dialog, locate and select the project, then click the **Open** button.

ADePT supports Web-based projects and datasets.

- *To open a Web-based project:*
  a. **Project ▶ Open Web Project...**
  b. In the **Open Web project** dialog, enter the project's URL, then click the **OK** button.
- *To add a Web-based dataset:*
  a. In the **Datasets** tab, SHIFT-click the **Add...** button.
  b. In the **Add Web Dataset** dialog, enter the dataset's URL, then click the **OK** button.

Adding Standard Errors or Frequencies to Outputs

- *To calculate standard errors:* Before clicking the **Generate** button, activate the **Standard errors** option.

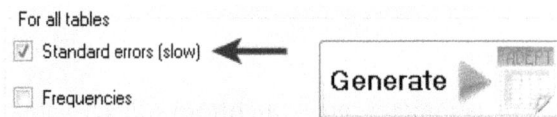

Calculating tables with standard errors takes considerably more time than calculating tables without them—possibly an order of magnitude longer. A good approach is to obtain the result you want without standard errors, then generate final results with standard errors.

- *To calculate frequencies:* Before clicking the **Generate** button, activate the **Frequencies** option.

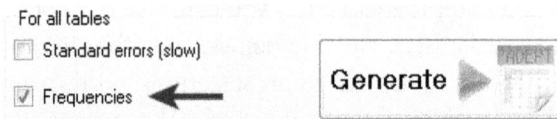

Tables with frequencies show the unweighted number of observations used to calculate a particular cell in a table. No significant additional time is needed to calculate frequencies.

Results of standard error and frequency calculations associated with a table are in separate worksheets, labeled **SE** and **FREQ**, within the output report.

Applying If-Conditions to Outputs

The purpose of if-conditions is to include observations from a particular subgroup of a population in the analysis. The inclusion condition is formulated as a Boolean expression—a function of the variables existing in the dataset. Each particular observation is included in the analysis if it satisfies the inclusion condition (the Boolean expression evaluates to value **true**). In many cases, the conditions we use are quite simple. Consider the following examples:

If-condition	Interpretation
urban=1	Only those observations having the value of variable **urban** equal to 1 will be included in the analysis.
region==5	Only observations from the **region** with code **5** are included in the analysis.
age_yrs>=16	Only those individuals who are 16 or older are included in the analysis.
sland!=0	Exclude from analysis those individuals who are not landowners (given that the variable **sland** denotes the area of the land owned).

1. In the list of tables and graphs, click the table or graph name.
2. Enter the if-condition at the bottom of the **Table description and if-condition** tab (see list of operators below).

If-condition operators:

Operator	Description
=	Equal
==	Equal
>=	Greater than or equal
<=	Less than or equal
!=	Not equal
&	Logical AND
|	Logical OR
inlist(<variable>,n_1,n_2,n_3,...)	Include only observations for which <variable> has values n_1, n_2, n_3, ...
inrange(<variable>,n_1,n_2)	Include observations for which <variable> is between n_1 and n_2
!missing(<variable>)	Exclude observations with missing values in <variable>

3. Click the **Set** button. A table or graph having an if-condition is highlighted.

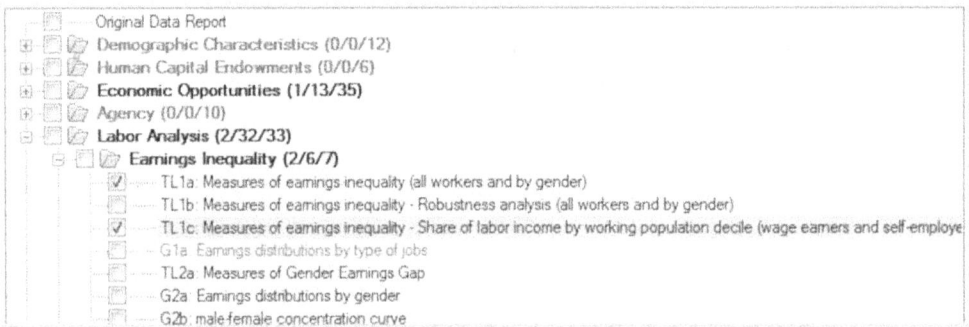

Generating Custom Tables

You can add a custom table to ADePT's output.

1. **Tools ▶ Show Custom table tab.**
2. In the lower left panel's **Custom table** tab, activate the **Define custom table** option.

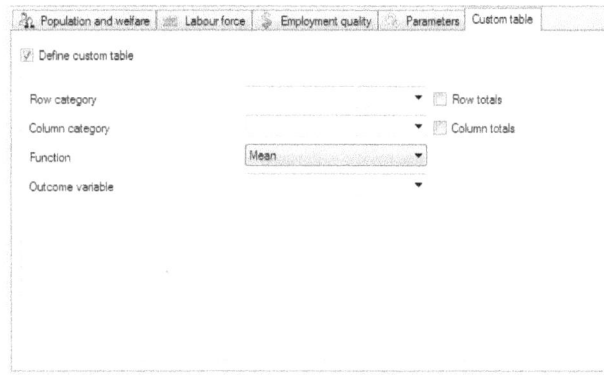

3. Design the table by selecting items in the drop-down lists and by activating the options as desired.

   The **Custom table** tab in the lower right corner of the ADePT main window displays a simple preview of your table design. This enables you to interactively modify the table to suit your needs.

4. In the upper right (outputs) panel:
   a. Scroll to the bottom of the list.
   b. Select **Custom table**.

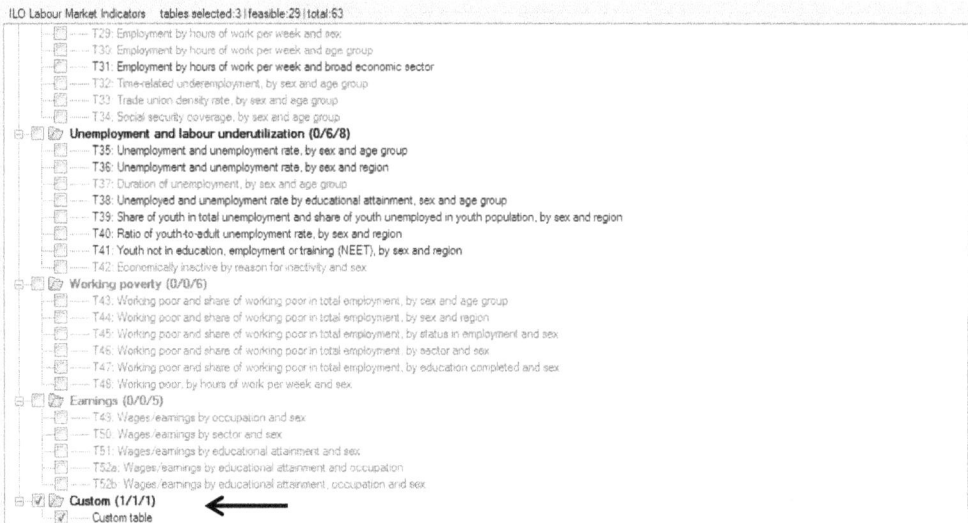

The custom table will be included in the report generated by ADePT.

Index

Boxes, figures, notes, and tables are indicated by *b*, *f*, *n*, and *t*, respectively, following page numbers.

www.ingramcontent.com/pod-product-compliance
Lightning Source LLC
Chambersburg PA
CBHW080539220326
41599CB00032B/6313